MW00636651

## The Guts of the Matter

*The Guts of the Matter* is a study of our oldest ecological problem: the transmission of infectious intestinal disease from human waste. Spanning the early hominin era to the present, this book explores the evolution of human waste disposal practices, the use of feces and urine as fertilizer, and the changing patterns of transmission of intestinal pathogens and parasites. Chapters trace the spread of viral, bacterial, and helminthic infections through the early processes of globalization and track the uneven successes of the sanitation revolution in recent centuries. The book also provides an overview of the cultural practices that influence the transmission of infectious intestinal disease and the impacts of biomedical advances such as oral rehydration therapy and vaccination. Webb's impressive breadth and meticulous research offer students of public health, environmental history, global history, and medicine new environmental perspectives on fundamental disease processes that have shaped the human past.

James L. A. Webb Jr. is Professor Emeritus of History at Colby College. His recent books include *The Long Struggle against Malaria in Tropical Africa* (2014) and *Global Health in Africa* (2013).

For Dick Guerrant,
with best wishes,

Jim Webb

# Studies in Environment and History

Editors

J. R. McNeill, *Georgetown University*
Ling Zhang, *Boston College*

Editors Emeriti

Alfred W. Crosby
Edmund P. Russell
Donald Worster

## Other Books in the Series

Maya K. Peterson *Pipe Dreams: Water and Empire in Central Asia's Aral Sea Basin*
Debjani Bhattacharyya *Empire and Ecology in the Bengal Delta: The Making of Calcutta*
Chris Courtney *The Nature of Disaster in China: The 1931 Yangzi River Flood*
Thomas Wickman *Snowshoe Country: An Environmental and Cultural History of Winter in the Early American Northeast*
Dagomar Degroot *The Frigid Golden Age: Climate Change, the Little Ice Age, and the Dutch Republic, 1560–1720*
Edmund Russell *Greyhound Nation: A Coevolutionary History of England, 1200–1900*
Timothy J. LeCain *The Matter of History: How Things Create the Past*
Ling Zhang *The River, the Plain, and the State: An Environmental Drama in Northern Song China, 1048–1128*
Abraham H. Gibson *Feral Animals in the American South: An Evolutionary History*
Andy Bruno *The Nature of Soviet Power: An Arctic Environmental History*
David A. Bello *Across Forest, Steppe, and Mountain: Environment, Identity, and Empire in Qing China's Borderlands*
Erik Loomis *Empire of Timber: Labor Unions and the Pacific Northwest Forests*
Peter Thorsheim *Waste into Weapons: Recycling in Britain during the Second World War*
Kieko Matteson *Forests in Revolutionary France: Conservation, Community, and Conflict, 1669–1848*
Micah S. Muscolino *The Ecology of War in China: Henan Province, the Yellow River, and Beyond, 1938–1950*
George Colpitts *Pemmican Empire: Food, Trade, and the Last Bison Hunts in the North American Plains, 1780–1882*
John L. Brooke *Climate Change and the Course of Global History: A Rough Journey.*
Paul Josephson et al. *An Environmental History of Russia*
Emmanuel Kreike *Environmental Infrastructure in African History: Examining the Myth of Natural Resource Management*
Gregory T. Cushman *Guano and the Opening of the Pacific World: A Global Ecological History*
Sam White *The Climate of Rebellion in the Early Modern Ottoman Empire*
Edmund Russell *Evolutionary History: Uniting History and Biology to Understand Life on Earth*
Alan Mikhail *Nature and Empire in Ottoman Egypt: An Environmental History*

Richard W. Judd *The Untilled Garden: Natural History and the Spirit of Conservation in America, 1740–1840*

James L. A. Webb, Jr. *Humanity's Burden: A Global History of Malaria*

Myrna I. Santiago *The Ecology of Oil: Environment, Labor, and the Mexican Revolution, 1900–1938*

Frank Uekoetter *The Green and the Brown: A History of Conservation in Nazi Germany*

Matthew D. Evenden *Fish versus Power: An Environmental History of the Fraser River*

Alfred W. Crosby *Ecological Imperialism: The Biological Expansion of Europe, 900–1900, second edition*

Nancy J. Jacobs *Environment, Power, and Injustice: A South African History*

Edmund Russell *War and Nature: Fighting Humans and Insects with Chemicals from World War I to Silent Spring*

Adam Rome *The Bulldozer in the Countryside: Suburban Sprawl and the Rise of American Environmentalism*

Judith Shapiro *Mao's War against Nature: Politics and the Environment in Revolutionary China*

Andrew Isenberg *The Destruction of the Bison: An Environmental History*

Thomas Dunlap *Nature and the English Diaspora*

Robert B. Marks *Tigers, Rice, Silk, and Silt: Environment and Economy in Late Imperial South China*

Mark Elvin and Tsui'jung Liu *Sediments of Time: Environment and Society in Chinese History*

Richard H. Grove *Green Imperialism: Colonial Expansion, Tropical Island Edens and the Origins of Environmentalism, 1600–1860*

Thorkild Kjærgaard *The Danish Revolution, 1500–1800: An Ecohistorical Interpretation*

Donald Worster *Nature's Economy: A History of Ecological Ideas, second edition*

Elinor G. K. Melville *A Plague of Sheep: Environmental Consequences of the Conquest of Mexico*

J. R. McNeill *The Mountains of the Mediterranean World: An Environmental History*

Theodore Steinberg *Nature Incorporated: Industrialization and the Waters of New England*

Timothy Silver *A New Face on the Countryside: Indians, Colonists, and Slaves in the South Atlantic Forests, 1500–1800*

Michael Williams *Americans and Their Forests: A Historical Geography*

Donald Worster *The Ends of the Earth: Perspectives on Modern Environmental History*

Robert Harms *Games against Nature: An Eco-Cultural History of the Nunu of Equatorial Africa*

Warren Dean *Brazil and the Struggle for Rubber: A Study in Environmental History*

Samuel P. Hays *Beauty, Health, and Permanence: Environmental Politics in the United States, 1955–1985*

Arthur F. McEvoy *The Fisherman's Problem: Ecology and Law in the California Fisheries, 1850–1980*

Kenneth F. Kiple *The Caribbean Slave: A Biological History*

# The Guts of the Matter

## A Global History of Human Waste and Infectious Intestinal Disease

JAMES L. A. WEBB, JR.

*Colby College*

CAMBRIDGE
UNIVERSITY PRESS

# CAMBRIDGE
## UNIVERSITY PRESS

University Printing House, Cambridge CB2 8BS, United Kingdom

One Liberty Plaza, 20th Floor, New York, NY 10006, USA

477 Williamstown Road, Port Melbourne, VIC 3207, Australia

314–321, 3rd Floor, Plot 3, Splendor Forum, Jasola District Centre, New Delhi – 110025, India

79 Anson Road, #06–04/06, Singapore 079906

Cambridge University Press is part of the University of Cambridge.

It furthers the University's mission by disseminating knowledge in the pursuit of education, learning, and research at the highest international levels of excellence.

www.cambridge.org
Information on this title: www.cambridge.org/9781108493437
DOI: 10.1017/9781108642323

© James L. A. Webb, Jr. 2020

First published 2020

Printed in the United Kingdom by TJ International Ltd, Padstow Cornwall

*A catalogue record for this publication is available from the British Library.*

ISBN 978-1-108-49343-7 Hardback
ISBN 978-1-108-73706-7 Paperback

To Alison

# Contents

Contents                                          xi

# Figures

# Acknowledgments

This book is a work of historical synthesis. It draws upon literatures in biology, medicine, public health, epidemiology, anthropology, and history, and it is supplemented with documents from the archives of the World Health Organization (Geneva), the London School of Hygiene and Tropical Medicine, and the National Archives of the United Kingdom (Kew).

The research for this book was funded in part by a sabbatical leave and by Social Science Research Grants from Colby College, and I gratefully acknowledge the former provost, Lori Kletzner, and my faculty colleagues for their support of this project. Over the course of the several years of researching and writing this book, other institutions also provided key support. During the fall semester of 2015, I was a member of the Institute for Advanced Study (IAS) in Princeton, where I received a stipend from the Willis F. Doney Fund. During the spring semester of 2016, I participated in the workings of the Centre Virchow-Villermé in Paris, affiliated with the Université de Paris IV (Descartes), as the Visiting Sanofi Chair in Public Health. During the spring semester of 2017, I was a Rachel Carson Fellow at the Rachel Carson Center at the Ludwig-Maximilians-Universität in Munich. During the spring of 2018, I was a visiting scholar at the University of Shanghai, through my participation in the People's Republic of China's High-End Foreign Expert program. During the 2018–19 academic year, I was a Fulbright Teaching and Research Professor in Gaborone at the University of Botswana.

I have given talks on various aspects of this research in university settings. For their kind invitations, I would like to thank my hosts Maitseo Bolaane and Fred Morton of the History Department at the

University of Botswana; Flurin Condreau of the Institute of Biomedical Ethics and Medical History at the University of Zurich; Nicholas Cosmo of the School of Historical Studies at the Institute for Advanced Study in Princeton; Jennifer Johnson of the History Department at Brown University; Greg Jones-Katz of the History Department at the Chinese University of Hong Kong, Shenzhen; Anwar Majid of the Center for Global Humanities at the University of New England in Tangier; Ismael Kasvosve, Tiny Masupe, Giacomo Paganotti, and Matshediso Zachariah of the Faculty of Health Sciences at the University of Botswana; Christof Mauch, director of the Rachel Carson Center in Munich; and Fei Sheng of the History Department at the Sun Yat-Sen University in Guangzhou.

I would like to thank Antoine Flahaut of the Institute for Global Health in Geneva and Patrick Zylberman of the École des Hautes Etudes en Santé Publique in Paris and Rennes for their invitation to a conference on global health history at the Brocher Foundation near Geneva. My article "Battling Intestinal Worm Disease: From the Hookworm Campaigns of the Rockefeller Foundation to Contemporary Mass Drug Administration," written for this conference, was published in *Generus: The Swiss Journal of the History of Medicine and Sciences* and draws upon some of the material that appears in Chapter 6. I am appreciative of the invitation of Marc Hall of the Department of Evolutionary Biology and Environmental Studies at the University of Zurich to appear on a panel with him at a meeting of the European Society for Environmental History in Versailles. I thank Urmi Engineer Willoughby of the Department of History at Murray State University for the invitation to join her panel at the annual meeting of the World History Association in Milwaukee and Simone Müller of the Rachel Carson Center for the opportunity to make a presentation at a workshop at the Rachel Carson Center in Munich. A double thanks goes to Iris Borowy of the Center for the History of Global Development at the University of Shanghai, who helped me organize the workshop "From Night Soil to Chemical Fertilizers: Transformations in Asian-Pacific Agriculture" and invited me to participate in other workshops at the University of Shanghai. In all of these settings, I am indebted to colleagues, too numerous to mention by name, for vigorous intellectual exchange and challenge.

Tamara Giles-Vernick, Jim McCann, John McNeill, and Randy Packard wrote letters of support for my grant applications. I greatly appreciate their confidence in this project. John provided incisive commentary that helped me reorganize an earlier draft of the manuscript.

# Introduction

*The Guts of the Matter* is a study of our oldest ecological problem: the transmission of infectious intestinal pathogens from human waste.[1] Over deep time, fecal pathogens have killed innumerable infants and young children and been a principal constraint on human population growth. Over the past several generations, we have gained increasing control over the transmission of infectious intestinal disease. These advances have contributed to an ongoing population explosion that is dramatically transforming global ecological systems.

I was drawn to this project by an apparently simple question: why were diarrheal diseases still killing so many children in the twenty-first century? In the course of research, the project deepened in time and broadened in scope. It grew into a global history ranging from the early hominin era to the present, exploring human waste disposal, infectious intestinal disease, and the uneven impacts of modern sanitation. It came to grapple with environmental perspectives on some foundational disease processes that have shaped the human past.

---

[1] I have defined the term *infectious intestinal disease* to mean the negative health consequences caused by the viral, bacterial, protozoal, and helminthic biological agents that are passed by a fecal route, ingested via an oral route, and then reinfect the intestines and, sometimes, reach other internal organs. I have expanded the reach of the term to encompass hookworm, which is passed by a fecal route and then is contracted by dermal exposure with feces-contaminated soils, from which hookworm larvae penetrate the skin and migrate to reinfect the intestines, because the epidemiology of hookworm is in many other respects similar to that of roundworm and whipworm, the other major soil-transmitted intestinal helminths, and co-infections are common.

In the course of writing the book, many friends and colleagues expressed some discomfort when they learned of its topic. The quasi-unmentionable nature of human waste underscores the fact that in the developed world, we carry out our excretory functions in private in special rooms devoted to this purpose, and many of us have little idea of what happens after we flush the toilet. Several times a day, we sit astride (or stand in front of) a section of the largest and most expensive environmental infrastructure in the world – the vast underground systems of sewers and wastewater treatment plants that are a defining feature of the developed world. Fully one-half of humanity squats today without these appurtenances, suffers the indignities of infectious intestinal disease, and mourns the diarrheal deaths of their infants and young children.

*The Guts of the Matter* is organized into eight chapters. Chapter 1, "Pathogens and Parasites," introduces the major helminthic, protozoal, viral, and bacterial intestinal disease agents, and it provides estimates of their current prevalence and contribution to the burden of human disease. The chapter discusses the biological and social determinants of infectious intestinal disease transmission, and it makes the point that, although a range of hygienic practices can have a significant influence on transmission, owing to a range of ecological and cultural variables, few universal rules apply. It discusses some recent findings from the microbiome project that provide new ways of thinking about infectious intestinal disease, and it makes the case that a deeper understanding of the historical epidemiology of infectious intestinal diseases can potentially improve the public health outcomes from contemporary interventions.

Chapter 2, "Early Change," explores what is known about environments in which intestinal disease transmission emerged. It marshals research in the biological sciences to discuss the settings in which early communities were able to transmit some intestinal pathogens and parasites, long before the agricultural revolution. It suggests that the construct of the "first epidemiological transition" needs to be revised. It explores the patterns of vulnerability to infectious intestinal disease associated with hunting, gathering, and fishing in an early era and those associated with early farming practices, settlements, and pastoral nomadism. It provides an historical overview of the evolution of zones of infectious intestinal disease; the various Eurasian attitudes toward human waste; regional patterns in the use or nonuse of human excreta in early agriculture; and early urban sanitation.

Chapter 3, "Diffusion and Amplification," discusses the long era in which pathogens and parasites were extended to new regions. As human communities became more complex, networks of trade expanded and became denser, allowing for the rapid, long-distance transmission of intestinal pathogens. Over the first millennium and a half of the Common Era, the disease pool of Eurasia and northern Africa became increasingly integrated. In the late fifteenth century, some Old World intestinal pathogens crossed the Atlantic and became established in the Americas. By the early nineteenth century, the integration had become global. Rapid urbanization in the industrializing North Atlantic states created a crisis of urban fecal pollution. In response, the first public health reform movements emerged. Beginning in the first half of the nineteenth century, cholera pandemics spread along global trade routes and infected all the inhabited continents. This provoked the first efforts at the international control of disease.

Chapter 4, "Innovations," discusses the environmental challenges in a rapidly urbanizing London, the capital of the largest empire of the modern period. It explores the early innovations in dealing with excreta disposal, including the creation of an underground sewer system and efforts to use the highly dilute sewer effluvia as fertilizer. The direct health benefits of modern sewerage alone were modest. Many smaller and less wealthy cities and towns opted for other methods of human waste disposal, including the tub-and-pail system. Much infectious intestinal disease was the result of pathogen-laden flies alighting on food and the contamination of the urban milk supply. The major reductions in mortality and morbidity from intestinal pathogens came about as a result of the filtration and chemical treatment of drinking water with chlorine or ozonation.

Chapter 5, "Adoptions and Adaptations," explores the evidence for the adoption of modern sewerage and water purification systems beyond the early centers in northern Europe and North America. The principal constraints to adoption of modern sanitation were fiscal, although ecological, political, and cultural forces also played large roles. The overall result was that the sanitation revolution beyond the North Atlantic was adopted piecemeal and that the benefits were generally concentrated in the core urban areas inhabited by those with political and economic power. Into the mid-twentieth century, the flush toilet and the disposal of human waste via water carriage made little impact on the overall problem of excreta disposal, and even the provision of piped water was generally limited to the cities and large towns in which Europeans, local elites of European ancestry, and/or non-European elites had an authoritative presence.

Chapter 6, "The Struggle against Hookworm Disease," examines the early campaigns of the Rockefeller Foundation to reduce transmission of the widespread helminthic infection. Launched in the southern United States and then extended southward in the western hemisphere and into the eastern hemisphere, the anti-hookworm campaigns became the very first global health initiative. Although the campaigns utilized chemical therapies to reduce the intestinal worm load, their primary focus was on changing defecation habits to encourage better sanitation. The campaigns failed to meet their goals, underscoring the limitations of mass drug treatment and the difficulties of changing entrenched defecation practices and the use of human waste as fertilizer.

Chapter 7, "An Era of Optimism," analyzes the new culture of sanitation practices that helped to define modernity. In the late nineteenth and early twentieth centuries, those living in the developed world became accustomed to wearing shoes, using toilet paper, bathing regularly with soap, and utilizing refrigeration systems to extend the life of foods. In the mid-twentieth century, populations in the Global North benefited from population-wide vaccination programs against poliomyelitis, whose prevalence seemed to have increased as a result of the implementation of better sanitation systems. Based on the "hygiene hypothesis," many specialists believed that poliomyelitis was rare in regions without modern sanitation. This was not the case. Regrettably, polio vaccination did not begin in the developing world until the 1970s. Oral rehydration therapy, a major breakthrough in the treatment of diarrheal disease, saved millions of lives.

Chapter 8, "Global Health and Infectious Intestinal Disease," explores the major challenges to and advances in the control of infectious intestinal diseases since 1970s, when new sets of actors took up the crusade against diarrheal diseases. Physicians and activists organized in response to a spike in infant deaths in the Global South linked to bottle-feeding. Nongovernmental agencies and national politicians encouraged behavioral change to end open defecation. Biomedical scientists developed additional vaccines against poliovirus and rotavirus. Epidemiologists threw new light on the global prevalence of diarrheal diseases and regional disparities in childhood survival rates. The new focus on biomedical interventions and programs of community- or national-level behavioral change constituted a new era in the control of infectious intestinal disease.

# I

# Pathogens and Parasites

It is a shitty world out there. Many hundreds of millions of people will fall ill this year from infectious intestinal pathogens passed in human feces. Just how many hundreds of thousands will die can only be reckoned roughly. Consider cholera. The World Health Organization estimates that most cholera outbreaks are not detected by public health agencies and that the officially reported cases of cholera probably represent 5 to 10 percent of the actual number of cases worldwide. Their experts guess at 2.8 million cases of cholera every year and an estimated 91,000 deaths, of which approximately half occur in children under the age of five years.[1] Typhoid fever probably afflicts annually more than 20 million, of which about a quarter of a million die.[2] Shigella infections take the lives of more than 200,00.[3] Each year, children suffer around 1.7 billion bouts of diarrheal disease from mostly undetermined causes.[4] From these bouts,

---

[1] Mohammed Ali, Anna Lena Lopez, Young Ae You, Young Eun Kim, Binod Sah, Brian Maskery, and John Clemens, "The Global Burden of Cholera," *Bulletin of the World Health Organization*, vol. 90 (2012), 209, 214.

[2] www.who.int/immunization/diseases/typhoid/en/.

[3] Ibrahim A. Khalil, Christopher Troeger, Brigette F. Blacker, Puja C. Rao, Alexandria Brown, Deborah E. Atherly, Thomas G. Brewer et al. "Morbidity and Mortality due to Shigella and Enterotoxigenic Escherichia coli Diarrhoea: the Global Burden of Disease Study 1990–2016," *Lancet Infectious Diseases*, vol. 18, no. 11 (2018), 1229–40.

[4] The burden of novel pathogenic agents that have yet to be discovered is high. Case studies of diarrheal illness in young children from low-income countries have determined that in fewer than 50 percent of the cases could researchers find any known pathogenic agents. Mihai Pop, Alan W. Walker, Joseph Paulson, Brianna Lindsay, Martin Antonio, M. Anowar Hossain, Joseph Oundo et al., "Diarrhea in Young Children from Low-Income Countries Leads to Large-Scale Alterations in Intestinal

more than a half a million children under five years of age die.[5] The number of deaths is appallingly high, yet it represents a major decline from just a generation ago, when the annual diarrheal death toll was estimated at more than 3 million.[6]

The pathogens that cause these illnesses and deaths are passed in human waste. When microscopically tiny particles of fecal matter contaminate hands, serving vessels, bowls, plates, tableware, liquids, or foods, the pathogenic agents – whether viruses, bacteria, or protozoa – travel to our intestines through the digestive tract. There, they disrupt the functioning of our guts, the incredibly complex universe known as the human microbiome. Another set of infections is caused by parasitic intestinal worms. In small numbers, some worms seem to contribute to the well-functioning of our immune systems, but in larger numbers, the same worms cause illness and, in rare cases, death. We can also become sick from contact with the fecal matter of wild or domesticated animals, but these infections are a relatively minor part of the story. Human beings transmit to each other the major infections that wreak illness and death. We are our own worst enemies.

### INTESTINAL VIRUSES, PROTOZOA, AND BACTERIA

Five intestinal viruses are particularly dangerous to human health: poliovirus, hepatitis A, hepatitis E, rotavirus, and norovirus. They are passed virtually exclusively by human beings to other human beings, and their range has been global. Immunization campaigns against poliovirus, which can cause muscular paralysis and, in rare cases, death, have been highly successful and have reduced the number of new poliovirus infections to twenty-two in 2017. Hepatitis A and hepatitis E attack the liver and remain global menaces. There are effective vaccines against both, but

Microbiota Composition," *Genome Biology*, vol. 15, no. 6 (2014), R76. http://genomebiology.com/2014/15/6/R76.

    For estimates of the impacts of the known intestinal pathogens, see Christopher Troeger, Mohammad Forouzanfar, Puja C. Rao, Ibrahim Khalil, Alexandria Brown, Robert C. Reiner Jr, Nancy Fullman et al., "Estimates of Global, Regional, and National Morbidity, Mortality, and Aetiologies of Diarrhoeal Diseases: A Systematic Analysis for the Global Burden of Disease Study 2015," *Lancet Infectious Diseases*, vol. 17, no. 9 (2017), 909–48.

[5] www.who.int/mediacentre/factsheets/fs330/en/.

[6] C. Bern, J. Martines, I. de Zoysa, and R. I. Glass, "The Magnitude of the Global Problem of Diarrhoeal Disease: A Ten-Year Update," *Bulletin of the World Health Organization*, vol. 70, no. 6 (1992), 705–14.

the public health systems are too weak in many countries to allow for population-level coverage. There are thought to be about 114 million infections of hepatitis A and 20 million infections of hepatitis E every year, although most cases are asymptomatic. More than 1 percent of those annually infected with hepatitis A (about 1.4 million people) and more than 15 percent of those afflicted with hepatitis E (about 3.3 million people) experience the characteristic symptoms of dark urine, jaundice, and extreme weakness. Those who recover from hepatitis A are immune to reinfection. There are multiple genotypes of hepatitis E, however, and the extent to which survivors enjoy any degree of protective immunity has not been determined. A high percentage of the population in the Global North is potentially susceptible because of the low levels of endemic transmission. In the Global South, virtually all adolescents and adults have been exposed to hepatitis A, and new cases are found almost exclusively among the young.[7] Hepatitis E affects a broader spectrum of the population and is a particular threat to adults with compromised immune systems.[8]

By contrast, until the first decade of the twenty-first century, rotavirus infections were nearly universal. Before the rollout of a vaccine in 2006, rotavirus infected virtually all children in the United States before their fifth birthday. Rotavirus continues to infect unvaccinated children around the world and kills 200,000 each year. Rotavirus transmission is principally via fomites, that is, surfaces on which we inadvertently deposit invisibly small viral particles from fecal matter, which are then inadvertently picked up by others. In the developed world, children's toys, doorknobs, and shared tableware are the usual culprits.[9] Norovirus is also a very bad actor, and because there is no vaccine, its prevalence is roughly equivalent to rotavirus earlier in the century. It is responsible for about 20 percent of all cases of diarrhea and vomiting in the United States. Indeed, norovirus is the leading cause of severe gastroenteritis worldwide.

[7] K. H. Jacobsen and S. T. Wiersma, "Hepatitis A Seroprevalence by Age and World Region, 1990 and 2005," *Vaccine*, vol. 28, no. 41 (2010), 6653–7. doi:10.1016/j.vaccine.2010.08.037.

[8] Lisa J. Krain, Kenrad E. Nelson, and Alain B. Labrique, "Host Immune Status and Response to Hepatitis E Virus Infection," *Clinical Microbiology Reviews*, vol. 27, no. 1 (2014), 139–65.

[9] Jacqueline E. Tate, Anthony H. Burton, Cynthia Boschi-Pinto, Umesh D. Parashar, World Health Organization–Coordinated Global Rotavirus Surveillance Network, Mary Agocs, Fatima Serhan et al., "Global, Regional, and National Estimates of Rotavirus Mortality in Children < 5 Years of Age, 2000–2013," *Clinical Infectious Diseases*, vol. 62, suppl. 2 (2016), S96–105.

It spreads when we ingest food and water contaminated with microscopically small specs of fecal matter.[10]

There are two major protozoa that infect the human intestinal tract: *Giardia lamblia* and *Entamoeba histolytica*.[11] These infections are infrequent in the developed world. They are introduced to humans via contamination from the feces and urine of other animals, such as dogs, cats, birds, sheep, deer, beaver, and cattle.[12] Hikers in remote areas who drink from streams and rivers are particularly at risk. Both protozoal intestinal infections produce diarrhea (and in the case of *Giardia lamblia*, sometimes severe constipation), but they are generally cleared within a matter of days or, at most, weeks. In the rural areas of the less developed world, these protozoal intestinal infections are common. The rural water supplies are frequently contaminated because human beings get their water from the same sources as do domesticated and wild animals. In many regions, the chains of infection are nearly continuous. Giardiasis is the most common cause of parasitic diarrhea in the world, although it does not kill. Amoebiasis from *Entamoeba histolytica* (also known as amoebic dysentery), however, is also widely distributed and causes about 50 million cases of diarrhea per year and kills about 100,000 people. It can be particularly destructive to the intestinal walls and open the gates to other infectious diseases.

Bacterial intestinal infections have been among the deadliest scourges of humankind. Two infections have killed large numbers of adults: typhoid fever (*Salmonella typhi* and *Salmonella paratyphi*) and cholera (*Vibrio cholerae*). Typhoid fever could exact a toll on the order of a 10–30 percent case fatality rate. It typically involved the passage of the bacteria from the intestine into the blood, producing sepsis. Cholera was even deadlier, with a case fatality rate that could reach 50 percent. Untreated cholera typically killed via severe diarrhea, which led to fatal dehydration.[13] A large number of additional pathogens could kill infants

---

[10] Sharia M. Ahmed, Aron J. Hall, Anne E. Robinson, Linda Verhoef, Prasanna Premkumar, Umesh D. Parashar, Marion Koopmans, and Benjamin A. Lopman, "Global Prevalence of Norovirus in Cases of Gastroenteritis: A Systematic Review and Meta-analysis," *Lancet Infectious Diseases*, vol. 14, no. 8 (2014), 725–30.

[11] Protozoa are similar to bacteria in that they are single celled, but they behave more like animals in that they typically have a sexual stage to their reproduction, whereas bacteria reproduce asexually.

[12] In the system of classification proposed by Thomas Cavalier-Smith, *G. lamblia* would be considered a member of the Archaea kingdom, rather than the Protozoa.

[13] The poor were particularly susceptible to infection by cholera and typhoid because many suffered from undernutrition, which is accompanied by low gastric acid activity in the

and young children whose immune systems were not fully developed. Even common, run-of-the-mill *E. coli* infections could pull into the grave infants and small children who were already weakened by malnutrition and/or other infections. They robbed the body of fluids and nutrients, causing severe diarrhea, dehydration, and, ultimately, death.

Today, typhoid fever, cholera, and amoebic dysentery are rare in communities that disinfect their water supplies with chlorine or ozone and maintain the physical integrity of the water delivery systems, from the reservoir to the tap. Even with this broad public health success, occasionally some bacterial pathogens, such as variants of *Escherichia coli*, *S. enterica*, and *Campylobacter*, enter the food supply and cause outbreaks of diarrheal disease and vomiting. But these are generally small-scale events that are easily contained, unless the local water supply system has become contaminated. For those who fall ill, the results are highly unpleasant but only temporarily debilitating, except in the case of the elderly and those with compromised immune systems, who are at greater risk for more serious consequences. The relative infrequency of bacterial infections is a positive reflection of our safe water treatment systems and our relatively high nutritional status. If bacterial pathogens are introduced only occasionally and the host's immune system is competent, the host is able to clear the infection and, generally, to kill or expel the pathogen. In the developed world, the risk of death from a bacterial pathogen is very low.

## INTESTINAL WORMS

The final group of unwelcome visitors to the human intestinal tract comprises intestinal worms known as helminths. Some of the worms attach themselves to the linings of the human intestines and draw their nourishment by sucking blood from their hosts. Most live from nutrients available in the intestinal tract. Some helminths, such as tapeworms and pinworms, are of minor public health significance. They spread via infinitesimally small eggs passed in human feces. The tapeworm eggs are ingested by cattle (*Taenia saginata*) or pigs (*T. solium* and *T. asiatica*),

---

stomach. This is one of the first lines of biological defense against *V. cholerae*, and normal gastric acid activity reduces the chances of the bacteria surviving its journey through the stomach to the small intestine. On the role of poverty and undernutrition in explaining the higher historical vulnerability of people of African descent in the Caribbean to cholera, see Kenneth F. Kiple, "Cholera and Race in the Caribbean," *Journal of Latin American Studies*, vol. 17, no. 1 (1985), 157–77.

where they develop into larvae, known as cysticerci, in the musculature of the animals and then are transferred to human beings who eat undercooked beef or pork, in which the taenia larvae survive. Once ingested, the cysticerci develop into adult tapeworms in the human intestine.[14] The pinworms (*Enterobius vermicularis* and *E. gregorii*) do not have a nonhuman host. They release tiny eggs that are deposited in tiny folds in the human anus, which becomes irritated and demands to be scratched. Sufferers from pinworm can then inadvertently transfer the eggs from hand to mouth, and once ingested, the cycle continues. It is also possible to transmit pinworm eggs via fomites – clothing, utensils, furniture, or other surfaces on which pathogens and parasites can survive – and a small proportion of the tiny eggs may become airborne and make their way to a human mouth and be inadvertently swallowed. They are remarkably common even in the developed world. An estimated 20 percent of the people in the United States will acquire a pinworm infection at some point in life.[15]

Far and away, however, the biggest intestinal worm challenges in global health are from a category known as soil-transmitted helminths (S-THs). A major difference is that the tiny eggs of the soil-transmitted helminths, after being passed through human feces, must mature in the soil. The three major S-THs are roundworms, whipworms, and hookworms. They are far and away most common of all the intestinal worms, and today they have a global distribution centered on the tropics and subtropics. The roundworms live from nutrients in the intestines. The hookworms and whipworms attach themselves to the human intestinal walls, where they grow to maturity, feeding upon human blood.

Researchers agree that roundworms, whipworms, and hookworms produce a large, global burden of disease. The difficulties in estimating the extent of the disease burdens are very considerable, because the data are not comprehensive or fully reliable. What seems clear, however, is that the likely total number of global deaths caused by complications from soil-transmitted helminths would be relatively small in comparison to the mortality caused by bacterial, protozoal, and viral infections.[16]

---

[14] It is also possible for human beings inadvertently to ingest *Taenia* eggs and host the development of the larvae in human tissues, such as the lung, liver, or brain.

[15] Edy Stermer, Igor Sukhotnic, and Ron Shaoul, "Pruritus Ani: An Approach to an Itching Condition," *Journal of Pediatric Gastroenterology and Nutrition*, vol. 48, no. 5 (2009), 513–16.

[16] Simon Brooker, "Estimating the Global Distribution and Disease Burden of Intestinal Nematode Infections: Adding Up the Numbers – A Review," *International Journal of Parasitology*, vol. 40, no. 10 (2010), 1137–44.

Somewhat paradoxically, it is more than likely that very light infections with these same worms have done us some good. There is evidence, for example, that populations with helminthic infections are less likely to suffer from allergic and autoimmune diseases. How can this be explained? According to the "hygiene hypothesis," because *Homo sapiens* co-evolved with intestinal worms until very recently, it seems likely that they have played a symbiotic role in our intestinal systems. The influence of helminths on the human immune system is under active investigation.

Roundworm (*Ascaris lumbricöides*) is the most widely distributed helminth in the world. It also afflicts the largest number of people, on the order of 1 billion. Adult worms live in the small intestine. The males grow to fifteen to thirty centimeters and the females to twenty to thirty-five centimeters. They are prolific. Each female can release up to 200,000 eggs per day, and both fertilized and unfertilized eggs are passed in feces. Where humans with roundworms defecate outdoors, the fertilized eggs – if the soil, moisture, and temperature conditions are suitable – develop in eighteen days to several weeks. Thereafter, they may be picked up by children playing outdoors or adults working on the land, and some eggs may become windborne and can be inadvertently ingested through the simple act of breathing, as well as via the fecal–oral route. When the mature eggs are ingested, they pass into the intestine, where they develop into larvae. They make their way from the intestine via the blood or lymphatic system to the lungs, from which they are then coughed up into the mouth and swallowed. They mature in the small intestine, attach themselves to the linings, and live on for one or two years. The cycle of infection must be ongoing for infections to be chronic. Most infections are relatively light, and many such sufferers do not experience any symptoms of infection. Heavy infections, on the other hand, can cause severe problems, including intestinal blockage.

Whipworm (*Trichuris trichiura*) infects perhaps three-quarters of a billion people. The worms live in the large intestine and produce eggs that are passed in feces. If the soil conditions are propitious, the eggs mature in fifteen to thirty days. They then become infective. These eggs, once ingested via the fecal–oral route, hatch in the small intestine and release larvae that attach themselves to the colon. They live for about one year. The adult female worm produces 3,000 to 20,000 eggs per day, which are passed in feces. Those with light infections may suffer no symptoms, while those with heavier infections may experience pain when passing stool and may even suffer rectal prolapse, when the lower part of the large intestine protrudes from the anus.

Hookworm (*Necator americanus* and *Ancylostoma duodenale*) infects about 500,000 to 600,000 people. Hookworms live in the small intestine, and the females produce eggs that are passed in feces. The eggs hatch quickly and turn into infective larvae – in six to twelve days under favorable conditions – and, unlike the other soil-transmitted helminths, the hookworm larvae live in the soil for three to four weeks. The larvae attach themselves to human skin – often the bare feet or hands of children or agricultural workers – and burrow under the skin, causing a rash. The larvae then enter the bloodstream and make their way to the heart and lungs, after which they ascend the pharynx and are swallowed. Most hookworms have a life-span of about one or two years, although some are much longer lived. *Ancylostoma duodenale* can become dormant in muscle tissue or in the intestine and may be able to be transmitted by an oral route or through breastfeeding.[17]

## DETERMINANTS OF DISEASE TRANSMISSION

The transmission of infectious intestinal pathogens is influenced by a large number of variables. Different societies have held different views about the appropriate means to dispose of human waste and whether or not to use excrement as a soil fertilizer, and different practices in different contexts have had epidemiological importance. Public health researchers have worked to establish firm relationships between "improved" systems of excreta disposal and better health, but they have found this difficult to do, because the relationships are complex and grounded in local ecological and cultural circumstances. Few universal rules apply.

The issue of sanitation – in the broadest sense, a range of behaviors that protect against the transmission of intestinal pathogens – is now recognized to be more complex than the "safe" disposal of human waste by modern sewerage and access to potable water. It is now clear that a range of hygienic practices can have a determinative effect. Some of our most basic and ancient practices, such as cooking food, not only make some foodstuffs more palatable and easy to digest but can kill viruses, bacteria, protozoa, and helminth eggs. Boiling drinking liquids can likewise

---

[17] The basic information about the biology and epidemiology of roundworm (*A. lumbricöides*), whipworm (*T. trichiura*), and hookworm (*N. americanus* and *A. duodenale*) was drawn from the website of the US Centers for Disease Control and Prevention: www.cdc.gov/parasites/ascariasis, www.cdc.gov/parasites/whipworm, and www.cdc.gov/parasites/hookworm.

dramatically reduce their pathogenic potential. Thus, access to energy supplies, such as firewood, dung cakes, and charcoal, has an enormous public health significance. Shortages of fuel can set off disease outbreaks, as can natural disasters that displace families from their energy resources. The use of soap to cleanse the hands after defecation or after cleaning up an infant's stool has been shown to sharply reduce the transmission of intestinal pathogens. Some of our basic understandings of the threats to children from infectious intestinal diseases are being reshaped by ethnographic research.

The transmission of intestinal pathogens is not, however, exclusively a function of access to "improved" sanitation, potable water, energy resources, or soap. Three basic biophysical factors set the parameters for some disease transmission processes. The first is temperature. Roundworm, whipworm, and hookworm eggs, for example, cannot survive when they are released in extremely cold temperatures, and for this reason, those who live in the Arctic regions do not suffer from these intestinal worms. Yet, extremely cold temperatures can militate against the washing of hands, and this enhances the possibilities for fecal–oral transmission of bacterial and viral pathogens. Extreme cold precludes the keeping of livestock and fowl and thus eliminates some sources of potential infection. Yet reliance upon hunting and fishing carries its own risks. Researchers have documented in the Arctic wide outbreaks of trichinosis, a helminthic infection with an enteric phase that causes prolonged diarrhea, and traced it to undercooked walrus meat. Communities in the Arctic also suffer occasional cases of diphyllobothriasis (fish tapeworm) from the consumption of undercooked fish and occasional cases of echinococcosis (tapeworms acquired from contact with dogs, reindeer, and elk).[18] At the other end of the temperature spectrum, a lengthy hot season is generally conducive to the survival and rapid maturation of the soil-transmitted helminth eggs and for the survival of bacterial and viral pathogens on fomites. There are decidedly greater risks to living in the tropics and subtropics.

Moisture is a second major factor. In dry deserts, such as the Sahara and the Gobi, the low humidity and near absence of rainfall combine with extreme diurnal temperature variations to kill some of the intestinal pathogens released into the environment. Feces desiccate quickly, and helminth

[18] Peter J. Hotez, "Neglected Infections of Poverty among the Indigenous Peoples of the Arctic," *PLoS Neglected Tropical Diseases*, vol. 4, no. 1 (2010), e606. doi:10.1371/journal.pntd.0000606.

eggs generally do not survive. It is possible, of course, to foul wells with human or animal waste and to transmit pathogens via the fecal–oral route, and for the populations of dry deserts, this can be a significant problem. In wet environments, high levels of moisture improve the survival of most intestinal pathogens. Rainfall runoff, if contaminated with human and animal feces, can distribute pathogenic materials widely and increase the possibilities for the transmission of disease.

Soil type is a third major biophysical determinant of intestinal pathogen transmission. Different soils have their most significant influence on the survival of helminth eggs. Hookworm eggs, for example, are able to germinate and produce larvae much more easily in sandy soils. Clayey soils are more impervious, and the survival rates of the helminth eggs are lower. As we will see in Chapter 6, the rates of hookworm infection in the US South in the early decades of the twentieth century were much higher in the coastal regions with sandy soils than in the upland regions with clayey soils.

Patterns of human lifestyle, particularly the practices of livestock keeping and herding, have also had a profound impact on the transmission of infectious intestinal disease. In societies that depend upon domesticated animals for milk, meat, hides, eggs, or furs, the close contact between animals and people increases the transmission of pathogens, such as the giardia protozoa, that have animal as well as human hosts. Whether or not the domesticated animals are held within enclosures is also epidemiologically significant. Enclosures such as barns or open-air pens concentrate the animal manure within the enclosure and ensure greater human contact with it, further enhancing the prospects for disease transmission. One of the most dangerous known practices is one of the most common: keeping free-ranging or penned chickens or other fowl close to the homestead. This is a prescription for the infection of young children who inadvertently contaminate themselves with pathogenic bacteria.

Cultural choices of where to defecate have also had epidemiological significance. A cultural preference for defecating in a stream or river, for example, principally put the communities downstream at risk. A cultural preference for defecating indoors – in the early twentieth-century United Kingdom, a usual spot for young children under the age of three or four was in the kitchen, eating room, or scullery – probably increased the contamination of foodstuffs, although the epidemiological consequences of this behavior were never quantified.[19]

---

[19] O. H. Peters, *Observations upon the Natural History of Epidemic Diarrhoea* (Cambridge: Cambridge University Press, 1911), 60–1.

Cultural practices of how to cleanse oneself after defecation have also been important. In Muslim societies, the religious requirement is to use the left hand to remove fecal matter and cleanse the anus with water. In Indonesia, for example, many Muslims met their obligation by defecating in waterways, which offered the immediate benefits of the submersion of feces and masking of its smell, as well as water for cleansing. In desert regions, Muslims have used sand to clean their left hands after defecation, thereby meeting the ritual requirement for ablution. These religiously sanctioned practices undoubtedly have their own deep histories that have not yet attracted the interest of cultural historians.

Across the globe, wherever human beings settled or congregated, their environments reeked. Both rural and urban life were permeated with the odors of urine and excrement. At night, to protect themselves from molestation by animals or other humans, many people relieved themselves nearby their homesteads or availed themselves of vessels within the homestead. By day, people relieved themselves on beaches and riverbanks; in fields, rivers, streams, forests, and grasslands; near schools, temples, and churches; in side yards, courtyards, barnyards, basement and outdoor cesspits, and privy vaults. Stench was pervasive. Daily encounters with one's own and others' shit and ammonia-reeking piss were inescapable, part and parcel of the lived world. (It is a measure of our distance from these experiences that in the "modern" Anglophone world, we have relegated the common nouns *shit* and *piss* to the realm of cusswords.) In environments permeated with bodily waste, it was hard to conceptualize feces as dangerous to health.

## CHANGING PERSPECTIVES ON CHILDHOOD DIARRHEAL DISEASES

In recent years, our understandings of the causes of childhood diarrhea and malnutrition have broadened. A major shift in thinking has been brought about by the appreciation of a condition known as environmental enteropathy. It is caused by the ingestion by young children of large quantities of fecal bacteria, principally from chickens raised nearby rural dwellings. The condition is characterized by poor growth, reduced intestinal barrier function, and chronic systemic inflammation.[20]

[20] Francis M. Ngure, Jean H. Humphrey, Mduduzi N. N. Mbuya et al., "Formative Research on Hygiene Behaviors and Geophagy among Infants and Young Children and

Researchers discovered that around homesteads where chickens were raised the possibilities for the ingestion of massive loads of bacteria were unmistakable.[21] In Zimbabwe, for example, the bacterial loads ingested by young children from homestead soils were estimated to be comparable or greater than the bacterial loads ingested from untreated drinking water. And these loads paled when compared with the inadvertent direct ingestion of chicken feces, which was roughly 4,000 times greater than from either untreated drinking water or from homestead soils. This revolutionary insight helped to refocus efforts in rural areas. Previously, the water, sanitation, and hygiene interventions had focused on improved disposal of human fecal matter, point-of-use water treatment, and maternal handwashing. There had been no interventions to interrupt the ingestion of contaminated soils and animal feces.[22]

A second major shift has occurred as a result of evidence that the (quantity) of water available is more important than its quality. Greater water availability encourages better hygiene – and more handwashing, in particular – and reduces the incidence of diarrheal disease. This evidence has challenged a foundational assumption that

Implications of Exposure to Fecal Bacteria," *American Journal of Tropical Medicine and Hygiene*, vol. 89, no. 4 (2013), 709; Jean H. Humphrey, "Child Undernutrition, Tropical Enteropathy, Toilets, and Handwashing," *Lancet*, vol. 374 (2009), 1032–35.

[21] Noel W. Solomons, Manolo Mazariegos, Kenneth H. Brown, and Kirk Klasing, "The Underprivileged, Developing Country Child: Environmental Contamination and Growth Failure Revisited," *Nutrition Reviews*, vol. 51, no. 11 (1993), 327–28.

Interestingly, researchers' attention to the link with chicken feces was drawn by the chicken breeders' maxim: "a dirty chicken is a poorly growing chicken." Chicken breeders had found that it was cheaper to add antibiotics to chicken feed than to build sanitary housing for the birds. The parallel with infants and children growing in highly unsanitary environments was far from exact. Some children – such as those who were infected or exposed to HIV and/or acutely malnourished – might be put on a regimen of antibiotics, if they had access to medical services, but the possibility to scale up to population level dosing with antibiotics was not in the cards. Such a program would have greatly accelerated antibiotic resistance. In addition, there were concerns that antibiotic use interfered with the microbiome and had been associated with antibiotic-associated diarrhea. Ethan K. Gough, Erica E. M. Moodle, Andrew J. Prendergast, Sarasa M. A. Johnson, Jean H, Humphrey, Rebecca J. Stoltzhus et al., "The Impact of Antibiotics on Growth in Children in Low and Middle Income Countries: Systematic Review and Meta-Analysis of Randomised Controlled Trials," *British Medical Journal*, Vol. 348 (2014).

[22] Francis M. Ngure, Brianna M. Reid, Jean H. Humphrey, Mduduzi N. Mbuya, Gretel Pelto, and Rebecca J. Stoltfus, "Water, Sanitation, and Hygiene (WASH), Environmental Enteropathy, Nutrition, and Early Child Development: Making the Links," *Annals of the New York Academy of Sciences*, vol. 1308 (2014), 121–24.

poor-quality drinking water was the primary cause of diarrheal disease.[23]

A third shift has evolved in linking the category of diarrheal disease with that of malnutrition. In many cases, the relationships are entwined. Malnutrition can cause diarrheal disease, and diarrheal infections can profoundly disrupt the body's ability to absorb and utilize nutrition.[24] The whys, hows, and wherefores of these dynamics are under investigation by scientists who are exploring the universe of the human gut.

## THE MICROBIOME

In recent years, biomedical scientists have launched major research projects to investigate the ecological world of the human microbiome.[25] These investigations promise to yield new understandings of our gut biota that will improve our abilities to treat intestinal infections, through improved drug uptake and better-targeted interventions. The human microbiome project will illuminate the chemical interactions between gut bacteria and the linings of our intestines; the transformational impact of diet on the microbiome; the relationship between the gut microbiome and other aspects of human health; and the roles that probiotics, fecal transplants, and microbiome vaccines can play in improving health outcomes. Some rather astonishing breakthroughs have already taken place. In 2017, for example, researchers discovered a new organ in the human body, known as the mesentery, that attaches the intestine to the wall of the abdomen, opening up the entirely new field of mesenteric science.[26] A revolution in biomedicine is in incubation.

[23] Valerie Curtis, Sandy Cairncross, and Raymond Yonli, "Domestic Hygiene and Diarrhoea – Pinpointing the Problem," *Tropical Medicine and International Health*, vol. 5, no. 1 (2000), 22–32.

[24] Jessica MacIntyre, Jennifer McTaggert, Richard L. Guerrant, and David M. Goldfarb, "Early Childhood Diarrhoeal Diseases and Cognition: Are We Missing the Rest of the Iceberg?," *Paediatrics and International Child Health*, vol. 34, no. 4 (2014), 295–307.

[25] The domain of investigation is broad, including the microbiome of the skin as well as the intestines. Most of the research, however, is focused on the gut. For an overview, see Jacques Ravel, Martin J. Blazer, Jonathan Braun, Eric Brown, Frederic D. Bushman, Eugene B. Chang, Julian Davies et al., "Human Microbiome Science: Vision for the Future, Bethesda, MD, July 24 to 26, 2013," *Microbiome*, vol. 2 (2014), 16, www.microbiomejournal.com/content/2/1/16.

[26] J. Calvin Coffey and D. Peter O'Leary, "The Mesentery: Structure, Function, and Role in Disease," *Lancet Gastroenterology & Hepatology*, vol. 1, no. 3 (2017), 238–47, https://doi.org/10.1016/S2468-1253(16)30026-7.

The research of the molecular scientists to date has resulted in new
characterizations of the bacterial assemblages within our intestinal systems. One set of findings has illuminated the fact that the composition of
the gut microbiota changes over the course of the human lifetime. The gut
biota of the newborn infant is strongly influenced by the gut bacteria of the
mother; the gut bacteria of breast-fed babies is less diverse, more stable,
and more protective than that of formula-fed babies; and the child's
bacterial assemblage will change dramatically over the first three years
of life.[27] The intestinal biota of pregnant women is different from women
who are not pregnant. The core intestinal biota of the elderly is markedly
different from younger adults.[28]

The microbiome research has also illuminated the fact that different
human communities possess rather different variants of a common microbiome. Researchers now think that there are three different types of
enterobacteria arrays or enterotypes.[29] These arrays may be determined
in part by genetic inheritance, although they are probably governed in
larger measure by the kinds and quantities of foods that we eat.[30]

In one sense, the research suggests the truism that we are what we eat.
There is a marked difference in the enterobacteria of those with a diet high
in protein and simple sugars (in the microbiome literature sometimes
referred to as the "Western diet") and those with a diet high in complex
carbohydrates. The histories of the major cultigens, farming systems, and
networks of international trade in foodstuffs have had a role in shaping
the microbial universes that we carry around within us. As have our
varying exposures to wildlife and domesticated livestock. As have our

[27] Wenguang Fan, Guicheng Huo, Xiaomin Li, Lijie Yang, Cuicui Duan, Tingting Wang, and
Junliang Chen, "Diversity of the Intestinal Microbiota in Different Patterns of Feeding
Infants by Illumina High-Throughput Sequencing," *World Journal of Microbiology and
Biotechnology*, vol. 29, no. 12 (2013), 2365–72.

[28] Marcus J. Claesson, Siobhán Cusack, Orla O'Sullivan, Rachel Greene-Diniz, Heleen de
Weerd, Edel Flannery, Julian R. Marchesi et al., "Composition, Variability, and
Temporal Stability of the Intestinal Microbiota of the Elderly," *Proceedings of the
National Academy of Sciences of the United States of America*, vol. 108, Suppl. 1
(2011), 4586–91, https://doi.org/10.1073/pnas.1000097107.

[29] Manimozhiyan Arumugam, Jeroen Raes, Eric Pelletier, Denis Le Paslier, Takuji
Yamada, Daniel R. Mende, Gabriel R. Fernandes et al., "Enterotypes of the Human
Gut Microbiome," *Nature*, vol. 473 (2011), 174–80, https://doi.org/10.1038
/nature09944.

[30] Studies in mice suggest that diet is the dominant factor in shaping gut microbiota.
Huizi Tan and Paul W. O'Toole, "Impact of Diet on the Human Intestinal
Microbiota," *Current Opinion in Food Science*, vol. 2 (2015), 71, https://doi.org/10
.1016/j.cofs.2015.01.005.

cultural inheritances of hygienic and nonhygienic practices. In the developed world, as these inheritances are at play, our profligate use of antibiotics is altering our gut bacteria.

We typically think of genetic variation between human populations as differences in the allele frequencies of our *Homo sapiens* genes. Yet because bacteria play such a significant role in regulating our basic metabolism of food and our immune responses to pathogens, we need to broaden our perspective to include the astounding genetic and metabolic diversity that can be found in the millions of genes and myriad gene functions within our gut microbial communities.[31] We are alive as a result of the vast and complex interactions that take place between our intestinal bacteria and our body organs.

Some of these interactions – perhaps the large majority of them – are mutually symbiotic, meaning that both human beings and our bacteria draw benefits from the interactions. Some may be commensal – that is, that the bacteria draw benefits from their colonization of our intestines while we do not – although this is more a theoretical possibility than an established fact. And some are clearly parasitic – that is, the bacteria draw energy resources from us. In doing so, they may weaken us or draw forth an immune response to an infection.

This typology of ecological associations – symbiotic mutualism, commensalism, and parasitism – is a useful as a heuristic construct, but it greatly simplifies our understandings of our relationship to our gut flora. This is because our gut flora interact within the intestinal microbiome, and they probably do so with bacteria elsewhere in the body.

The sheer number of bacteria in the human gut is astounding – on the order of 100 trillion or ten times the number of human body cells. And their variety is impressive, too. There are about 500 different species of bacteria in the gut, as well as some fungi, protozoa, and archaea. The bacteria in our intestines weigh up to about two kilograms, and they make up about 30 percent of our feces. They produce vitamins. They modulate our immune responses to intestinal challenges. They are critically determinative in our ability to fight off infectious pathogens. This has come into popular appreciation through the once unthinkable and now accepted

---

[31] Tanya Yatsunenko, Frederico E. Ray, Mark J. Manary, Indi Trehan, Maria Gloria Dominguez-Bello, Monica Contreras, Magda Magris et al., "Human Gut Microbiome Viewed across Age and Geography," *Nature*, vol. 486, no. 7402 (2012), 222–27, https://doi.org/10.1038/nature11053.

procedure of using fecal implants to bolster the immune response to *Clostridium difficile*, a particularly nasty bacterium that can cause devastating diarrhea in the elderly and others with compromised immune systems.

Our knowledge of the mysteries of the microbiome will develop as more research discoveries are made. It seems likely that the different enterotypes exercise an influence on the immunological response of the intestinal system to pathogenic challenge, and thus help to determine just how severe is our illness when we do get sick. And it is possible that they have a significant influence on the pathogens to which we are susceptible and thus help to determine whether or not we get sick at all.

The human microbiome is also, of course, made up of a vast number of viruses, many of which are highly beneficial to us, and most of which have not been studied. In years to come, the virologists, who are lining up for the microbiological study of the human biome, will certainly come to play a significant role. The human microbiome project will continue for decades, and over time it will revolutionize our understandings of our bodies and the internal environments that nourish us. It will open up a new field of medical interventions that can use this knowledge to improve human health. Already, it is increasingly accepted that we have a second "brain" located in our intestines that sends signals to the brain in our skulls and that we make decisions – for example, about what and what not to eat and how much – in response to these gut signals, without any conscious reflection.[32]

The preliminary discovery of three different human enterotypes suggests that fundamental environmental influences such as diet help to structural the bacterial and viral environments of our guts. Because our intestinal universes are extraordinarily complex and have changed over time with our changing diets and with our species' expansion into new biomes, our guts have had to adapt to our changing gut biota. This is an epitomic example of the physical incorporation of environmental influences into our bodies to which our genes must necessarily respond. The study of these epigenetic processes will open new paths for genomic study of the influence of intestinal flora on nutrition and growth and for pathogenic challenge and response.

---

[32] The best popular introduction to these perspectives is Guilia Enders, *Gut: The Inside Story of Our Body's Most Underrated Organ* (Vancouver, BC: Greystone Books, 2015).

## HISTORICAL EPIDEMIOLOGY AND CONTEMPORARY
## INTERVENTIONS

Infectious intestinal diseases are central to understanding the human past because they have played such a large role in our species' demographic history. Over millennia, they have quietly killed infants and young children and put a brake on population growth. They have also chronically sickened older children, adolescents, and adults, and in occasional epidemic outbreaks, they have scourged the populations of army encampments, refugee camps, prisons, and besieged towns. In recent centuries, infectious intestinal diseases have circulated globally as a result of the increased speed and volume of international trade and travel. Around the globe, they have afflicted populations whose water sources, excreta disposal systems, and access to energy supplies have been compromised through warfare, failed maintenance, or natural disaster.

Common infectious intestinal diseases have long been accepted as a natural part of the human condition. Most couples accepted the sad fact that they might lose children to one infectious disease or another, and the loss of children to diarrheal disease was unexceptional. It is only in the last few generations in developed countries with "improved" water supplies and excreta disposal systems that we have come to view childhood death as unnatural and exceptional.

In the twentieth century, public health investigations began to reveal the large dimensions of global childhood mortality and morbidity beyond the developed countries. There were two major lines of explanation for the high rates of childhood mortality and morbidity outside the developed countries and the falling rates within. One explanation was that decreasing childhood mortality was the result of increasing incomes and standards of living in the "modern" states. Another held that the so-called third epidemiological transition of lengthening life expectancy at birth and declining childhood mortality was principally a result of improvements in the quality of the water supply and in human waste disposal practices. Some analysts blended these understandings together, linking improvements in childhood survival either to access to more nutritious food, better clothing, and shelter made possible by improved economic circumstances or to investments in basic infrastructure made possible by improved state resources. These were useful perspectives from the domain of neoclassical development economics, but they were hardly comprehensive.

In the late twentieth century, new frames of reference were forged. Many thinkers came to understand intestinal diseases as diseases of the poor, and poverty was understood as the result of power relations between classes, ethnic groups, and state actors rather than as a "natural" condition of humanity. From this perspective, the historical power relations between colonizer and colonized; master and slave; and middle and upper classes versus lower classes were seen to be the most critical social determinants of health or illness that had left long legacies of inequality in their wakes. From this vantage point, the privileged classes could be seen to have largely allocated services to themselves; the underprivileged classes received modest services, if any. Sometimes the power differential between classes matched up closely with race or ethnicity, as, for example, throughout the European colonial world and in apartheid-era (and post-apartheid) South Africa and in the early and mid-twentieth-century US South (and in poorer US urban areas today). Virtually everywhere, power and income differentials were correlated with differential access to clean water, sanitation, and general health care. This was expressed in higher rates of childhood and adult mortality and morbidity.

This book explores the historical epidemiology of infectious intestinal disease, sanitation, and health interventions with the goal of illuminating a wide range of historical experiences with disease control. It takes the position that differing perspectives should be understood as different truths that can be usefully invoked to illuminate specific epidemiological contexts and that an exclusive insistence on any one set of perspectives can distort our broader appreciation of epidemiological processes in human history.

Depending on one's perspective, the fact that hundreds of thousands of children die every year from intestinal pathogens that are transmitted by a fecal–oral route might be seen to be a chronic problem that will improve with the passage of time if countries develop, a global public health crisis that must be prioritized in order to focus international programs and financial resources on it, or an ongoing challenge that can only be addressed by engaging local populations to find locally appropriate solutions. The fact that large numbers of children are infested by soil-transmitted worms can be seen as a minor public health problem that will ultimately be solved by economic growth, as a chronic problem that should continue to be addressed through the mass administration of deworming drugs, or as prima facie evidence of the need to end the practice of open defecation.

The assessment of differing critical perspectives is important because it is on this basis that we form our understandings of the nature of contemporary intestinal disease challenges and weigh the feasibility of proposed efforts to reduce the burden of disease. Our knowledge about the successes and failures of past interventions constitutes a foundation for planning new interventions.

# 2

# Early Change

In an almost unimaginably distant past, our early hominin ancestors shared the same intestinal biota as the nonhuman primates from which they were ever so slowly evolving. The bacteria, viruses, protozoa, and worms of our ancestors' intestinal systems – the early hominin enterotype – had developed to handle an omnivorous diet. Our early proto-human ancestors ate fruits, nuts, leaves, and insects, much as our evolutionary cousins, the nonhuman primates, do today. Then our hominin ancestors learned to share knowledge, and they embarked on an entirely new evolutionary path.

A first phase began when early hominins mastered fire and began to cook, perhaps as long as 1.8 million years ago. Over time, as our ancestors made good use of cooked animal proteins, their brain sizes began to increase. They began to be more selective in their food choices. As their diet changed, so did their guts. Their small and large intestines became much shorter, their stomachs more efficient. Our ancestors' bodies accommodated different assemblages of bacteria that broke down protein-rich foods easily, and their bodies evolved to hold digested foods in their guts for a shorter time before they were expelled as waste.

Our ancestors acquired their gut biota from their immediate environments – from their mothers during the passage through the birth canal, their kin with whom they were in intimate contact, and the animals, insects, plants, soils, and waters that made up the natural worlds in which they lived. Across the African biomes, during the course of the daily activities of hunting, gathering, scavenging, fishing, defecating, having sex, and eating they introduced a universe of bacteria, archaea, protozoa, helminths, and viruses to their intestinal tracts. Some of the microscopic guests took up residence in our ancestors' guts, and of those that did, the vast majority lived in mutually symbiotic relationships with them. Yet our ancestors also took on pathogens and parasites that either stripped nutrients or interrupted metabolic processes and made them sick. Some infections were transient, others debilitating or fatal.

## RETHINKING THE FIRST EPIDEMIOLOGICAL TRANSITION

Ongoing research across a range of scientific disciplines is reshaping what we know about the deep history of human disease. Until recently, the construct known as the first epidemiological transition has been broadly influential. It acknowledges an early history of "heirloom" diseases inherited from our hominin ancestors that includes parasites such as the *Taenia* tapeworms that we acquired from eating meat scavenged from the kills of other carnivorous predators.[1] Its core ideas are that during the era of the Neolithic agricultural revolution, beginning about 10,000 BCE and continuing into the late eighteenth and early nineteenth centuries CE, new agricultural practices allowed for unprecedented demographic growth and that the greater population densities in permanently settled communities allowed for the circulation of pathogens, many of which had jumped species from domesticated animals to human beings. The beginning of the Neolithic agricultural revolution thus is taken as the breakpoint between a deep human past of hunting and gathering and an ongoing transition to permanent settlement. The first epidemiological transition initiated an era of pestilence and famine that contrasted with an earlier, less disease-prone epoch of hunting and gathering.

This postulation of a first epidemiological transition, however, has recently become complicated by new scientific evidence. The evidence is not all of a piece, but it is broadly consilient with a revised understanding of early patterns in human history. Physical archaeologists, for example, have discovered that some early human groups lived from maritime resources, at least on a seasonal basis.[2] The finding challenges long-held

---

[1] Eric P. Hoberg, Nancy L. Alkire, Alan de Queiroz, and Arlene Jones, "Out of Africa: Origins of the Taenia Tapeworms in Humans," *Proceedings of the Royal Society of London B: Biological Sciences*, vol. 268 (2001), 781–87.

[2] Archaeologists have found the earliest evidence of dense seasonal settlement, dated to approximately 90,000 years ago, along the banks of the Zaire River in central Africa. John E. Yellen, Alison S. Brooks, Els Cornelissen, Michael J. Mehlman, and Kathlyn Stewart, "A Middle Stone Age Worked Bone Industry from Katanda, Upper Semliki Valley, Zaire," *Science*, vol. 268, no. 5210 (1995), 553–56.

assumptions that early human groups were hunters and gatherers. The evidence of seasonal riverine settlement in the deep past suggests new ways for understanding the epidemiological significance of early seasonally settled communities. It seems likely, for example, that settled sites near bounteous fish and/or shellfish resources may have been more or less continuously inhabited for extended periods of time. It seems likely that the coastal, lacustrine, and riverine settlements may have allowed for population densities sufficiently high to permit the ongoing transmission of falciparum malaria, for which the chains of transmission are much harder to maintain than for vivax malaria.[3] Some molecular evidence, for example, suggests that the transmission of falciparum malaria took place much earlier than the Neolithic agricultural revolution. This could only happen if some human population groupings were larger and less mobile than hunting and gathering groups.[4] Moreover, it seems likely that some groups engaged in the paracultivation of tubers, that is, in planting of tubers such as yams that are self-propagating, and that they may well have been seasonally settled in order to take better advantage of the harvests.[5]

Evidence from molecular science is also generating new perspectives on the history of extended settlement. Because the eggs of soil-transmitted intestinal worms must mature in the soils before they become infective, ongoing transmission requires that human beings are locally resident for weeks at a time (at a minimum) in order to become exposed to the mature eggs. Until recently, it was thought that during the earliest phases of the Neolithic agricultural revolution, when our ancestors domesticated the wild boar, human beings acquired the roundworm (*Ascaris lumbricöides*) from pigs that suffered from a nearly identical roundworm, *Ascaris suum*. The logic of the domestication was based upon the idea of mutualistic

---

[3] The lifecycle of the *Plasmodium falciparum* parasite does not have a latent liver phase. This means that new attacks of malaria can only come from infective mosquito bites and that in order to sustain an chain of infection the parasite must be transmitted on an ongoing basis. The *Plasmodium vivax* parasite, by contrast, has a dormant liver phase, which means that new attacks of malaria can reoccur months or even years after an infective bite. For this reason, vivax infections plagued human communities in tropical Africa deep in time, and the vivax malarial pressure selected for a genetic mutation, known as Duffy antigen negativity, that protected against vivax infections. See James L. A. Webb Jr., *Humanity's Burden: A Global History of Malaria* (New York: Cambridge University Press, 2009), 18–29.

[4] James L. A. Webb Jr., "Early Malarial Infections and the First Epidemiological Transition," in Michael Petraglia, Nicole Boivin, and Rémy Cressard (eds.), *From Colonization to Globalization: Species Movements in Human History* (New York: Cambridge University Press, 2017), 477–93.

[5] Webb, *Humanity's Burden*, 29–32.

exchange. The pigs cleaned up our ancestors' feces, which contained an estimated 8 percent of caloric value of the food that we consumed.[6] Our ancestors got a proximate environment somewhat less fouled by their own excrement and closer contact with the pigs that we slaughtered for meat as needed. One consequence of this domestication was that our ancestors became infected with the roundworm through ongoing contact with pig excrement, and eventually the human roundworm *Ascaris lumbricöides* became a separate species, distinct from the porcine roundworm *Ascaris suum*.

New molecular evidence indicates, however, that the species jump took place in the opposite direction. Pigs acquired their roundworm infections from us, indicating that we had roundworm infections long before our ancestors' domestication of the wild boar and before the transition to permanent settlements.[7] These intestinal worms seem to have been human parasites of long standing, and they traveled immense distances inside human bodies to populate new continents. Indeed, the presence of *Ascaris* eggs, detected in human coprolites in Brazil and Chile dated to 8,800 BP, confirms that human beings continued to carry roundworm infections long after some groups made their exodus from Africa.[8] This was true as well of tapeworm infections. We acquired them deep in the Pleistocene era, and much later we passed on tapeworms to cattle in which they speciated to become *Taenia saginata* and to swine in the separate lineages *T. asiatica* and *T. solium*.[9]

These bits and pieces of evidence are consonant with the view that the Neolithic agricultural revolution may not have constituted as sharp a break with the deeper patterns of disease transmission as has been

[6] David Waltner-Toews, *The Origin of Feces* (Toronto: ECW Press, 2013), 18.

[7] Gonçalves et al., "Human Intestinal Parasites in the Past," 106.

[8] Daniela Leles, Adauto Araújo, Luiz Frenando Ferreira, Ana Carolina Paulo Vincente, and Alena Mayo Iñiguez, "Molecular Paleoparasitological Diagnosis of *Ascaris* sp. from Coprolites: New Scenery of Ascariasis in Pre-Columbian South America Times," *Memórias do Instituto Oswaldo Cruz*, vol. 103, no. 1 (2008), 106–8.

[9] Hoberg et al., "Out of Africa: Origins of the Taenia Tapeworms in Humans," 786. Tapeworm eggs are passed in human feces. When the feces are eaten by pigs or cattle, the larvae develop inside the pig or cow and form cysts in the musculature. When human beings eat undercooked pork or beef, they swallow the cysts which develop into adult tapeworms in the human gut. These infections are called taeniasis.

Human beings also can become infected by drinking fluids or eating foods contaminated with tapeworm eggs or by putting contaminated fingers in their mouths. Tapeworm infections are not grouped as soil-transmitted helminthic infections because the tapeworm eggs do not mature in the soil. These infections are called cysticercosis. See www.cdc.gov /parasites/taeniasis/epi.html and www.cdc.gov/parasites/cysticercosis/epi.html.

presumed by the construct of the "first epidemiological transition." They also force us to consider our biological roles as disseminators of pathogens and thereby to move away from a more purely anthropocentric perspective that focused exclusively on what other animals' pathogens had done to us. Our distant ancestors seem to have had more varied ways of life than we had previously imagined, some of which predisposed them to new types of infections, and the dynamics of disease transmission, including those of some parasitic worms, seem to have been made possible by larger population groupings than we had previously imagined.

## PATTERNS OF VULNERABILITY

Early human beings had extensive exposure to human feces. This was not only because our ancestors had to deal with their own evacuations. It was because caregivers had to deal with the evacuations of infants and young children who, of course, were physiologically unable to control their bowels. This was a matter of epidemiological significance for all human groupings. It was, of course, possible to wash one's hands or wipe one's fingers on soil, leaves, or bark after cleaning an infant, but this was largely inefficacious in reducing the exposure to fecal pathogens. From earliest times, we were parties to a chain of infections that resulted in the early death of a large percentage of children.[10] Although human beings may not have realized that human feces were dangerous, even if they had there were limits to what they could do to minimize their exposure. Shit was a ubiquitous part of the human landscape.

Yet there were also benefits to human wastes. Human beings had long realized that human feces and urine, like those of other animals, were potent fertilizers. Plants generally grew more rapidly and larger when the soils from which they drew nutrients were manured with dung or urine. This knowledge had undoubtedly encouraged experiments with these natural materials for tens of millennia. Yet with the advent of agricultural settlements, the conservation of human excrement and urine became of practical value.

[10] Many societies used human excrement and urine for ritual purposes. The nineteenth-century naturalist John Gregory Bourke was fascinated by these practices and compiled evidence from a wide range of texts. See his *Compilation, Notes, and Memoranda Bearing upon the Use of Human Ordure and Human Urine* (Washington, DC, 1888) and *Scatologic Rites of All Nations* (Washington, DC: W. H. Lowdermilk, 1891).

Both could be applied to the soils, although most of the chemicals useful to promote plant growth are in human urine.[11] If human excrement and urine were separated, urine needed to be diluted in order to avoid "burning" the plants. Feces alone or in combination with urine and/or refuse products could be worked directly into the soils. Human excrement by itself was not abundantly rich in nutrients, but in most agricultural settings its use paid dividends. When applied to soils either prior to planting or after the seedlings matured, our natural solid waste would produce more robust plant growth and higher yields. When manures from farmyard animals were available and entered into the mix, they, too, boosted productivity. These practices, while rudimentary, were an integral part of what we would consider today sustainable agriculture.

The long human apprenticeship to vegeculture and agriculture launched a fundamental paradox in human history. As more communities were drawn away from fishing, gathering, and hunting as their core activities, their working of the land in good years yielded a bounty of calories from the tubers and grains and their practice of keeping domestic animals secured sources of fats and proteins. The strategies of storing foodstuffs and moving animals between pastures allowed for human populations to expand faster than ever before.

Yet the population increases had a decided downside. Higher human population densities in combination with the keeping of animals eventually facilitated the circulation of pathogens of numerous sorts. Many infections were zoonotic, that is, they vaulted over the species barriers from other animals to humans. Of the zoonoses, many of the most lethal were viral – such as chickenpox (ancient origins likely, with evolution in primates), smallpox (evolved from cattlepox, circa second millennium BCE), and measles (evolved from ungulates such as cattle, sheep, and goats, early second millennium CE).[12] Other zoonoses were

---

[11] The percentages vary with diet, but somewhere in the range of 70–88 percent of the nitrogen, 25–67 percent of the phosphorus, and 80–90 percent of the potassium of our bodily wastes are in urine, with the remainder in feces. James R. Mihelcic, Lauren M. Fry, and Ryan Shaw, "Global Potential of Phosphorus Recovery from Human Urine and Feces," *Chemosphere*, vol. 84, no. 6 (2011), 833; H. Kirchmann and S. Pettersson, "Human Urine – Chemical Composition and Fertilizer Use Efficiency," *Fertilizer Research*, vol. 40, no. 2 (1995), 149–54.

[12] Timothy R. Wagenaar, Vincent T. K. Chow, Chantanee Buranathai, Pranee Thawatsupha, and Charles Grose, "The Out of Africa Model of Varicella-Zoster Virus Evolution: Single Nucleotide Polymorphisms and Private Alleles Distinguish Asian Clades from European/ North American Clades," *Vaccine*, vol. 21, no. 11–12 (2003), 1072–81, https://doi.org/10 .1016/S0264-410X(02)00559-5; S. Shchelkunov, "How Long Ago Did Smallpox Virus

bacterial – such as brucellosis (acquired from unpasteurized milk or undercooked meat) and salmonellosis (also from milk, milk products such as cheese, or undercooked meat). And as had been the case with some parasites, other pathogens, known as anthroponoses, jumped from humans to domesticated animals. It is possible that this was the case of tuberculosis.[13] The estimates of the onset of the earliest human infections with tuberculosis vary widely. According to some specialists, it is possible that early human beings may have become infected with tuberculosis during the distant epoch in which they domesticated fire, or perhaps in the late Mesolithic era, or even the early Neolithic era and then infected cattle in the process of animal domestication.[14]

Many of the infectious diseases, particularly viral infections such as measles, mumps, chickenpox, and smallpox, eventually spread through settled populations without much regard for class or gender. If the populations were large enough that the infections were continuously transmitted, the viruses afflicted only those who had not yet developed immunities – the youngest members of the societies. These new "childhood diseases" put the brakes on what would have been even more rapid population growth.

The burden of infectious intestinal diseases fell unevenly on the settled populations, producing different impacts on the social hierarchy of priests (and others who eschewed agricultural labor) and farmers and slaves. Infectious intestinal diseases certainly were not unknown in the higher classes, but they heavily burdened those who toiled in the fields, walked across shit-laden expanses in bare feet, plunged their hands into soils to plant, weed, and harvest, drank from contaminated water sources, and worked with domesticated animals. Those who used their own excrement along with animal manure to fertilize the crops more fully exposed themselves and their families to bacterial, viral, protozoal, and helminthic infections. Acute afflictions typically caused diarrhea. Chronic infections

---

Emerge?," *Archives of Virology*, vol. 154, no. 12 (2009), 1865–71; Yuki Furuse, Akira Suzuki, and Hitoshi Oshitani, "Origin of Measles Virus: Divergence from Rinderpest Virus between the 11th and 12th Centuries," *Virology Journal*, vol. 7, no. 52 (2010), https://doi.org/10.1186/1743-422X-7-52.

[13] Iñaki Comas and Sebastien Gagneux, "The Past and Future of Tuberculosis Research," *PLoS Pathology*, vol. 5, no. 10 (2009), e1000600.

[14] Rebecca H. Chisholm, James M. Trauer, Darren Curnoe, and Mark M. Tanaka, "Controlled Fire Use in Early Humans Might Have Triggered the Evolutionary Emergence of Tuberculosis," *Proceedings of the National Academy of Sciences*, vol. 113 (2016), 9051–56.

could be more insidious, causing anemia and worse. Those who kept animals in or near their compounds exposed their infants and young children to both animal and human feces. The pathogens ingested by the young caused enteropathy with physical and mental stunting. The physical condition and stature of the agricultural laboring classes came to be distinguishable from that of their rulers. In this manner, the first chapter in the book of the "diseases of poverty" was written.

Over long millennia, population growth in the river basins forced out-migration. New communities formed where water and soil resources beckoned and where grasses and shrubs could support domesticated livestock. Eventually, here and there, populations that practiced mixed farming reached a critical mass, and the lifestyle of pastoral nomadism began to emerge. Settlers with skills in animal husbandry broke away from their settlements with their herds of sheep, goats, and cattle to explore new pasturelands. From a hearth in the northeastern Mediterranean zone, cattle, sheep, and goat herders pioneered transhumance patterns that allowed them to move their animals to fresh pastures at different seasons of the year. (Pigs could not be herded; they were penned.) Some cattle herders and their animals drifted into new regions, southward to the Nile valley and into a relatively verdant Sahara and then eventually farther south into eastern Africa and westward across the southern shore of the Sahara. Others herders drifted eastward toward the Tigris–Euphrates, Indus, and Yellow River (Huang-He) valleys and floodplains.[15]

In some ecological zones, other animal species were domesticated and new forms of pastoralism developed. In a region to the north of the Black and Caspian Seas, hunters domesticated the horse and organized themselves into effective raiding groups. In the alpine settings of northern Tibet, hunters domesticated the yak, and in northeastern Afghanistan or southwestern Turkestan, the Bactrian camel. The dromedary camel was broken to service in arid lands. Hunters learned to herd reindeer in the northern wastes of Eurasia.

[15] Melinda A. Zeder, "Domestication and Early Agriculture in the Mediterranean Basin: Origins, Diffusion, and Impact," *Proceedings of the National Academy of Sciences*, vol. 105, no. 33 (2008), 11597–604; Jonathan Ethier, Eszter Bánffy, Jasna Vuković, Krassimir Leshtakov, Krum Bacvarov, Mélanie Roffet-Salque, Richard P. Evershed, and Maria Ivanova, "Earliest Expansion of Animal Husbandry beyond the Mediterranean Zone in the Sixth Millennium BC," *Scientific Reports*, vol. 7, no. 1 (2017), 7146, https://doi.org/10.1038/s41598-017-07427-x; Jared E. Decker, Stephanie D. McKay, Megan M. Rolf, JaeWoo Kim, Antonio Molina Alcalá, Tad S. Sonstegard, Olivier Hanotte et al., "Worldwide Patterns of Ancestry, Divergence, and Admixture in Domesticated Cattle," *PLoS Genetics*, vol. 10, no. 3 (2014), e1004254.

Along the southern shore of the Sahara, early immigrants had introduced sheep, goats, cattle, and camels in the first millennium CE and created a zone of pastoralism that abutted dryland farming. The practice of livestock keeping could not be extended farther to the south because of the presence of the tsetse fly. It transmitted the disease trypanosomiasis that was lethal to the breeds of animals that had been domesticated in the Fertile Crescent. The tsetse fly effectively prevented the evolution of mixed farming systems. This constraint was surmounted in the eastern African "cattle corridor" that stretched from western Kenya south to Zimbabwe, in which herders burned out the brush habitats of the tsetse fly and established a long, narrow north–south pastoral zone. It was not integrated, however, with the local systems of farming. The success of the pastoral economy in eastern Africa depended on moving the herds to grasslands that sprouted after the seasonal burns rather than on pasturing the herds on farmers' fields.

The lifestyles of pastoral nomadism had many rigors, but from the point of view of disease transmission, they marked a major improvement over the class-dominated worlds of the incipient civilizational centers. To be sure, the pastoral nomads, like the densely settled agricultural communities, could be devastated by the introduction of viral and bacterial pathogens. But these disease encounters happened less frequently, particularly as many groups migrated to greener pastures and lived at distance from the civilizational zones. The herders who moved north from the original centers of domestication in the Fertile Crescent toward the interior of Eurasia received something of a respite from disease, because the Eurasian winters killed off some of the bacterial and viral pathogens. The herders who moved south into tropical Africa were not so lucky, and there they encountered the range of disease challenges that early human communities had faced before historic out-migration many tens of thousands of years earlier. From their domesticated livestock, however, the infectious intestinal diseases challenges were relatively minor – principally from *E. coli* and *Salmonella enterica* bacteria that could cause acute food poisoning, but were rarely life-threatening.

All pastoral nomads, however, were mobile, and this meant that they moved away from their defecations (rather than living in close proximity to them). Without close contact with agricultural fields, soil-transmitted helminthic infections were almost impossibly difficult to sustain. The nomadic ways of life had additional consequences for the pastoral microbiome. Animal herders adapted to subsist directly from the milk, blood, and meat of their herds. This meant the accommodation of a different bacterial assemblage to facilitate the digestion of a diet rich in animal products.

## ZONES OF INFECTIOUS INTESTINAL DISEASE

As settled communities became incorporated into the spheres of influence of the core civilizational centers, distinctive zones of infectious intestinal disease formed. Within these zones were gradients of disease transmission that tailed away from the major river basins of the Nile, Tigris–Euphrates, Punjab, Ganges, and Huang-He (Yellow) Rivers into the surrounding hinterlands. The core areas were characterized first and foremost by higher population densities, which facilitated the transmission of pathogens to produce what are known as crowd diseases. The more distant villages participated less intensively in trade and had less exposure to crowd diseases. Those living within the settled areas, either in the core or peripheral communities, lived with ongoing exposure to their own excrement. This amplified the burden both of fecal–oral transmitted disease and helminthic infections.

Distinctive differences emerged in the styles of agriculture in the Old World agricultural zones. One important difference was between the subtropical and the temperate zones. In temperate northern China, for example, early farmers began to domesticate common millet about 10,000 years ago, in the same era that they domesticated chickens and pigs, their principal barnyard animals.[16] Cattle were present, but they do not appear to have ever formed part of the core farm economy. The northern soils were not rich, but they were adequate for growing millet.[17] The early farmers learned that fertilizers could boost yields, and they took to conserving adult human bodily waste, mixing it with pig manure, and then adding straw, debris, and soil, humus, or clay. The logic of the practice was so dominant that some historians think that these practices must have begun several thousand years ago.[18] If so, the result

---

[16] Hai Xiang, Jianqiang Gao, Baoquan Yu, Hui Zhou, Dawei Cai, Youwen Zhang, Xiaoyong Chen, Xi Wang, Michael Hofreiter, and Xingbo Zhao, "Early Holocene Chicken Domestication in Northern China," *Proceedings of the National Academy of Sciences*, vol. 111, no. 49 (2014), 17564–69.

[17] Houyuan Lu, Jianping Zhang, Kam-biu Liu, Naiqin Wu, Yumei Li, Kunshu Zhou, Maolin Ye et al., "Earliest Domestication of Common Millet (*Panicum miliaceum*) in East Asia Extended to 10,000 Years Ago," *Proceedings of the National Academy of Sciences*, vol. 106, no. 18 (2009), 7367–72.

[18] Donald Worster, "The Good Muck: Toward an Excremental History of China," *RCC Perspectives: Transformations in Environment and Society*, no. 5 (2017), 25–27.

might be considered a first apex of recycling and sustainability. In central China, wet rice cultivation seems to have developed in approximately 8,000 to 10,000 BP, and spread into northern China and perhaps to Japan by 6,000 BP. Rice also diffused south and west, eventually hybridizing with an independently cultivated rice in India perhaps in the fourth millennium BCE.[19] In the wet rice cultures, too, human waste, supplemented with animal wastes from the semi-domesticated water buffalo (which was harnessed to work but never bred in captivity), eventually became a core component of the agronomic system.

The routine handling of human waste came at a cost to human health. The utilization of human manures spawned a wide distribution of all three soil-transmitted helminthic infections throughout the Eurasian tropics, subtropics, and temperate regions. Roundworm was the most widely recognized because it was large enough to be seen by the unpracticed eye. Representations of it appear in early Egyptian hieroglyphics, Greek and Roman literature, the Babylonian Talmud, the Indic Vedas, early Arab and Persian literature, and early Chinese texts.[20] In the prehistory of the Americas, however, there seem to have been relatively few soil-transmitted helminthic infections. The reasons for this disparity are not well understood. It is possible that it is owing to the efficacy of Native American medicine, settlement patterns, fecal avoidance, and/or lower population densities.[21]

## EURASIAN ATTITUDES TOWARD HUMAN WASTE

Although there is much that has been lost to the historical record, across the length of Eurasia cultural attitudes toward human excrement and urine had developed by the first millennium CE. These were expressed in the manuring practices that were the foundations of the agricultural economies. The differing attitudes toward human waste seem to have

[19] Dorian Fuller, "Pathways to Asian Civilizations: Tracing the Origins and Spread of Rice and Rice Cultures," *Rice*, vol. 4, no. 3 (2011), 78–92; Briana L. Gross and Zhijun Zhao, "Archaeological and Genetic Insights into the Origins of Domesticated Rice," *Proceedings of the National Academy of Sciences*, vol. 111, no. 17 (2014), 6190–97.

[20] Representations also appear in the Spanish postconquest literatures on Peru and Mexico. For a survey, see R. Hoeppli, "The Knowledge of Parasites and Parasitic Infections from Ancient Times to the 17th Century," *Experimental Parasitology*, vol. 5, no. 4 (1956), 398–419.

[21] Adauto Araújo, Karl Reinhard, and Luiz Fernando Ferreira, "Paleoparasitology – Human Parasites in Ancient Material," *Advances in Parasitology*, vol. 89 (2015), 21–22.

reflected in part the influences of various religious and philosophical traditions.

At one end of the spectrum were the societies in East and Southeast Asia that were influenced by Buddhist, Daoist, and Confucian thought. There, human excreta were valued, scrupulously collected, and dedicated to agricultural use. In Japan, Korea, and China, human wastes, either raw or composted with vegetable refuse and animal dejecta, were deemed critical to agricultural productivity. In these societies, the work of human waste collection was reviled, but not the workers themselves.[22]

At the other extreme, in the wider Indic world, cultural beliefs about purity and pollution discouraged but did not exclude the use of human excreta in agriculture. According to Hindu doctrine – with its core notion of a hierarchical caste system maintained through the inheritance of caste identity at birth – members of the upper castes needed to avoid exposure to the human waste of those in the lower castes. At least by the time of the expansion of Islam in the eleventh century CE, the tasks of feces disposal fell upon the Dalits, the "untouchables" theoretically outside of the caste system whose work was considered so defiling that they perforce defiled everything that they touched beyond the cesspits.[23] Most of the excrement of the Indic world was disposed of in bodies of water or at dump sites, rather than used in agriculture. The consequence was that many farmers in India made do with animal dung principally from cattle that were considered sacred.[24]

Societies in the Muslim and Christian zones of western Eurasia had a nuanced appreciation of human manure, and nowhere in western Eurasia was the use or non-use of human waste an important cultural or religious signifier. In the Qur'an, there was no reference concerning the permissibility of using human excrement for manure. Some Arab agricultural texts offered explicit advice on how and where to deploy human feces, although the excreta were regarded as impure and their

---

[22] S. B. Hanley, "Urban Sanitation in Preindustrial Japan," *Journal of Interdisciplinary History*, vol. 18, no. 1 (1987), 1–26; Yong Xue, "Treasure Nightsoil as If It Were Gold: Economic and Ecological Links between Urban and Rural Areas in Late Imperial Jiangnan," *Late Imperial China*, vol. 26, no. 1 (2005), 41–71.

[23] For this view, see B. N. Srivastava, *Manual Scavenging in India: A Disgrace to the Country* (New Delhi: Concept, 1997), 16–17.

[24] Vanaja Ramprasad, "Manure, Soil and the Vedic Literature: Agricultural Knowledge and Practice on the Indian Subcontinent over the Last Two Millennia," in Richard Jones (ed.), *Manure Matters* (Surrey: Ashgate, 2012), 173–84. Tellingly, there appears to be no mention of the use of human excreta as manure in the Vedic literature.

use required ablutions.[25] Nor in the Old nor New Testament was there a religious prohibition against the use of human waste as fertilizer.[26] Within the Greek and Roman regions that became Christianized, human excreta were just one of several materials for soil enrichment. Farming systems that integrated sheep, goats, pigs, and oxen had a lot of natural material to work. The patterns of use were local and sub-regional. Some landowners fertilized with human waste; others did not.[27]

EARLY URBAN SANITATION

The inhabitants of the earliest permanent settlements were by necessity directly dependent upon surface waters. Farmsteads, compounds, villages, towns, and early cities were all located along rivers, streams, or lakes. The early coastal settlements were found in the river deltas. The core logistical imperative was ready access to potable water, the elixir of life itself.

Early villagers dug wells in a few areas with underground water resources that they could burrow through the soils to reach. The earliest wells discovered by archaeologists were rudimentary affairs, shored up by wood scaffolding and bound with raffia nets. They were also relatively shallow, because the workers only had bronze and wooden digging tools. The early wells were unlined and could be polluted by fecal matter that percolated into the subsoils.

[25] Daniel Varisco, "Zibl and Zira'a: Coming to Terms with Manure in Arab Agriculture," in Richard Jones (ed.), *Manure Matters* (Surrey: Ashgate, 2012), 134–36.

[26] Jews and Muslims looked upon dogs and pigs with disgust, owing to the fact that they consumed human and other animal feces, and they banned the consumption of these animals by religious law. Christians, on the other hand, did consume swine (domesticated pigs and wild boar), although they did not eat dogs (as was done in much of mainland eastern Asia and in the pre-Columbian Americas). André G. Haudricourt, "Le role des excrétats dans la domestication," *L'Homme*, vol. 17, no. 2–3 (1977), 125–26.

This probably reflected the legacy of early, pre-Christian hunting traditions to the north of the Mediterranean, the natural habitat of the wild boar, and the practice of keeping of pigs in the Aegean region, where in some areas such as mainland Greece, the pig was considered a sacred animal, suitable for sacrifice. Frederick J. Simoons, *Eat Not This Flesh: Food Avoidances from Prehistory to the Present*, 2nd ed. (Madison: University of Wisconsin Press, 1994), 29–32.

[27] Richard Jones, "Why Manure Matters," in Richard Jones (ed.), *Manure Matters* (Surrey: Ashgate, 2012), 1–11; Robert Shiel, "Science and Practice: The Ecology of Manure in Historical Retrospect," in Richard Jones (ed.), *Manure Matters* (Surrey: Ashgate, 2012), 13–23.

In the early Neolithic, significant threats to health began to emerge in the village and town clusters. Communities in the socially stratified, urbanizing settlements not only drew their water from their immediate environs, but they dumped their waste back into the rivers and lakes or deposited it nearby, and it could be swept into the water sources during heavy storms. The overall results were clear enough: the emerging urban areas were the most stratified and most lethal environments.[28]

How did early village and town dwellers attempt to counter these threats to health? The first written strategies for the control of infectious intestinal diseases counseled the purification of water. Sanskrit inscriptions from the first millennium BCE in the corpus of Ayurvedic medical knowledge and from the Suśruta Samhita recommended the boiling of water, exposure of water to sunlight, filtering it through charcoal or sand and coarse gravel, or repeatedly dipping a heated iron into a container of water. In the Mediterranean region, many philosophers and medical writers from the first millennium BCE onward advised letting water settle to remove impurities, filtering water through cloth or porous vessels, and boiling water to improve its taste or to render it more healthful.[29] Boiling water, in particular, was time consuming and fuel intensive, and it seems likely that other purification strategies were not regularly available to the nonelite population.

Quite apart from the threats to health was the problem of stench. All early agricultural communities innovated, designating terrains such as fields, woods, and beaches as appropriate sites for defecation, where the repulsive odors of concentrated human waste could be localized, although farmers, workers, and children often had to relieve themselves when and where opportunities permitted. The localization of stench was not possible in the more densely settled, urban environments where, regardless of the rudimentary arrangements for human excreta disposal, a pall of shit and urine permeated the streets.

---

[28] Researchers have identified hookworm in some of the earliest farming sites (4000–2800 BCE) in Europe. Interestingly, hookworm is not found in later sites during the Bronze and Iron Ages. This may be an artefact of the decomposition of the sites or, possibly, evidence that farmers made greater use of latrines. Piers D. Mitchell, "Human Parasites in Medieval Europe: Lifestyle, Sanitation, and Medical Treatment," *Advances in Parasitology*, vol. 90 (2015), 1–32.

[29] Moses N. Baker, *The Quest for Pure Water: The History of Water Purification from the Earliest Records to the Twentieth Century* (Denver, CO: American Water Works Association, 1981), 1–8.

A few of the emerging civilizational centers addressed the problem of human waste pollution through civic engineering. Archaeologists discovered at Habuba Kabira, on the Euphrates River in Syria, an Uruk settlement dating to the fourth millennium BCE with cylindrical pipes that appear to have been used for wastewater; there does not seem to have been a system to bring water to the households. In ancient southern Mesopotamia, there was no infrastructure either to remove waste or to provide clean water, although some households had deep pit toilets and some larger buildings had sloped-drain toilets that emptied into the street. Toilets of any kind, however, were few in number, and most urban residents must have either defecated on a culturally designated terrain or used a container within the house that would be emptied outside.[30] Practices undoubtedly varied. In Egypt, defecation in the open was the rule. The torrid environment caused human shit, if not first consumed by scavenging dogs, to desiccate and become less offensive.[31]

The first truly major advance seems to have taken place in the third millennium BCE at Mohenjo-Daro in Pakistan. The city had 700 brick-lined wells in the city, one for every three houses or so. The urban residents emptied their waste into open sewer drains. Rainstorms flushed the household effluent into soak pits. Because the availability of well water and sewer drainage in Mohenjo-Daro is strikingly different from other early urban environments, some scholars have speculated that the commonly shared practices may be related to the apparent absence of a sharply delineated social hierarchy.[32]

Eventually storm sewers and open pits for human waste became the universal hallmarks of early towns and cities.[33] Their degree of

[30] Augusta McMahon, "Waste Management in Early Urban Southern Mesopotamia," in Piers D. Mitchell (ed.), *Sanitation, Latrines and Intestinal Parasites in Past Populations* (Surrey: Ashgate, 2015), 19–40.

[31] D. M. Dixon, "A Note on Some Scavengers of Ancient Egypt," *World Archaeology*, vol. 21, no. 2 (1989), 193–97.

[32] M. Jansen, "Water Supply and Sewage Disposal at Mohenjo-Daro," *World Archaeology*, vol. 21, no. 2 (1989), 177–92; D. M. Dixon, "Population, Pollution and Health in Ancient Egypt," in P. R. Cox and J. Peel (eds.), *Population and Pollution* (New York: Academic Press, 1972), 29–36.

In this regard, Mohenjo-Daro was not a unique outlier. Early settlements along the banks of the Niger Bend, organized in what appear to be occupational or caste divisions, show no evidence of an absolutist hierarchy. Roderick J. McIntosh, *Ancient Middle Niger: Urbanism and the Self-Organizing Landscape* (Cambridge: Cambridge University Press, 2005).

[33] Soak pits handled human excreta and other household liquid wastes. Today, underground septic systems that allow household effluent to drain into the soil are generally

elaboration varied considerably. Engineers in the ancient cities of the Harappa civilization in the Indus River valley, such as those in the port city of Lothal, designed latrines that were emptied by tidal action. Some of the Minoan palaces of the second millennium BCE, such as Knossos, had sophisticated sewerage that served the elite.[34] Aegean engineers designed urban systems similar to Harappa, with household connections to dump wastewater into the storm sewers. The Aegean sewers typically were underground and, at least in some cases, had been constructed by war captives. If the cities were sited near rivers, the wastewater could be routed there.

Innovation continued in classical Greece. The Greeks built public lavatories with expanded capacities, the largest of which could accommodate dozens of users at a time. Most residents of the cities did not have access to them. Portable vessels were probably the most common private accommodations.[35] The Romans also built public latrines, but they, too, served a small percentage of urban dwellers. The Romans valued human excrement as fertilizer and carted much of the urban excreta deposited in cesspits to nearby fields. Household latrines, for example, were often sited in kitchens, probably because of convenience. From there, the excreta could be thrown out with other kitchen wastes to compost.

The Romans, with their enormously powerful state and vast public resources, designed the most advanced systems of storm sewers in the world in the late centuries of the first millennium BCE and the first centuries of the first millennium CE. (On the eastern rim of Eurasia, the early Chinese dynasties also constructed urban storm drainage systems, but they were rudimentary by comparison.) The core urban centers of

referred to as leach fields. Cesspits were generally reserved for the deposition of human excreta and solid household wastes such as food scraps. Cesspits lined with brick or stone are sometimes referred to as privy vaults.

Latrines could be simple pits or trenches for defecation, either open-air or protected for privacy and against the weather by walls and/or roofs.

[34] The total extent of the sewerage system within the Knossos palace ran to 150 meters. Most palaces did not, however, have either bathrooms or sewers. They were a convenience not a necessity. A. N. Angelakis, D. Koutsoyiannis, and G. Tchobanoglous, "Urban Wastewater and Stormwater Technologies in Ancient Greece," *Water Research*, vol. 39 (2005), 210–20.

[35] Georgios P. Antoniou and Andreas N. Angelakis, "Latrines and Wastewater Sanitation Tehnologies in Ancient Greece," Piers D. Mitchell (ed.), *Sanitation, Latrines and Intestinal Parasites in Past Populations* (Surrey: Ashgate, 2015), 53.

Roman world had underground networks that funneled rainwater, over-
flow from the fountains and public basins, and wastes into the adjoining
rivers or seas. The networks did not, as a rule, feature drainage connections to houses. Private owners could undertake this expense if they
desired, although apparently few did. The sewers carried away some of
the bulky road excreta swept off by rainstorms but did little to reduce the
overall urban exposure to human and animal wastes. Fecal smears covered the roadsides. Moreover, as would be the case in settlements all over
the world, the exposed animal and human fecal matter was fertile ground
for the breeding of flies, and the domestic flies spread the filth to food
supplies.

The Romans complemented their storm sewers with the world's most
sophisticated water delivery system. In a major engineering triumph, the
Romans built aqueducts that stretched for miles across the countryside to
bring water to urban areas from distant protected sources, including
springs and lakes. The aqueduct water was available from urban fountains
for drinking, cooking, and bathing. The health impact of this extraordinary civic accomplishment was apparently slight. According to the historian Alex Scobie, the public basins and fountains were almost certainly
contaminated with wastes, offal, and the carcasses of dead animals.[36] Life
expectancies in the Roman world remained low, and childhood mortality
rates high, as in the rest of the world.

The overall picture of the impacts of early urban settlements on health
is thus rather dark. As populations gradually pushed into new ecological
zones, and as settlements increased in number and size across the Old
World, there was scant overall improvement in human health, and likely
none at all in the urban settlements. As historians and demographers have
documented, even as late as the early twentieth century, cities typically
experienced a net negative rate of population growth. To the extent that
urban populations grew, it was a result of in-migration. Some of this
urban human wastage was attributable to the phenomena of crowd diseases. Epidemics could cause enormous loss of life and general panic. But
much loss of life was so commonplace that it barely warranted mention in
the surviving historical record. In infancy and the early years of childhood,
when insidious bacterial and viral intestinal pathogens caused diarrhea,
death was a frequent visitor. Infants and small children died from dehydration in vast numbers. Their deaths helped to keep the overall global life

[36] Alex Scobie, "Slums, Sanitation, and Mortality in the Roman World," *Klio*, vol. 86, no. 2
(1986), 399–433.

expectancy at birth to roughly twenty-five years of age until the eighteenth century.[37]


Our earliest ancestors participated in a long chain of infectious disease transmission that they shared with other great apes because their infants required intimate caregiving and defecated in intimate proximity to their caregivers. Yet the first *Homo sapiens*, and the precursory hominin species from which they emerged, were already biologically distinct in their brains, intestinal systems, and intestinal biota from other great apes. They had been transformed by culture.

Ongoing cultural evolution continued to propel us into new domains. Some distant forebears settled seasonally along the seacoasts, riverbanks, and lakesides to harvest shellfish or to fish. These groups were larger and had a greater potential to transmit infectious intestinal pathogens, because more people were living in close proximity and fecal pollution increased in scale. Later, when more recent ancestors took up agriculture and some eventually congregated in urban settlements, disease transmission intensified. Infants and small children – whose immune systems had not yet developed – bore the lion's share of the burden. Their deaths were a brake on human population growth.


[37] James C. Riley, *Rising Life Expectancy: A Global History* (New York: Cambridge University Press, 2001).

# 3

# Diffusion and Amplification

Over most of the last two and a half millennia, infectious intestinal pathogens quietly took their toll, principally on infants and children. Many outbreaks in both rural settings and towns were limited in scale, contracted in households where fecal matter had inadvertently contaminated food and household water supplies. Among the communities that practiced floodplain agriculture, such as those in the area of contemporary Bangladesh, the infections were frequently widespread because during the high-water seasons, highly diluted human waste flooded dwellings, fields, and wells. In cities, the prevalence of intestinal disease was elevated, because of close quarters that facilitated transmission and the fecal contamination of rivers from which residents drew their water. During times of warfare, these dynamics were reenacted on the fields of battle. Military encampments were mobile cities where the abysmal hygienic conditions sickened warriors and transferred intestinal pathogens to noncombatants.

Only in recent centuries – following the discovery of the Americas and the rise of transoceanic trade – did outbreaks of infectious intestinal diseases get recorded more frequently and is it possible to appreciate their significance more exactly. In the early centuries of global maritime trade, the groundwork was laid for more extensive infectious intestinal disease transmission.

## THE EARLY DIFFUSION OF INFECTIOUS INTESTINAL DISEASE TO THE AMERICAS

During the sixteenth century, Spanish conquistadors, clerics, merchants, soldiers, and sailors introduced to the Caribbean islands and the densely populated Aztec and Incan Empires some diseases that were common in the Mediterranean region. The Portuguese did the same in coastal Brazil. The tsunami of pathogens proved exceptionally lethal because the peoples of the Americas had had no prior experience with them and thus no hard-earned immunological defenses. The timing could not have been worse. The pathogens were unleashed in the midst of Spanish military campaigns that ignited civil warfare within the Aztec and Incan Empires. The war-torn populations were exposed to severe trials, scarcities, the nightmare of living through societal disintegration, and later the rigors of labor service under the conquerors' whip. Over the first century of contact with Europeans, the regional populations plummeted by 90 percent, the largest such demographic decline in world history.[1]

Historians had long thought that the principal biological killers were smallpox and measles. But diarrheal disease must now be added to the list. Recent research in Mexico indicates that *Salmonella enterica* serovar Paratyphi C – one variant of the pathogen that causes typhoid fever – was deeply implicated in the carnage. The discovery of this pathogen in a mid-sixteenth-century mass cemetery in Mexico associated with an epidemic locally known as *cocoliztli* suggests that typhoid fever may have been one of the important killers of Native American populations.[2]

In a later phase, the currents of international trade, gaining strength in the seventeenth century, swept other intestinal pathogens into the Americas. These produced patterns of endemic infections rather than horrifying epidemics, in part because the pathogens were generally not lethal and because they principally affected European and African immigrants, some of whom had prior experience with them. Native American populations at the time were in full collapse.

---

[1] The absolute sizes of the precontact populations of the Aztec and Incan worlds are not known with certainty.

[2] Å. J. Vågene, M. G. Campana, N. M. R. García, C. G. Warinner, M. A. Spyrou, A. Andrades Valtueña, D. Huson et al., "*Salmonella enterica* Genomes Recovered from Victims of a Major 16th Century Epidemic in Mexico," *bioRxiv* (2017), 106740, https://doi.org/10.1101/106740.

Not all agree. The anthropologist Sandra Guevara, in her presentation "Images and Words: An Approximation to Cocoliztli's Diagnosis through Indigenous Codices" at the 2018 annual meeting of the American Association for the History of Medicine, contended that the indigenous documentary evidence depicting the mid-sixteenth-century epidemic does not suggest the symptoms associated with infectious intestinal diseases and that the human remains investigated by the molecular scientists come from a cemetery that is not associated with the 1545–50 epidemic.

In the late sixteenth and early seventeenth centuries, as Europeans began to expand the cultivation of sugar, tobacco, and coffee on New World plantations, they scrambled to find workers. There were two principal sources: the European poor who sold themselves into indentured service and African captives who were sold into slavery to European traders. Both Europeans and Africans were put to hard labor on the same plantations. For a generation or two, they worked side by side under the tropical sun. But by the second half of the seventeenth century, after European trading companies had inadvertently introduced yellow fever and falciparum malaria to the Americas, plantation owners noticed that many of the European indentured servants met an untimely death.[3] As a result, the European trading companies turned decisively toward the slave-trading ports on the western coast of Africa. Over the next three centuries, the transatlantic trade reduced millions of Africans to misery. The historical records are not sufficiently detailed to sort out the relative importance of overwork, poor nutrition, physical abuse, torture, and disease to net population decline. These factors collectively created an environment that was toxic to working age adults as well as infants and young children. Africans whose cultures celebrated fertility could not produce enough surviving children to replace themselves.

The Africans' suffering began well before they landed in the Americas. The hygienic conditions on the slave ships were grim. Many contracted dysentery, a generic descriptor of a painful intestinal infection that caused abdominal cramps and watery stools, passed with blood, mucus, or pus. Dysentery was the single most lethal affliction for those crammed beneath decks, responsible for approximately 40 percent of the deaths of African captives.[4]

Suffering from dysentery was not restricted to the Africans in transit to the Americas. There was also a demand for laborers on similar plantations developed on the small islands off the African coasts, in the Indian Ocean, and on the islands and mainland of Southeast Asia.[5] In the Indian Ocean and Southeast Asia, most of the Asian laborers were indentured, drawn

[3] On yellow fever, see John R. McNeill, *Mosquito Empires* (New York: Cambridge University Press, 2010); on malaria, James L. A. Webb Jr., *Humanity's Burden: A Global History of Malaria* (New York: Cambridge University Press, 2009).
[4] Richard H. Steckel and Richard A. Jensen, "New Evidence on the Causes of Slave and Crew Mortality in the Atlantic Slave Trade," *Journal of Economic History*, vol. 46, no. 1 (1986), 57–77.
[5] David T. Courtwright, *Forces of Habit: Drugs and the Making of the Modern World* (Cambridge, MA: Harvard University Press, 2002), 9–30.

from southern India and Southeast Asia. As on the slave ships, dysentery haunted the oceanic passage for indentured servants and free migrants.[6] During the era of the long-distance transport of unfree and free laborers, dysentery was off-loaded at every port of call. The "bloody flux" became a deep stratum of infection in the maritime networks that ringed the globe.

The African slave trade also introduced a major intestinal parasite to the New World. Many Africans, before departing from the western coasts of Africa, were parasitized with an endemic hookworm that would later be named *Necator americanus*. They introduced it to the Americas, where the nematode found soils in which it could propagate. Over time, it became widely prevalent in Meso-America, South America, North America, and the Caribbean – wherever people worked the soils without shoes. It infected virtually all who came within the orbit of the plantation or mine, and over time, hookworm infected a high percentage of rural dwellers in all areas with sandy soils. It became one of the most widely shared infections in the Americas.

### THE USES OF HUMAN AND ANIMAL WASTES

Beginning in the sixteenth century, the tropical plantation economies and then slowly some other agricultural regions began to participate in widening networks of trade. In an era before the invention of chemical fertilizers, agriculturalists who enriched their soils did so with natural fertilizers – principally human and animal manures. The global practices were diverse, and our knowledge about them is far from comprehensive. The available evidence, however, can be organized to suggest a spectrum of use.

The societies that did not make use of natural fertilizers were typically less productive (unless they were "mining" virgin soils) and were typically ensconced in subsistence agriculture. At one end of the spectrum was tropical Africa. South of the Sahara and beyond the eastern African cattle corridor, the agricultural fields went without human or animal manures. Farmers set their fields afire to incinerate unwanted vegetation, spread the ash, broke the soils with the hoe, and sometimes worked leaves and other natural vegetation ("green manures") into the soils. The abstention from the use of human manure was also practiced in

---

[6] Dysentery was also the principal killer of migrant laborers brought to the Pacific islands in the nineteenth century. Ralph Shlomowitz, "Epidemiology and the Pacific Labor Trade," *Journal of Interdisciplinary History*, vol. 19, no. 4 (1989), 585–610.

some other regions in which cultivators labored without the benefit of draft animals. Societies on the Pacific islands, for example, opted not to compost or use human shit as fertilizer. The Maori of New Zealand viewed human excreta as unclean and refused to defile their sweet potato plots. They built communal latrines that hung over the sides of cliffs or were situated at the edges of lagoons or creeks.[7] Elsewhere in Micronesia and Polynesia, the islanders likewise did not value human shit as fertilizer. Eighteenth-century European visitors to the Society Islands reported that the inhabitants defecated at night on paths through the islands. On Tahiti, the inhabitants left their stools for rats to consume. In the Marquesas, the inhabitants buried their individual night soil deposits.[8]

This abstention was not universal in the tropics. In Amazon basin, before the era of European colonization, rainforest farmers used animal manures, charcoal, and other organic materials to create the *terra preta* soils with elevated carbon concentrations, and there is firm evidence that the soil-makers used human excreta in their mix.[9] The enriched soils were more productive and facilitated intense cultivation.[10] This process of soil creation was unusual: *terra preta* soils do not occur elsewhere in the Americas, and there appear to be only limited analogs elsewhere in the world.[11]

At the other end of the spectrum were the East and Southeast Asian farmers who made the use of human shit integral to their cultivation of calorie-rich wet rice that supported growing populations. Consider the

---

[7] Craig Pauling and Jamie Ataria, "Tiaki Para: A Study of Ngai Tahu Values and Issues Regarding Waste," *Landcare Research Contract Report Science Series*, no. 39 (Lincoln, NZ: Manaaki Whenua Press, 2010), 7–9.

[8] John Gregory Bourke, *Scatologic Rites of All Nations* (Washington, DC: W. H. Lowdermilk, 1891), 135–36, citing Hawkesworth's *Voyages* (1773) and Forster's *Voyage Round the World* (1777).

[9] Bruno Glaser and Jago Jonathan Birk, "State of the Scientific Knowledge on Properties and Genesis of Anthropogenic Dark Earths in Central Amazonia (*terra preta de Índio*)," *Geochimica et Cosmochimica Acta*, vol. 82 (2012), 46–47.

  The *terra preta* soils have inspired some projects to recreate comparable soils using human excrement in the service of sustainable agriculture. See H. Factura, T. Bettendorf, C. Buzie, H. Pieplow, J. Reckin, and R. Otterpohl, "Terra Preta Sanitation: Re-discovered from an Ancient Amazonian Civilisation – Integrating Sanitation, Bio-waste Management and Agriculture," *Water Science and Technology*, vol. 61, no. 10 (2010), 2673–79.

[10] Charles C. Mann, *1491: New Revelations of the Americas Before Columbus* (New York: Vintage Books, 2006), 306–10.

[11] Ben Pears, "The Formation of Anthropogenic Soils across Three Marginal Landscapes on Fair Isle and in the Netherlands and Ireland," in Richard Jones (ed.), *Manure Matters: Historical, Archaeological, and Ethnographic Perspectives* (Surrey: Ashgate, 2012), 109–27.

case of southern China. During the Tang Dynasty (618–907), wet rice cultivation was introduced into southern China so successfully that it displaced slash-and-burn (swidden) agriculture. Farmers initially cultivated in the lowlands, where water control was essential to success, until the Song Dynasty (960–1279) encouraged early-maturing, drought-resistant *champa* wet rice. Farmers could grow champa on hillsides as well as the lowlands, and this multiplied the arable rice lands. From the mid-eighth century to the late eleventh century, the Chinese population doubled in size, with the fastest rates of increase in the south. Wet rice depleted the soil nutrients, and farmers applied human waste, mixed with straw, to the rice fields before replanting. By the late eleventh century, the population of southern China, previously something of a regional backwater, totaled 50 million, half of the total population of China.

The demographic growth in southern China, despite the extensive utilization of human and animal manures, indicates that the Chinese had developed hygienic practices to protect themselves against diarrheal diseases. Dietary and culinary practices had major significance. The Chinese only drank beverages that had been boiled, cooked with *congee* (rice broth) rather than milk, and avoided uncooked food of any kind.[12] Indeed, it was only when warfare displaced populations that Chinese sources record the outbreak of epidemic dysentery and other diseases.[13] In less violent times, the diarrheal scourges apparently were kept in check. Indeed, in the early twentieth century, visitors to both southern and northern China expressed astonishment at the relative absence of intestinal disorders. Even helminthic infections were kept at low or moderate levels, except in the mulberry groves, where workers

[12] Anonymous, "Enteric or Typhoid Fever in the Hot Climates," *Journal of Tropical Medicine*, January 15, 1904, 27–30.
[13] The population of southern China was further increased by the mass influx of millions of peasants provoked by the twelfth century CE Jurchen invasion of northern China that caused the Song Dynasty itself to relocate southern China. By the late twelfth and early thirteenth centuries, the center of Han Chinese population was in the south. Then, famines and epidemics struck the Southern Song regions. In weakened condition, the population suffered epidemics of dysentery, probably smallpox, and perhaps typhus. The Mongol invasion of the late thirteenth century devastated the Jurchen (Jin) and the Southern Song Dynasties and brought about a demographic decline on the order of 50 percent. Joseph P. McDermott and Shiba Yoshinobu, "Economic Change in China, 960–1279," in John W. Chaffee and Denis Twitchett (eds.), *The Cambridge History of China*, vol. 5, part II, *Sung China, 960–1279* (Cambridge: Cambridge University Press, 2015), 321–436.

deposited human waste in order to enhance the productivity of the trees.[14]

To the north of the wet rice zone, the grain farmers of northern and central China and Korea likewise utilized human excrement and urine as a fertilizer. They mixed human excreta with animal dungs, grasses, and other vegetation to develop organic fertilizers, composts, and/or soil mixtures that would produce the highest agricultural yields and were tailored to specific crops and intercropping practices.[15] In northern China, peasants dug an outdoor manure pit near their dwellings and after use covered it with soil. (By contrast, peasants in southern China applied their waste directly to the paddy fields.) When the pit was full, the farmers scooped out the night soil and heaped it into piles to compost.[16] It was a world in which the droppings of farm and draft animals were recycled and in which receptacles for human urine and feces were placed along the roads for the convenience of travelers. As the eminent twentieth-century parasitologist Norman R. Stoll noted:

[14] The close contact with human and pig excrement, however, came at the cost of extensive roundworm infections of both the farmers and their swine. One blessing of the northern Chinese agricultural zone was that neither the soils nor the climate facilitated the transmission of hookworm and whipworm.

Twentieth-century epidemiologists found that the single most important factor in explaining the presence of very heavy infections of roundworm in some families was the defecation practices of the children. Children who did not defecate in the pig-pen /latrine polluted the immediate courtyard environs, and dogs ate their feces and widely disseminated the roundworm eggs. G. F. Winfield, "On the Use of *Ascaris lumbricoides* as a Public Health Standard in the Study of Problems of Rural Sanitation," *Transactions of the Ninth Congress of the Far Eastern Association of Tropical Medicine of Nanking*, vol. 2 (1934), 794–95; W. W. Cort and N. R. Stoll, "Studies on *Ascaris lumbricoides* and *Trichuris trichiura* in China," *American Journal of Hygiene*, vol. 14, no. 3 (1931), 663.

[15] The use of human manure on the wet rice fields produced a roughly comparable pattern of helminthic infections as in northern China. When the first studies of intestinal worms were carried out in the early twentieth century, most of the southern Chinese rice farmers were infested with roundworm, but there were few whipworm and hookworm infections. A major exception was in the sub-regions in which, according to genetic scientists, mulberry groves had been cultivated for silkworms at least since 5000 BP, and where hookworm infestations eventually became rife. Marian R. Goldsmith, Toru Shimada, and Hiroaki Abe, "The Genetics and Genomics of the Silkworm, *Bombyx mori*," *Annual Review of Entomology*, vol. 50 (2005), 74. Human manure was used to fertilize the trees, and the warm climate and draining soils allowed for the hookworm larvae to mature. Those who worked barefoot underneath the mulberry trees got hookworm infections.

[16] Yu Xinzhong, "The Treatment of Night Soil and Waste in Modern China," in Angela Ki Che Leung and Charlotte Furth (eds.), *Health and Hygiene in Chinese East Asia* (Durham, NC: Duke University Press, 2010), 53–58.

FIGURE 3.1 Chinese farmer with night soil.
Source: Wellcome Collection

A part of this tremendous economic value of nightsoil to the Chinese farmer is reflected in the intensive use of the soil and the abundant crops secured. In the Soochow (Suzhou, to the immediate northwest of Shanghai) region, for instance, two crops, such as wheat and rice, follow each other each year from the same soil, a practice which according to report has been going on continuously for over two thousand years in this area. Vegetable plots often produce three crops annually. It would appear that such procedures are the rule throughout the well-watered parts of Central and South China. Other fertilizers, of course, are used, as is the system of crop rotation. The use of night soil seems, nevertheless, to be the principal factor in the maintenance of fertility.[17]

[17] Norman R. Stoll, "On the Economic Value of Nightsoil in China," in W. W. Cort, J. B. Grant, and N. R. Stoll (eds.), *Researches on Hookworm in China: Embodying the*

The Japanese also used human waste as fertilizer and were exceptionally discerning about its qualities. They judged excrement from diets rich
in fish as superior to that from simpler food regimens. Overall, urban shit
was prized for producing bountiful harvests of rice and vegetables.
Surprisingly, there were different regional assessments of the value of
human urine. In western Japan, urine was highly valued. In eastern
Japan, in the hinterlands of Edo (Tokyo), farmers did not even bother to
collect it. Remarkably, even within discrete regions, farmers expressed
local preferences. In the hinterland of Osaka, for example, the inhabitants
of some villages bought night soil but not urine, others bought urine but
not night soil, and yet others bought both.[18]

In Japan, the role of human shit in the agricultural sector was too
central to be considered polluting. It did not jeopardize the farmer's
standing. Handling shit was entirely unlike handling livestock carcasses,
a job which marked one's standing as an outcaste. The transport of
human waste from the cities to the farms went on like clockwork, except
during extraordinary outbreaks of disease such as the cholera epidemic
of 1877, when peasants refused to come into the cities to empty the
privies.[19]

In Southeast Asia, some of the same practices obtained. In northern
Vietnam, farmers applied night soil and urine to their rice fields and
vegetable gardens. In central Vietnam, by contrast, farmers had an aver-
sion to using human waste, and in many rural areas, wild pigs were
permitted to scavenge human excrement. In southern Vietnam, where
practicable, human waste was deposited in the fishponds.[20] Similarly, in
Java, human excrement enriched the fishponds, and where draft animals
were plentiful, and their dung was widely valued as a fertilizer. In Malaya
and the Straits Settlements, night soil was considered too valuable for use
in fishponds, and it was allocated to vegetable production. The application of an excreta slurry on vegetable plots, however, promoted

*Results of the Work of the China Hookworm Commission, June, 1923 to November,*
*1924,* Monographic Series no. 7 (Baltimore: The American Journal of Hygiene, 1926),
262.

[18] David L. Howell, "Fecal Matter: Prolegomenon to a History of Shit in Japan," in Ian
Jared Miller, Julia Adeney Thomas, and Brett L. Walker (eds.), *Japan at Nature's Edge:*
*The Environmental Context of a Global Power* (Honolulu: University of Hawaii Press,
2013), 140, 144–45.

[19] Howell, "Fecal Matter," 146.

[20] Greg Berry, "Agricultural Sanitation: From Waste to Resource" (PhD thesis, University
of Tasmania, 2000), 51.

hookworm infection, because the gardeners worked on their hands and knees in the enriched soils.[21]

In India, a bewildering complexity of local rules governed the agricultural use of human feces. It was common practice for farming families to defecate in their own fields. (Men could defecate in the fields at any hour; women did so only under the cover of darkness.) In some locales, for example, higher-caste Jat farmers required members of the outcaste Dalits to defecate in the Jat fields. In other locales, the Jat farmers prohibited the Dalits from doing so.[22] In a broad sense, however, it is clear that farmers in India did not venerate human night soil, as was the case in East and Southeast Asia. There was no large-scale commerce in human waste from the city to the countryside, and as a general rule, farmers neither stored nor composted human as a fertilizer. As a consequence, in the wet rice growing areas such as Bengal and Bangladesh, the rice yields were lower than in China. In the late nineteenth century, there were breaks with past practice. In the Bombay Presidency, for example, human excreta began to be mixed with other manures to boost the yields of the sugarcane and tobacco cash crops.[23]

In southwest Asia and Europe, customary practices varied. In northern Pakistan, farmers conserved human waste and spread it on their fields. In Iraq and Iran, farmers fertilized their vegetable gardens with night soil.[24] Many British farmers, particularly those with fields in close proximity to large towns and cities, applied human excrement to their holdings. In Continental Europe, variation was the rule. The Flemish carefully collected both urine and feces for their fertilizer value. Farmers near Valencia and Paris used human manures; farmers near some other cities did not. Put broadly, Europeans neither venerated the agricultural virtues of shit nor reviled its use.[25]

---

[21] The Muslim communities on Java, for example, considered that the impurities in human excreta could be removed by dilution and the flow of water, and they considered it religiously acceptable to use untreated excreta to fertilize fishponds. Duncan Mara and Sandy Cairncross, *Guidelines for the Safe Use of Wastewater and Excreta in Agriculture and Aquaculture. Measures for Public Health Protection* (Geneva: World Health Organization, 1989), 91.

[22] Assa Doron and Robin Jeffrey, "Open Defecation in India," *Economic and Political Weekly*, December 6, 2014, 3.

[23] Government of India, *Gazetteer of the Bombay Presidency*, vol. 12, *Khándesh* (Bombay: Government Central Press, 1880), 147, 161.

[24] Berry, "Agricultural Sanitation," 28–30.

[25] Alan Macfarlane, *Savage Wars of Peace: England, Japan, and the Malthusian Trap* (London: Palgrave Macmillan, 2003), 169–70.

FIGURE 3.2 Dung cake preparation in Brittany, circa 1900.
Source: public domain

The expanding Euro-American agricultural frontier along the eastern
seaboard of North America traced a different trajectory. For decades, the
largely virgin soils did not require fertilization, and into the first half of the
nineteenth century, the colonists were resistant to using even animal
manures, let alone human waste. Only when the soils became less productive did the colonists change their ways. By the 1840s, north of
Virginia and east of the Appalachians, Euro-Americans had taken up the
use of animal manures, and in short order created a market for imported
South American guano and a compost of dried human waste produced in
the cities.[26]

In communities that did not have ready access to supplies of wood,
charcoal, or peat, the dung of large animals served as their principal fuel
for cooking and heating.[27] Across the great zones of pastoral nomadism,
the dried dung of the cow, camel, yak, llama, alpaca, and water buffalo,
and, to a lesser degree, horse, mule, and donkey were used for fuel, and
scavenged dung from wild herds such as the bison herds on the great plains

[26] Joel A. Tarr, "From City to Farm: Urban Wastes and the American Farmer," *Agricultural
History*, vol. 49, no. 4 (1975), 603.
[27] Cattle dung, diluted with water, could also be used to plaster walls, although the
quantities needed were small compared to the daily demand for cooking and heating fuel.

of North America could put to the same purpose. Some mixed farming communities also used dung for cooking, as did some impoverished villagers and city dwellers. These practices came at a cost to human health. The close contact with animal dung increased the transmission of *E coli* 0157, a bacterium that causes no harm to its nonhuman animal host, and *Salmonella spp.*, both of which cause severe diarrhea in humans.

## URBAN SANITATION REDUX

In Eurasia, in the wake of the fourteenth-century bubonic plague, towns and cities received an influx of rural workers seeking better opportunities. As urban populations increased, they produced a commensurate volume of human waste. Some governments legislated rudimentary sanitation with modest success. In the era before the industrial revolution, some British cities, for example, required the removal of human waste from cesspools under the sanction of regulation. These efforts succeeded in creating more aesthetically pleasing urban environments.[28] It is unlikely, however, that they produced much of an impact on health. Typhoid fever, amoebic dysentery, and a host of other maladies were common. The death rates in cities ran higher than in rural areas.[29]

In some regions, in the post-plague era new ecological relationships began to be forged between city and countryside. Consider for example the case of China. Beginning during the Ming period (1368–1644), commercial firms in some of the southern cities organized workers to collect night soil and sold it directly to the farmers for use in their paddy fields. The night soil collection workers, however, had at best a modest impact on urban pollution because city dwellers generally practiced open defecation throughout the urban areas, with some waste making its way into the rivers. The unsanitary conditions remained so banal that writers rarely commented upon them. As the writer Bao Shichen (1785–1855) noted of the Qing Dynasty's (1644–1912) southern capital of Nanjing: "Hardly any

---

[28] See, for example, Leona J. Skelton, *Sanitation in Urban Britain, 1560–1700* (Routledge: New York, 2016), which demonstrates the effectiveness of regulation in producing less polluted urban environments.

[29] There are formidable problems with data on mortality in urban and rural areas in the premodern era, but the preponderance of evidence suggests higher mortality in urban areas, with perhaps a smaller differential between cities and the countryside in Japan as compared to England. See Robert Woods, "Urban-Rural Mortality Differentials: An Unresolved Debate," *Population and Development Review*, vol. 29, no. 1 (2003), 29–46.

FIGURE 3.3 "John Hunt, nightman and rubbish carter." Eighteenth-century advertising flyer.
Source: Wellcome Collection

ditch in the city is not blocked. Night soil and waste find no way out and pollute wells, making well water bitter and salty. During the summer and autumn, waves wash into inner city waterways. Along these river banks are many brothels, which clean bins and stools in the river. The polluted water flows down and is used by residents living downstream."[30]

Similar conditions prevailed in the northern cities. There, too, night soil workers picked up some of the human waste and brought it to night soil plants where the material could be composted and sold to farmers. Sanitation conditions in the cities remained execrable. As the writer Fang Bao (1668–1749) described the fouled ditches and roads in the Qing Dynasty's northern capital of Beijing: "Humans live side by side with livestock, crowding this place. People feed on raw and stale food. No toilets are found in households, leaving excrement polluting and fouling ditches and roads."[31]

In contrast with China, Japan during the era of the Tokugawa Shogunate (1603–1868) may have had the most advanced system of

[30] Xinzhong, "Treatment of Night Soil and Waste in Modern China," 58; Donald Worster, "The Good Muck: Toward an Excremental History of China," *RCC Perspectives: Transformations in Environment and Society*, no. 5 (2017), 29–31.

[31] Xinzhong, "Night Soil and Waste in Modern China," 53.

urban feces disposal in the world. In part, this may have had an economic as well as cultural logic. Japanese farmers paid a premium for the shit of city dwellers. Commercial firms amassed the waste of the city populations, loaded it on barges and floated to farming communities. In Japan, human feces were deemed too valuable to dump in rivers, and indeed, there was sufficient profit in trafficking shit that Japan was very late in adopting modern sewage systems. As late at 1985, only 34 percent of Japanese communities had modern toilets and sewerage. It may well have been the very success of the premodern night soil practices that discouraged the commitment to modernity.[32]

The North American practices were among the most rudimentary, because the agricultural market for human feces was very late to develop. As the filth piled up, cities created jobs for "scavengers" who cleaned cesspits and privy vaults and who carted away dead horses, dogs, and other animals that lay rotting in the streets.[33] The scavengers simply dumped the filth on the nearest beach or into the nearest river, lake, bay, or gutter.[34]

## URBAN CRISIS OF SCALE AND THE EMERGENCE OF PUBLIC HEALTH MOVEMENTS

The industrial revolution accelerated urbanization, and the rapid growth of cities created a crisis for urban feces disposal. There was more shit to move, and it overwhelmed the capacity of the cities to move it and for local markets to absorb it. The crisis was one of scale.

In some regions of the United States, an agricultural market for urban feces developed, if belatedly, that absorbed some of the urban fecal matter. By 1887, scavengers removed human waste from 103 of the 222 cities listed in the Tenth Census of the United States for agricultural use. The shit either was either deposited directly on the fields, composted with earth and other materials, or sold for manufacture into fertilizer. Most of the cities that moved urban feces to farms were in New England and the Midwest; a smaller percentage of the cities in the South or West did so; the patterns were highly uneven.[35]

---

[32] See S. B. Hanley, "Urban Sanitation in Preindustrial Japan," *Journal of Interdisciplinary History*, vol. 18, no. 1 (1987), 1–26.

[33] Boston appointed a scavenger as early as 1666–67. John Duffy, *The Sanitarians: A History of American Public Health* (Urbana: University of Illinois Press, 1990), 13.

[34] John Duffy, *The Sanitarians*, 73.   [35] Tarr, "From City to Farm," 600–601.

Britain's industrial cities also grew rapidly in the nineteenth century and experienced the same elemental crisis. There was simply too much shit concentrated in a small area. Some shit was returned to the land as fertilizer, but much of it rotted in place. Consider the condition of Manchester in the 1820s, the premier center of textile manufacturing in Great Britain:

Whole streets ... are unpaved and without drains or main-sewers, are worn into deep ruts and holes, in which water constantly stagnates, and are so covered with refuse and excrementious matter as to be almost impassable from depth of mud, and intolerable from stench. In the narrow lanes, confined courts and alleys, leading from these, similar nuisances exist, if possible, to a still greater extent ... In many of these places are to be seen privies in the most disgusting state of filth, open cesspools, obstructed drains, ditches full of stagnant water, dunghills, pigsties, &c, from which the most abominable odours are emitted. But dwellings perhaps are still more insalubrious in those cottages situated at the backs of the houses fronting the street, the only entrance to which is through some nameless narrow passage, converted generally, as if by common consent, into a receptacle for ordure and the most offensive kinds of filth. The doors of these hovels commonly open upon the uncovered cesspool, which receives the contents of the privy belonging to the front house, and all the refuse cast out from it, as if it had been designedly contrived to render them as loathsome and unhealthy as possible. Surrounded on all sides by high walls, no current of air can gain access to disperse or dilute the noxious effluvia, or disturb the reeking atmosphere of these areas. Where there happens to be less crowding, and any ground remains unbuilt upon, it is generally undrained, contains pools of stagnant water, and is made a depôt for dunghills and all kinds of filth.[36]

From this urban crisis, the early public health movements in France and Britain were born. They expressed different philosophies, but they shared a commitment to reforms in river water distribution, storm sewer extension, the suppression of refuse and waste dumping, and sewer and street cleaning – all in an effort to reduce stench. The French movement formed first, in the early nineteenth century.[37] The French reformers' mission was expressed diffusely in the idea of hygienism that held that a broad

[36] Report of Dr. Baron Howard on Manchester, England, reproduced in Edwin Chadwick, *Report on the Sanitary Condition of the Labouring Population of Great Britain*, edited by M. W. Flinn (Edinburgh: Edinburgh University Press, 1965), 38.
[37] In France, there was a continuity of ideas about public health that extended back to the eighteenth century. In 1829, the journal *Annales d'hygiène publique et médicine légale* was founded. This can serve as a convenient marker of the birth of the early nineteenth century French public health movement. Ann F. La Berge, *Mission and Method: The Early-Nineteenth Century French Public Health Movement* (New York: Cambridge University Press, 1992), 19.

spectrum of modernizing activities – from housing reform to improved sewerage – could prevent disease and promote public health. Over the course of the nineteenth century, hygienism proved to be a shifting constellation of policies and politics that embraced the necessity of state control.[38] In Britain, the mission of the reformers was expressed as sanitarianism. As in France, the British movement embraced the theory of miasmas that held that diseases were born of putrid airs carried through the immediate atmosphere. In policy, the sanitarians were far narrower in their scope than the hygienists. They focused on the reform of sewers and drainage to accomplish the evacuation of refuse and excrement. In practical terms, rather than have the cesspits and privy vaults mucked out by hand and the contents loaded on to carts, they advocated for a system of sewers that would drain the filth into the adjoining bodies of water. There, the waters would render the obnoxious material no longer dangerous.[39]

The early modern sanitation system of London was under severe stress in the early nineteenth century. Before 1815, London had exported much of its excrement to local fields. (It had been, in fact, illegal to discharge human waste into the sewers that were built to evacuate rainwater.) As the rapid growth of London, however, overwhelmed the capacity of the local farms to utilize the urban shit, London's poor took to dumping their wastes into the streets. As the wealthier households began to adopt the use of the indoor water-flushed toilet (known euphemistically as the water closet) in the first half of the nineteenth century, they connected their indoor facilities directly to the sewer lines.[40]

The rapid increase in urban populations was not the sole factor that drove the urban environmental crisis of the industrial era. Throughout the greater North Atlantic region, draft animals made the urban economy function, by bringing goods to market and carrying passengers through muck-laden streets. The waste products of the transport animals made their own impressive contributions to urban filth. In 1900, in New York

---

[38] Fabienne Chevallier, *Le Paris moderne: Histoire des politiques d'hygiène, 1855–1898* (Rennes: Presses Universitaires de Rennes, 2010).

[39] Chadwick estimated that two-thirds of the expense of "street cleansing" was in the expense of cartage. Chadwick, *Report on the Sanitary Condition*, 54.

[40] As an 1857 report put it: "We believe that the introduction of water-closets in the metropolis, to any extent, may be dated from about the year 1810, from which time until 1830 their increase was only gradual; but since 1830 the increase has been very rapid and remarkable. The number of cesspools which has been discontinued in London, is stated to be not far short of two hundred thousand." *Parliamentary Papers* (1857), vol. 36, 4, note 3, cited by Stephen Halliday, *The Great Stink of London: Sir Joseph Bazalgette and the Cleansing of the Victorian Metropolis* (Phoenix Mill: Sutton, 1999), 42.

City, for example, 100,000 horses discharged 1,250 tons of manure and 400,000 gallons of urine every day on the city streets and in urban stables.[41]


### GLOBAL CHOLERA

In the early nineteenth century, during the early phases of rapid North Atlantic urbanization, the industrializing metropolitan centers and their overseas colonies fueled an increase in overland travel and maritime trade. The most spectacular consequence in terms of human mortality was the dispersion from British-controlled India of a deadly intestinal pathogen: *Vibrio cholerae*. The bacillus began a new phase in its long career, far beyond the zone of endemic infection in coastal northeastern India, and in the process wrote a new chapter in the global history of disease.

Cholera had undoubtedly long stalked the maritime routes of southern Asia, with documented outbreaks in the Dutch East Indies in the sixteenth century, China in the seventeenth century, and in southern India in the eighteenth century. The cholera bacillus may well have reached populations in other reaches of the Indian Ocean or mainland South Asia in even earlier centuries.[42] But in 1817–18 it scourged Delhi and much of the South Asian subcontinent. It arrived with Hindu pilgrims who participated in enormous religious gatherings, from which it branched off to distant communities with the devout as they returned home. Epidemic cholera traveled overland on the subcontinent. It sailed on shipboard to infect the islands of the Indian Ocean, the Arabian Peninsula, and the eastern coast of Africa.[43] It eventually reached Southeast Asia, China, and Japan in the east and Mauritius, the eastern coast of Africa, and the Arabian Peninsula in the west, and then traveled up through the Persian Gulf to Persia, Syria, and Armenia, and then north to Astrakhan, at the gates of Russia.[44]

---

[41] Joel A. Tarr, "The Horse: Polluter of the City," in Joel A. Tarr (ed.), *The Search for the Ultimate Sink: Urban Pollution in Historical Perspective* (Akron, OH: University of Akron Press, 1996), 323–33.

[42] The expansion might have taken place in an earlier epoch, such as the Chinese fifteenth-century voyages of discovery that brought Chinese fleets to the eastern coasts of Africa, but there is no historical evidence to support this.

[43] Myron Echenberg, *Africa in the Time of Cholera: A History of Pandemics from 1817 to the Present* (New York: Cambridge University Press, 2011), 15–18.

[44] J. N. Hays, *Epidemics and Pandemics: Their Impacts on Human History* (Santa Barbara, CA: ABC Clio Press, 2005), 193–200.

The cholera pandemic of 1817–26 was the first of seven and may have been the most destructive of human lives. The second (1828–36) and third (1839–61) pandemics had an even more extensive reach. From South Asia, they passed overland through Russia to reach Europe and then crossed the Atlantic to North America. They, too, caused great destruction. The numbers of lives lost can only be roughly estimated. In Russia, during the first pandemic the czar's government imposed strict quarantine measures but still lost nearly 290,000 individuals. The Russians became convinced that quarantines were useless and did not invoke these measures during the second pandemic and went on to lose more than 880,000.[45]

In Europe, the arrival of cholera caused a panic that recalled the time of the Black Death. The case fatality rates varied greatly from one locale to another, and this contributed to the view that environmental conditions must be critical to the disease. Physicians disagreed as to whether or not cholera was a result of emanations from the atmosphere, poison in the soil, or bad water. It was clear that poor communities were struck more severely than the wealthy, but this fact could be interpreted in various ways. Some took it to be a consequence of moral failure and depraved behaviors. In the United States, when cholera struck during the second and third global pandemics, it was taken to emanate from the atmosphere, and to be an expression of God's judgment on a sinful society.[46]

The second and third pandemics sailed on larger, more efficient ocean-going ships and arrived at their destinations more rapidly, before the disease could burn its way through the crews and passengers and leave the survivors with immunity.[47] This helps to explain the increasing range of

[45] Norman Howard-Jones, *The Scientific Background of the International Sanitary Conferences, 1851–1938* (Geneva: World Health Organization, 1975), 15.

[46] Charles Rosenberg, *The Cholera Years: The United States in 1832, 1849, and 1866* (Chicago: University of Chicago Press, 1962).

Cholera outbreaks were intensely frightening, because cholera could kill within hours, sending an individual who felt fine in the morning into a shroud by evening. Moreover, it produced ghastly symptoms such as blue and shrunken skin. It was a nightmare come to life. Cholera outbreaks ripped at the social order, as panicked commoners sought out religious, ethnic, or class scapegoats, and the ruling classes struggled to manage the unleashed disorder. For an exploration of the social, cultural, and scientific meanings of the disease in several different contexts, see Christopher Hamlin's *Cholera: The Biography* (Oxford: Oxford University Press, 2009).

[47] The larger context in which these cholera epidemics broke out was an increase in international trade in the aftermath of the Napoleonic Wars (1803–15). Thereafter, oceanic shipping rates in the North Atlantic declined, particularly on long haul routes,

FIGURE 3.4  Cholera in Palermo, 1835.
Source: US National Library of Medicine

successive pandemics. The third pandemic reached Latin America. It was a complex, spiraling disaster, exacerbated by warfare and new patterns of global trade. The United States' decision to open Japan to Western trade by coercion during the 1850s inadvertently facilitated the introduction of *Vibrio cholerae* to the Japanese islands. More than 100,000 died in the Nagasaki region alone.[48]

The fourth pandemic (1863–79) retraced some familiar patterns, spreading into East Asia as well as Europe, North America, and the Caribbean, but sparing South America. It also covered new ground.

and this coincided with an increase in international passenger travel across the North Atlantic. In the middle to late nineteenth century, the construction of railroad networks – first in the United Kingdom, Continental Europe, and the United States and then unevenly in other areas of the wider world – allowed for the lower cost movement of goods whose transport costs had been prohibitively high in the age of draft animals and river and canal boats. The new railroad systems expanded the regions that participated in the thickening webs of international commerce. Railroads, like the oceangoing vessels, moved people farther, more quickly, and more inexpensively than ever before. Douglass North, "Ocean Freight Rates and Economic Development 1730–1913," *Journal of Economic History* 18, no. 4 (1958), 537–55.

[48] Ann Bowman Jannetta, *Epidemics and Mortality in Early Modern Japan* (Princeton, NJ: Princeton University Press, 1987).

FIGURE 3.5 The Old Quarters of Cairo, during the prevalence of the cholera, 1865.
Source: US National Library of Medicine

Cholera spread by caravan across the Sahara from North Africa to Senegal, from whence it diffused in West Africa, and it spread from the Horn of Africa down the eastern coast, as far south as Mozambique. It was also devastating in mainland India, where in 1867, during and following the Hindu pilgrimages at Hardwar, cholera took 125,000 lives. Cholera also moved along the routes of Muslim pilgrimage, reaching Mecca with the congregants for the Hajj, and traveling with them as they left.

The fifth pandemic (1881–96) hit East Asia with particular vengeance and was probably the worst pandemic to date for that region. The Russian Empire also suffered grievously. By one estimate, the Russians buried some 254,000 from cholera in 1892 and 1893.[49] During the sixth pandemic (1899–1923) most of the destruction initially centered on South Asia, Southeast Asia, and East Asia. Perhaps 8 million Indians died of cholera in the two decades between 1900 and 1920. It did not strike during World War I, but it broke out in fury

---

[49] Nancy Friedan, "The Russian Cholera Epidemic, 1892–1893, and Medical Professionalization," *Journal of Social History*, vol. 10, no. 4 (1977), 551.

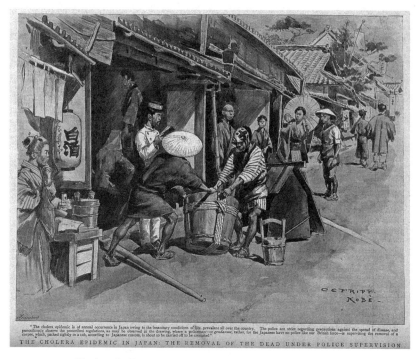

"The cholera epidemic is of annual occurrence in Japan owing to the insanitary conditions of life prevalent all over the country. The police are strict regarding precautions against the spread of disease, and punctiliously observe the prescribed regulations, as may be observed in the drawing, where a policeman—or *gendarme*, rather, for the Japanese have no police like our British force—is supervising the removal of a corpse, which, packed tightly in a tub, according to Japanese custom, is about to be carried off to be cremated."

THE CHOLERA EPIDEMIC IN JAPAN: THE REMOVAL OF THE DEAD UNDER POLICE SUPERVISION

FIGURE 3.6  Cholera in Japan.
Source: US National Library of Medicine

during the chaos of the Russian Revolution and the ensuing Russian Civil War.[50]

The enormous disruption, fear, and outright panic that struck the trading nations affected by the successive cholera pandemics called forth efforts to arrest their progress. Earlier in the century it was clear to most observers that cholera was somehow portable and that it was linked to the movement of people. As early as the second cholera pandemic, the European and North American public health reformers had begun to generate new insights about the value of disinfection and quarantine, embracing scientific, secular interpretations of the pandemics that competed with religious explanations.[51]

The clear and present danger of cholera, in league with the new scientific understandings about disease control, in 1851 initiated the first of

---

[50]  Hays, *Epidemics and Pandemics*, 345–47.
[51]  Charles Rosenberg, *The Cholera Years: The United States in 1832, 1849, and 1866* (Chicago: University of Chicago Press, 1962).

a succession of international meetings to determine the causes of the cholera outbreak and the rules that ought to regulate the quarantining of ships and the denial of entry at frontier overland checkpoints. The first International Sanitary Conference agreed to report on the different national sanitary regulations.[52] There were successive meetings in 1859, 1866, 1874, 1881, and 1885, but the participants had great difficulty in achieving consensus on what to do, in part because the imposition of quarantine raised the costs of shipping and thus business interests opposed it. Finally, at the seventh conference in 1892, the participants agreed on an International Sanitary Convention. It was effective (or, at the least, was coincident) in preventing further cholera epidemics in Western Europe, with the exception of Italy, where the sixth pandemic (1899–1923) struck in 1910–11.[53]

Over more than a century, global cholera epidemics created havoc and killed millions. Out of this chaos, international treaties to control disease eventually emerged. They were the precursors to the League of Nations Health Organization and, later, the World Health Organization, the major international disease control organizations of the twentieth century.[54]

As human communities became more complex, networks of trade expanded and thickened allowing for the rapid, long-distance transmission of intestinal pathogens. Over the first millennium and a half of the Common Era, the disease pool of Eurasia and northern Africa became increasingly integrated. In the late fifteenth century, some Old World intestinal pathogens crossed the Atlantic and became established in the

---

[52] Austria, Great Britain, Greece, Portugal, Russia, Spain, France, Turkey, and the four Papal States participated. Norman Howard-Jones, *The Scientific Background of the International Sanitary Conferences, 1851–1938* (Geneva: World Health Organization, 1975).

[53] In the late 1890s, Waldemar Haffkine developed an anticholera vaccine. It was used with considerable success in India. It reduced cholera mortality by 50 percent in those who were vaccinated, in comparison with control groups, although it did not reduce the case fatality rate among those who contracted the disease. See Ilana Löwy, "From Guinea Pigs to Man: The Development of Haffkine's Anticholera Vaccine," *Journal of the History of Medicine and Allied Sciences*, vol. 47, no. 3 (1992), 270–309; Barbara J. Hawgood, "Waldemar Mordecai Haffkine, CIE (1860–1930): Prophylactic Vaccination against Cholera and Bubonic Plague in British India," *Journal of Medical Biography* vol. 15, no. 1 (2007), 9–19.

[54] Mark Harrison, *Contagion: How Commerce Has Spread Disease* (New Haven, CT: Yale University Press, 2012).

Americas. By the early nineteenth century, the integration had become global. Rapid urbanization in the industrializing North Atlantic states created a crisis of urban fecal pollution. In response the first public health reform movements emerged. Beginning in the first half of the nineteenth century, cholera pandemics spread along global trade routes and infected all the inhabited continents. In response the first efforts at the international control of disease were promulgated.

# 4

## Innovations

In the first half of the nineteenth century, a "sanitarian" movement in Great Britain gained traction. The movement was rooted in the dominant medical paradigm of the day, known as miasmatic theory, whose roots reached back to early Greek and Roman thinkers. It held that where there was stench, there was the possibility of contracting disease. According to miasmatic theory, individuals became susceptible to diseases through exposure to rotting feces, animal carcasses, and stinking vegetable matter, and all the more so if they had experienced lapses in moral behavior such as drunkenness, gluttony, or sexual debauchery.

The sanitationists' approach to cleansing the polluted urban environments advanced with impeccable logic: when most night soil and animal carcasses were removed from the cities, the overweening stench would dissipate, and there would be fewer outbreaks of disease. The solution was compelling on aesthetic, moral, and medical grounds. In the late 1850s, they secured commitments to fund the construction of a vast underground sewer system in London, the first in the world. This laid the foundation for a "sanitation revolution" in public health that would eventually go global.[1]

---

[1] During a mid-nineteenth-century cholera epidemic in London, Dr. John Snow investigated why some neighborhoods suffered high mortality from cholera and others did not. He discovered that the principal determinant of the large differences in mortality among subdistricts in south London was a badly contaminated water supply provided by one of London's major water companies. Snow's critique, however, cut against the grain of the sanitationists' scientific understanding, and it was largely ignored. The appreciation of John Snow as the founder of modern epidemiology developed several generations after his death.

### EARLY SEWERAGE

Before the sanitation revolution, the sewerage and drainage system of London had grown organically and locally. Open surface-level drains had been laid in streets and in basements to channel away downpours. They functioned poorly. The drains clogged with fecal matter, offal, bones, and household refuse. In principle, the filth would be discharged into the Thames River and carried away from London. But because the Thames was tidal, the sewers got tide-locked between low tides. During high tides, sewage gushed backward, and during rainstorms polluted water rose through the drains and flooded streets and basements. Beginning in the 1830s, wealthier households began to connect their new-fangled water closets to the street drains by means of household pipes. This was a rudimentary affair: the pipes frequently clogged and conveyed sewer gases into the houses.

Most of the population of London did not have water closets, and they dumped their excrement into the vast number of cesspools (estimated at 200,000 in the 1840s) that adjoined the houses and tenements of London. The population of London – and their fecal deposits – more than doubled between 1801 and 1841, and an ever increasing volume of human waste made its way directly into the Thames, facilitated by the lifting of earlier statues that had prohibited connecting house drains to sewers.[2] Some of the shit could be conveyed to the local farms by cart and by canal boat, but because human manure was of relatively low quality as a fertilizer, the cost of haulage from London limited the demand to nearby farms, and supply soon outstripped demand.[3]

Just a few years after the sanitationist Edwin Chadwick in 1842 published his *Report on the Sanitary Condition of the Labouring Population of Great Britain*, the conditions of human waste disposal worsened under successive shocks of competition. Nitrogen-rich bird excrement known as guano from the Pacific coast of South America reached the British market and the footing slid out from underneath the muckrakers. Guano was less expensive and more potent than human shit. By mid-century, the German inventors of nitrogen-rich synthetic fertilizers delivered a second shock. When their products reached the market, the jig was up for human

---

[2] Stephen Halliday, *The Great Stink of London: Sir Joseph Bazalgette and the Cleansing of the Victorian Metropolis* (Phoenix Mill: Sutton, 1999), 45–46.

[3] The demand for human manure did not entirely cease for decades. As late as 1904, barges were hauling some 45,669 tons of manure from Paddington Basin to be applied to the Hertfordshire countryside. Halliday, *Great Stink*, 41.

manures in many British regions. Although advocates for the agricultural use of human manure trumpeted that profits from human shit were there for the taking, the flow of London's human excrement to local fields slowed to a dribble. Britain was at the vanguard of a modernizing club of nations that had embarked on a radical restructuring of agricultural ecology based on the use of nonrenewable mineral fertilizers or, in the case of guano, natural stockpiles that would be rapidly depleted.[4]

As London was coping with bottlenecks to human waste disposal, improvements to the city's supply of water created additional challenges.[5] Following an outbreak of cholera in 1831–32, some London water companies installed filtration mechanisms and built settling reservoirs in which organic sediments would precipitate out. A few companies shifted their sources of supply away from the sewage outflows that fed into the Thames.[6] This was an ongoing process, and it was only in 1849 that local legislation required that the entire water supply of London be filtered.[7] The water companies also increased the volume of water supplied to the city. They installed street-level public hydrants for the poor and residential connections for the well-off, who built "water closets" and flushed their bodily wastes into adjoining cesspools or storm drains. The volume of wastewater began to overwhelm the city's sewer system.[8]

From the late 1840s it became clear that a new sewer system would have to be built, and several commissions advanced proposals that were rejected because of high costs. But in the hot and dry summer of 1858, when summer rains were scant, the sewage-laden Thames barely flowed,

---

[4] Gregory T. Cushman, *Guano and the Opening of the Pacific World: A Global Ecological History* (New York: Cambridge University Press, 2013); Halliday, *Great Stink*, 41, 109.

[5] Water companies had supplied customers in London since about 1600. By 1820, roughly half of the buildings in the metropolis had water piped to them. Leslie Tomory, *The History of the London Water Industry, 1580–1820* (Baltimore: Johns Hopkins University Press, 2017), 3–5.

[6] Peter Vinten-Johansen, Howard Brody, Nigel Paneth, Stephen Rachman, and Michael Rip, *Cholera, Chloroform, and the Science of Medicine: A Life of John Snow* (New York: Oxford University Press, 2003), 254–55.

[7] William L. D'Olier, *The Sanitation of Cities* (New York: Sanitation Corporation of New York, 1921), 45.

[8] Dr. John Snow, the pioneering epidemiologist, took a stance against the abolition of cesspools and the growing preference for indoor toilets ("water closets"). He considered the water closets to be an epidemiological disaster, because the wastes flushed from the house to the cesspool were highly dilute and percolation from the cesspools poisoned the nearby wells. Vinten-Johansen et al., *Cholera, Chloroform, and the Science of Medicine*, 254–56, 343.

F U N.—August 18, 1866.

DEATH'S DISPENSARY.
OPEN TO THE POOR, GRATIS, BY PERMISSION OF THE PARISH.

FIGURE 4.1 "Death's dispensary."
Source: George J. Pinwell, *Fun*, August 16, 1866

and an utterly noxious stench shut down government offices at Westminster. The "Great Stink of London" provided cover for politicians to cast aside earlier concerns about expense and to endorse a grand solution – an integrated underground network that would shunt the city's raw sewage into the lower Thames, from whence it would flow to the sea.

This design posed formidable engineering and political challenges. It involved massive excavation beneath a city already in place. The gifted engineer and political adept Joseph Bazalgette guided the project through to success in 1875. In most of London, the aesthetic results were impressive. Most cesspools disappeared. In the better neighborhoods, the stench of human feces dissipated. In the poorest neighborhoods, however, shit continued to pile up in yards and in cesspits into the early twentieth century. The public health results were far less impressive. Typhoid fever and other diarrheal diseases continued to take their toll, with higher infant and childhood mortality in poorer communities than wealthier ones.[9]

## DEATH BY SEWAGE

In the broader North Atlantic region as in London, early urban sanitation had advanced in stages. In the United States, for example, as early as the late eighteenth century, a few cities had storm sewers to channel rain and snow melt into nearby rivers or lakes. In the first half of the nineteenth century, private companies began to channel water to urban residents and install fire hydrants in the larger cities along the eastern seaboard, and by 1860 the sixteen largest cities in the United States had waterworks.[10] By 1875, hundreds of cities and towns had them. Yet the water services had limited reaches. Until well into the second half of the nineteenth century, most city dwellers drew their water from ponds, streams, rainwater cisterns, or wells.

Few cities had underground sewerage, because the systems seemed unnecessary, unproved, or too expensive. Yet as the supply of piped water began to overwhelm the cesspits and privy vaults, human sewage began to flow into the storm sewers and ultimately into rivers, lakes, and seas.[11] When cities adopted sewer systems with outfalls of raw sewage into rivers, they became noxious. Once the organic matter settled in the

---

[9] Diarrheal diseases and dysentery were estimated to be the cause of 46 percent of all infant and childhood deaths in the early twentieth century. Infant and childhood mortality rates increased in Britain in the 1880s and 1890s, and began to decline in 1899. The decline was national and appears largely unrelated to improvements in sewerage. Poorer communities suffered higher rates of infant and childhood mortality than did wealthier communities. See R. I. Woods, P. A. Watterson, and J. H. Woodward, "The Causes of Rapid Infant Mortality Decline in England and Wales, 1861–1921 Part I," *Population Studies*, vol. 42, no. 3 (1988), 343–66, and "The Causes of Rapid Infant Mortality Decline in England and Wales, 1861–1921 Part II," *Population Studies*, vol. 43, no. 1 (1989), 113–32.

[10] The systems of water hydrants in cities served the dual purpose of providing water to extinguish house fires and of washing fecal matter and offal off the streets and into the sewers. George Edwin Waring, *Earth Closets and Earth Sewage* (New York: The Tribune Association, 1870), 7, quoting an essay by Prof. S. W. Johnson of Yale College.

[11] Joel A. Tarr, James McCurley III, Francis C. McMichael, and Terry Yosie, "Water and Wastes: A Retrospective Assessment of Wastewater Technology in the United States, 1900–1932," *Technology and Culture*, vol. 25, no. 2 (1984), 228–31.

river channels, it released sulfur and phosphorus compounds that bubbled up in gases. The stench was choking.[12]

The rivers also ran rich with pathogens. The dumping of untreated excreta sickened or killed some of those who drew their drinking water from the contaminated sources. Some victims were city dwellers from whom the excreta originated. Others lived downstream. It is not possible to estimate the number of deaths from the ingestion of water contaminated by the discharges of the flush toilet, because the historical data do not distinguish between intestinal disease deaths by water source, and many died from intestinal disease before the era of engineered sewage. In England in the 1860s – before the completion of London's sewer system – an estimated 140,000 fell ill from "night soil fever" (typhoid fever) every year, with approximately 20,000 deaths.[13]

One solution was to filter river water before supplying the cities. English engineers developed a sand filtration method for the London water supply and exported it to the continent in 1860. In Germany, English engineers installed sand filters for Altona, and later Berlin and some other German cities, but the patterns of adoption were idiosyncratic. Hamburg, opposite Altona on the Elbe River, did not use sand filters, and in 1892, cholera struck Hamburg with epidemic force and spared Altona.[14] It was strong evidence that the rudimentary late nineteenth-century methods could drastically reduce the pathogen load.

[12] Charles Meymott Tidy, *The Treatment of Sewage* (New York: D. Van Nostrand, 1887), 43.

[13] Waring, *Earth Closets and Earth Sewage*, 57, citing the report of the committee established to investigate the epidemic of typhoid fever at the Maplewood Young Ladies Institute at Pittsfield, Massachusetts, in 1864 that quoted Dr. E. D. Mapother, Professor of Health, and Medical Officer of Health of the city of Dublin.

[14] In 1884, Robert Koch, the German scientist who would become celebrated as the founder of bacteriology and win the Nobel Prize in Physiology or Medicine in 1905, discovered the pathogenic agent responsible for cholera, which he named *Vibrio cholerae*. It seemed to make good logical sense that the bacillus caused cholera. Empirical observation suggested, however, that not all those who were exposed to cholera-infected water came down with cholera, and thus scientific opinions differed as to whether or not there were other important modes of transmission beyond a polluted water supply and if there were other infectious agents that caused cholera in addition to *Vibrio cholerae*.

After the "natural experiment" in cholera took place in northern Germany, the comparative evidence from Altona and Hamburg proved convincing to many scientists, and the germ theory of cholera gained adherents. Richard J. Evans, *Death in Hamburg: Society and Politics in the Cholera Years, 1830–1910* (Oxford: Oxford University Press, 1987).

A full scientific consensus in favor of germ theory did not emerge, however, until the early decades of the twentieth century, after the sanitation revolution had been embraced by affluent communities in the North Atlantic region.

Cost often proved the deciding factor in whether or not to adopt filtration.[15] In the United States, the cities of Atlanta, Pittsburgh, Trenton, and Toledo (among many others) opted not to do so and suffered increases in typhoid deaths. Late in the 1890s, some US municipalities began to build sand and mechanical filters that treated sewage-laden waters at the point of intake, and the cases of typhoid fever began to fall off dramatically.[16] The goal was to achieve a water supply that was "reasonably insured against water-borne disease."[17]

## THE "DRY EARTH" AND "TUB-AND-PAIL" SYSTEMS

In farming settlements and many of the smaller and less wealthy cities and towns in the North Atlantic region, underground sewerage systems were cost-prohibitive. In the late 1850s, the Rev. Henry Moule devised a household or institutional system for covering excreta with sifted soil and called it the "dry earth system." At its simplest, it was a chair with a large hole in the seat, under which was situated a pail. Behind the chair's back was a metal reservoir filled with earth with a release opening that would dump the soil onto the excreta. The dry earth system was adopted in schools and barracks in the United Kingdom and exported abroad. It was employed in the hospitals, asylums, and jails of British India for several years where it was credited with preventing outbreaks of cholera or typhoid fever.[18] By the 1860s, the dry earth system was extended to the Straits Settlements and Canada.[19]

Sifted earth acted as a natural deodorizer and desiccator, and once it was fully saturated, after six, eight, or even ten procedures, the enriched soil could serve as a fertilizer. Advocates for the dry earth system hoped that it would find acceptance in urban households served with piped water and water closets connected with sewers.[20] The water closet, however, proved

[15] D'Olier, *Sanitation of Cities*, 45–46.

[16] Joel A. Tarr, James McCurley III, Francis C. McMichael, and Terry Yosie, "Water and Wastes: A Retrospective Assessment of Wastewater Technology in the United States, 1900–1932," *Technology and Culture*, vol. 25, no. 2 (1984), 239, 242.

[17] D'Olier, *Sanitation of Cities*, 53–54.

[18] Waring, *Earth Closets and Earth Sewage*, 71–73. The use of the dry earth system continued to expand. See Tidy, *Treatment of Sewage*, 28.

[19] The Under Secretary of State for the Provinces (Canada) reported in 1868 that the Canadian Board of Inspectors of Prisons and Asylums in Canada was the first on the North American continent to adopt the system. E. A. Meredith, "Preface," in Henry Moule, *Earth Sewage versus Water Sewage or National Health and Wealth Instead of Disease and Waste* (Ottowa: G. E. Desbarats, 1868), vi.

[20] As Waring noted: "There can be no doubt whatever that earth which has been used five times in the Closet will find a ready sale at $50 per ton (for it is usual in England to

a formidable competitor. It was an appurtenance of the wealthier classes, and this helped to spur acceptance among middle class households.

A municipal level system, known as the tub-and-pail, won adherents in cities and towns that found cesspits unacceptably noxious. Householders collected their excrement in pails and then emptied the pails into tubs with airtight lids. Sanitation workers collected the tubs, dumped the contents into a common midden, and mixed the wastes with coal ash.

For the communities that adopted the tub-and-pail system, other innovations followed. Local farmers did not want to use excreta in a raw state, and new industries emerged to manufacture a dry manure product. In the UK Borough of St. Helens, for example, the raw excreta were mixed with ash and then ground up. In Nottingham, the householders themselves mixed coal ash with the wastes in their tubs, and every three months the tubs were collected and taken to the manure wharf where they were sold. In Birmingham, workers emptied the tubs into a drying machine. In Paris, the wastes from "water-tight" municipal cesspools were hauled to the suburb Villette to be powdered into *poudrette*.[21] In the United Kingdom, The Native Guano Company produced a human-source competitor to imported guano, using its "ABC" method of adding alum, blood, and clay.[22]

The tub-and-pail was a British innovation. The United States and the rest of the Americas and Europe transitioned from the use of cesspits and privy vaults to waterborne sewerage, without an intermediate stage. It was, however, a slow and uneven process. Of the 222 cities listed in the *Tenth Census of the United States* (1880), for example, only 102 had any system of sewerage.[23]

### SEWAGE FARMING AND TRENCHING

Late nineteenth-century thinkers about sanitation diverged sharply over what to do with the new volumes of liquid human waste. One group believed that it could be dumped more or less safely into rivers. Another held that the sewage should be detoxified before disposal, and yet a third argued for returning the human waste to agricultural fields. The challenge

---

estimate its value after seven uses as equal to that of Peruvian guano, which sells at about $80 in New York). This will allow $2 per ton for the original cost of the earth, and $6 for each handling, which would be fully three times its actual cost, including the rent of proper storage-room." Waring, *Earth Closets and Earth Sewage*, 75.

[21] Tidy, *Treatment of Sewage*, 19–23.     [22] Tidy, *Treatment of Sewage*, 143.

[23] Joel A. Tarr, "From City to Farm: Urban Wastes and the American Farmer," *Agricultural History*, vol. 49, no. 4 (1975), 600–603.

for the advocates of the "sewage farm" was how to cope with the vast mass and volume of dilute waste.[24] The effluent from households was approximately 200 times the weight of human waste alone.[25]

The Germans were in the vanguard. In 1869, Danzig became the first European city to irrigate with sewage; Berlin followed in 1874.[26] For either surface irrigation or trenching for subsurface deposition, there were significant capital costs. For surface irrigation, the sewage had to be pumped up to elevation, surface channels dug, and the fields leveled and drained. The sewage had to be plowed into the soils in preparation for planting, and compared with non-sewage irrigated agriculture, this involved more horses and double the number of man-hours.[27]

Surface irrigation was problematic. The supply of sewage was constant, but the demand was not. Farmers did not want irrigation during rainy spells or when their crops were ripening. Excess sewage ran off the fields and polluted the local surface waters, particularly when the ground was frozen. (The severe winter cold more or less foreclosed the possibility of creating sewage farms in Scandinavia.) Moreover, to keep transport costs low, the sewage farms had to be nearby the city sewage systems, and they required a lot of land – one acre of land for every 500–1,000 people who flushed their wastes into the sewers.[28]

As the health costs of dumping raw sewage into water sources became understood, the trenching of sewage emerged as a reasonable alternative. The Germans investigated the options over a period of fifteen years, and the epidemiologist Rudolf Virchow concluded, after considering alternatives such as the chemical treatment of waste, that trenches were best. Berlin's sewage farms grew more than tenfold from 2,026 acres in 1876 to 22,881 in 1895, at which point they were larger than the city itself.[29]

[24] In the eighteenth century, a few experimentalists had added water to human waste and used the slurry for irrigation. Beginning in 1740, an early trial was undertaken in Bunzlau (Prussian Silesia) and from 1760, there were ongoing applications to the Craigentinny meadows at Edinburgh. These experiments had been limited in scope and import. H. Alfred Roechling, "The Present Status of Sewage Irrigation in Europe and America," *Journal of the Sanitary Institute*, vol. 17 (1896), 484.

[25] Daniel Schneider, *Hybrid Nature: Sewage Treatment and the Contradictions of the Industrial Ecosystem* (Boston: MIT Press, 2011), xxi.

[26] H. Alfred Roechling, "The Berlin Sewage Farms (43,009 Acres)," *Journal of the Sanitary Institute*, vol. 32 (1912), 178–206.

[27] Tidy, *Treatment of Sewage*, 43, 58–61.

[28] Daniel Schneider, *Hybrid Nature: Sewage Treatment and the Contradictions of the Industrial Ecosystem* (Boston: MIT Press, 2011), 15.

[29] Roechling, "Present Status of Sewage Irrigation," 488–89. The city of Paris exported a part of its sewage to a small farm of 126 acres held in private hands at Gennevilliers, beginning in

TANK AT THE SEWAGE FARM, NEAR BARKING.

FIGURE 4.2   Tank at the sewage farm near Barking, UK.
Source: Wellcome Collection

They doubled again to 43,009 by 1910. Much, perhaps half, of the acreage was devoted to livestock raising, orchards, and the establishment of convalescent homes. The Berlin sewage farms frequently made money, but not enough to pay the interest and sinking fund charges on the farm capital. Financial success in the sewage farm sector was rare.[30]

1872. The Gennevilliers sewage farm grew to 1926 acres by 1895. Not until the late 1880s did legislation authorize the extension of the disposal of sewage onto other lands, envisioned to be conveyed by aquaduct, and not until 1894 was the water carriage of sewage in all of Paris mandated. Roechling, "Present Status of Sewage Irrigation," 491–92.

[30] H. Alfred Roechling, "The Berlin Sewage Farms (43,009 Acres)," *Journal of the Sanitary Institute*, vol. 32 (1912), 178, 186ff.

In the late nineteenth and early twentieth centuries, the easiest and least expensive means of disposal was still to funnel raw sewage into waterways. Coastal cities dumped excreta into the oceans with impunity, secure in the belief that the currents swept most of the discharge out to sea. As late as 1914, the authorities piped the raw sewage of some 6 million inhabitants of New York City directly into the harbor.[31] When the stench became obnoxious and it was suspected that the fecal load might be too great to dilute adequately, the engineers proposed to dredge the waterway and deepen the channels. This provided a boon to commerce and obviated the need for investments in sewage treatment. Some inland cities were forced to more expensive options. The city of Chicago, for example, invested in a canal to reverse the flow of the Chicago River away from Lake Michigan. The city treated its sewage and released it into the reverse flow, to join the Des Plaines River which then flowed into the Illinois and Mississippi Rivers.[32]

For cities situated along lakeshores, dumping their wastes risked fouling their drinking water. Some municipalities innovated. Rochester, New York, for example, had a steamboat transport in buckets the sewage and garbage from the summer resorts along Hemlock Lake to the foot of the lake and then had carried it by tram to a trenching ground, where it was layered into trenches, covered with soil, and mounded. After a period of one or two years, the same lands could be retrenched to the same purpose.[33]

## FLIES, HOUSEHOLD HYGIENE, AND CONTAMINATED MILK

Even with the improved methods of feces disposal, infectious intestinal disease transmission continued apace. Some of the means of transmission proved difficult to address. Consider the problem of flies. In urban areas, flies propagated in horse manure, a near-perfect medium. Work horses were often in poor health, and their feces carried the pathogens for the bacterial infection salmonellosis and the parasitic infection cryptosporidiosis. Those who worked directly with horses were at particular risk, but the larger health problem resulted from the billions of flies that buzzed

[31] Duffy, *Sanitarians*, 177.
[32] D'Olier, *Sanitation of Cities*, 101; Martin V. Melosi, *The Sanitary City: Urban Infrastructure in America from Colonial Times to the Present* (Baltimore: Johns Hopkins University Press, 2000), 163–64.
[33] Broom, "Tub and Pail," 667–69.

from mountainous piles of horse manure and the remaining urban cesspits into homes and then flitted from one household serving bowl to another. Fly-borne diseases brought death into the kitchen. The brutal reality was that the early improvements in urban sanitation did not reduce urban childhood deaths.[34]

In the early twentieth century, the issue came into clearer focus, and the struggle against flies was enjoined. Initially, reformers stressed the importance of the regular mucking out of stables and the elimination of cesspits in which flies bred. Aggressive habitat-reduction programs enjoyed some success. Until the arrival of the motor car, truck, and bus, the principal means of local transport was the horse, and wherever there were horses, there was horse shit. As late as the second decade of the twentieth century, in the US fly-borne disease caused an estimated 70,000 deaths per year.[35]

Hygiene within the household was another major problem. The flush toilet kept human excreta out of the yards and off the streets, but it did little to stem the high death rates of children and the overall incidence of serious attacks of diarrhea in both adults and children.[36] Indeed,

---

[34] Bacteriological studies in the late 1880s and 1890s had demonstrated that flies could feed on the bowel evacuations of cholera patients and then on sterilized milk, and when the milk was cultured, there would be a rich harvest of cholera bacilli. Studies showed that flies could spread typhoid directly from feces to food. Nancy Tomes, *The Gospel of Germs: Men, Women, and the Microbe in American Life* (Cambridge, MA: Harvard University Press, 1998), 99.

[35] Dawn Day Biehler, *Pests in the City: Flies, Bedbugs, Cockroaches, and Rats* (Seattle: University of Washington Press, 2013), 28, citing C. F. Hodge and Jean Dawson, *Civic Biology* (Boston: Ginn, 1918), 234.

[36] Intestinal disorders were looked upon as natural. As an early twentieth century British epidemiologist noted: "Constipation on the one hand, and diarrhea on the other, are regarded as disorders suitably adapted for home treatment, and not requiring special medical advice. The idea of infection is of course never entertained, and in laying about for a cause it is customary to seize upon the first suggestion that comes to hand. In infants it is invariably the teeth; in adults, since it cannot be the tooth, it is fruit; and of the different kinds of the latter, plums for preference. In the early summer, when plums are not available the cause is generally referred to strawberries. Among the causes assigned to demonstrably typical attacks of epidemic diarrhea were medicine, currants, chocolates, fruit, teething, heat, and cold. It is true there seems to be a generally recognised obligation to name a cause for the attack, but having discharged that duty in the manner above indicated, and generally it appears with great mutual satisfaction to all concerned, patients and friends lapse into complete indifference upon the matter. Moreover, this not incorrectly sets for the attitude of the general public, educated and uneducated alike, to what is in reality a very great scourge and a great sanitary reproach to the community at large." O. H. Peters, *Observations upon the Natural History of Epidemic Diarrhoea* (Cambridge: Cambridge University Press, 1911), 21–22.

FIGURE 4.3 "Kill the fly and save the child."
Source: *The Medical Officer* (1920)

a detailed epidemiological study of diarrheal disease in the town of
Mansfield, England found that there were no substantial improvements
in the districts in which pails and privies had been entirely replaced by
flush toilets. There was, in fact, a slightly greater incidence in the
"improved" neighborhoods. The core variables that explained disease

transmission were the density of the infant population and the corresponding wholesale fecal contamination within the house. Flies were implicated in disease transmission, but in Mansfield the flies transmitted the infections from human fecal matter, not from animal manure.[37]

The contamination of foodstuffs – particularly milk – also played an important role in disease transmission. For millennia, because milk spoiled quickly and was difficult to transport, it had been consumed locally. Rich in bacteria when drawn directly from an animal's udder, milk was commonly contaminated with hair, urine, and animal fecal matter, and thus many societies either boiled their milk before use or allowed it to ferment in order to neutralize the pathogens. It was quintessentially a rural foodstuff, and in some areas – such as northern Europe – it was a drink of the poor.

In the nineteenth century, the growth of European and North American cities, fueled by rural in-migration, created a new demand for milk. The farm insinuated itself into the city. Urban dairies fed their milch cows on the grain wastes of the urban breweries and distilleries that met other key demands of the working poor. Confinement in the dairy stalls and the diet of fermented and highly acidic grain waste took its toll. The cows developed disease and led short lives.

Human avarice took its toll as well. Dairymen scooped cream and most of the nutrients from the milk. They then added water, chalk, thickeners (including cow brains), and other materials to produce what was known as swill milk, the staple of the urban market. As cities grew larger, the urban dairies were unable to meet the demand, and with the construction of new railroad spurs into the countryside, rural dairies began to produce for the cities. They too adulterated their milk, and a combination of unhygienic practices and the lack of refrigeration resulted in high rates of contamination. This poor-quality product killed a few urban adults and sickened many others. Its principal impact, however, was on children. It sent many to the grave.[38]

---

[37] Peters, *Observations Upon the Natural History of Epidemic Diarrhoea*, 52, 58, 64–65.

[38] For a short, lucid history, see Hannah Velten, *Milk: A Global History* (London: Reaktion Books, 2010). For a careful examination of the role of milk in the UK, see P. J. Atkins, "White Poison? The Social Consequences of Milk Consumption, 1850–1930," *Social History of Medicine*, vol. 5, no. 2 (1992), 207–27.

   Interestingly, in the late nineteenth century, studies on both sides of the North Atlantic found that children who were breastfed rarely were victims of "summer diarrhea." See, for example, T. Clarke Miller, "A Contribution to the Etiology, Pathology, and Therapeutics of Cholera Infantum," *American Journal of Obstetrics and Diseases of Women and Children*, vol. 12 (1879), 236–51; John A. Henning, "The Summer Diarrhea of Children," *Ohio Medical Recorder*, vol. 4 (1879–80), 152–54; L. Emmett Holt,

Childhood diarrheal deaths from contaminated milk, however, remained a low-profile issue for decades, in an era when childhood mortality from all causes was high. The principal preoccupation of urban adults was tuberculosis, the "white plague" that was said to be the "scourge of the race."

Childhood deaths from diarrhea peaked during the summer months.[39] In Baltimore, summer diarrhea killed three times as many individuals as did TB.[40] There was a simple solution to the problem – to heat the milk in order to kill the pathogens. The virtues of "pasteurization" had been known since the 1870s, but vested interests, fearing the expense and burden of government regulation, fought long and hard against milk ordinances.[41]

### THE TYPHOID FEVER VACCINE

In the years following Louis Pasteur's elaboration of the germ theory of disease and his revolutionary experiments with the use of live attenuated bacilli and viruses to produce immunizations against anthrax and rabies, other researchers, inspired by Pasteur's successes, explored the possibilities of a protective vaccination against typhoid fever. Typhoid fever was a major threat to colonial tropical empire. During the Spanish American War (1898), for example, the rate of typhoid fever admissions to field hospitals among US military forces ran an extraordinary 140 per 1,000 troops.[42] Laboratories in Germany and Britain went to work on

---

"The Antiseptic Treatment of Summer Diarrhea," *Archives of Pediatrics*, vol. 3 (1886), 726–51. These studies marked a significant advance in understanding summer diarrhea. Earlier writers identified hot weather as a major cause.

[39] The phenomenon of summer diarrhea in urban settings had been discussed as early as the 1790s. See Charles Caldwell, *An Attempt to Establish the Original Sameness of Three Phenomena of Fever (Principally Confined to Infants and Children), Described by Medical Writers under the Several Names of Hydrocephalus Internus, Cynanche Trachealis, and Diarrhea Infantum* (Philadelphia: Thomas Dobson, 1796), 42–48.

[40] In Baltimore at the turn of the twentieth century, summer diarrhea accounted for roughly one half of the annual childhood deaths. J. H. M. Knox Jr. and V. H. Bassett, "An Examination of Milk Supplied to Infants Suffering with Summer Diarrhea, with a Plea for a Purer Milk Supply Accessible to the Poor of Baltimore," *Maryland Medical Journal*, vol. 45, no. 6 (1902), 242.

[41] On the decline of the protective practice of breastfeeding, see Jacqueline H. Wolf, *Don't Kill Your Baby: Public Health and the Decline of Breastfeeding in the Nineteenth and Twentieth Centuries* (Columbus: Ohio State University Press, 2001), 65–70.

[42] Research Laboratories of the Army Medical School, *Immunization to Typhoid Fever* (Baltimore: Johns Hopkins University Press, 1941), 15–16; Vincent J. Cirillo, *Bullets and Bacilli: The Spanish-American War and Military Medicine* (New Brunswick, NJ: Rutgers University Press, 2004).

a typhoid fever vaccine in the late 1890s.[43] In 1900, the British researcher Almroth Wright pioneered a killed typhoid vaccine that was administered to troops in India and South Africa and inmates of an asylum in Dublin, reducing the incidence of morbidity in all groups by 50–96 percent and the case fatality rate roughly by half.[44] Not all British troops received this protection. During the Second Boer War (1899–1901), British troops suffered epidemic typhoid fever. Admissions to hospital ran 114 per 1,000 per annum, with a death rate of 13.77 percent.[45]

The Germans, French, and Americans also developed typhoid vaccines, and their usage eventually became widespread.[46] The US Army adopted a vaccine in 1909 on a voluntary basis, and in 1911 it became the first army to make vaccination compulsory. The policy paid dividends. During the First World War, US typhoid cases were an astonishingly low 37 per 100,000.[47] The British administered more than a million doses to protect British soldiers during the First World War, and the vaccine is credited with saving a half million lives.[48] The Germans also used the vaccine and reduced the number of typhoid fever deaths among their troops to low

---

[43] Dieter H. M. Gröschel and Richard B. Hornick, "Who Introduced Typhoid Vaccination: Almroth Wright or Richard Pfeiffer?," *Reviews of Infectious Diseases*, vol. 3, no. 6 (1981), 1251–54.

[44] Almroth E. Wright, *A Short Treatise on Anti-Typhoid Inoculation* (Westminster: Archibald Constable, 1904), 62–64.

[45] Joseph F. Siler and John S. Lambie Jr., "Typhoid and the Paratyphoid Fevers," in *The Medical Department of the U.S. Army in the World War*, vol. IX, *Communicable and Other Diseases* (Washington, DC: US Government Printing Office, 1928), 17. Today, typhoid fever, if untreated, can result in up to 10 percent mortality in adults; and even if treated successfully, some infections become chronic and asymptomatic. Fatality rates in children under four years of age may be even higher, ranging between 10 and 20 percent. A. Anwar, E. Goldberg, A. Fraser, C. J. Acosta, M. Paul, and L. Leibovici, "Vaccines for Preventing Typhoid Fever," *Cochrane Database of Systematic Cochrane Reviews*, no. 1 (2014): Article CD001261, https://doi.org/10.1002/14651858.CD001261.pub3, 5.

About 1–6 percent of those infected develop chronic gall bladder infections that are a reservoir of infections that maintain ongoing transmission. Thomas Ruby, Laura McLaughlin, Smita Gopinath, and Denise Monack, "Salmonella's Long-Term Relationship with Its Host," *FEMS Microbiology Reviews*, vol. 36, no. 3 (2012), 600.

[46] Derek S. Linton, "Was Typhoid Inoculation Safe and Effective during World War I? Debates within German Military Medicine," *Journal of the History of Medicine and Allied Sciences*, vol. 55, no. 2 (2000), 106–7,

[47] Research Laboratories of the Army Medical School, *Immunization to Typhoid Fever*, 15–16.

[48] The efficacy of this vaccine was only established in 1960. It is estimated at 73 percent. Anwar et al., "Vaccines for Preventing Typhoid Fever," 6. Check Mark Harrison, *The Medical War: British Military Medicine in the First World War* (Oxford: Oxford University Press, 2010).

levels.[49] By contrast, the French troops were only partially protected during the first two years of the conflict and suffered high rates of infection.[50]

The threat of typhoid infections also loomed in nonmilitary settings. In the United States, during the Great Depression, living conditions in the Civilian Conservation Corps camps were highly unsanitary. When the typhoid vaccine for these government workers was finally adopted in 1936, hospital admission rates dropped by about 90 percent.[51] The lesson was clear. Typhoid fever could be contained in the North Atlantic region, when and if the political will was mobilized to do so.[52]

### WATER FILTRATION AND DISINFECTION

Sanitary engineers had built sand filtration systems to reduce turbidity and algae in drinking water supplies well before the discovery of pathogenic bacteria in the late nineteenth century. The sand filters were highly effective in removing the visible objectionable characteristics of the water and, depending upon local variables, were to a greater or lesser extent effective in reducing the invisible microbial threats to health. The natural filters, however, had two significant drawbacks: they required large plots of dedicated land, and water moved slowly through them. Sand filters had been pioneered in Europe, mostly in England, and cities in the United States experimented with them. In the eastern United States, they had problems. The high clay content of the soils, in combination with higher rainfalls and a greater number of violent storms, meant that the filters had to be cleaned more frequently and that the water required pretreatment with anticoagulants and sedimentation in settling basins.[53] Water engineers in the United States developed a system of mechanical filtration that would work after the larger solid particles had been removed, and when this was combined with alum anticoagulation and sedimentation, the hybrid technologies achieved something of a milestone in the safety of

[49] On the complexities of determining the effectiveness of the typhoid fever vaccine during the war and the debates within the German military, see Derek S. Linton, "Was Typhoid Inoculation Safe and Effective during World War I? Debates within German Military Medicine," *Journal of the History of Medicine and Allied Sciences*, vol. 55, no. 2 (2000), 101–33.

[50] Siler and Lambie, "Typhoid and Paratyphoid Fevers," 22.

[51] Research Laboratories of the Army Medical School, *Immunization to Typhoid Fever*, 28.

[52] Research Laboratories of the Army Medical School, *Immunization to Typhoid Fever*, 18.

[53] Michael J. McGuire, *The Chlorine Revolution: Water Disinfection and the Fight to Save Lives* (Denver, CO: American Water Works Association, 2013), 89–91.

urban water supply. The design was first worked out at Little Falls, New Jersey. Bacterial counts of the water passed through the system showed that the bacterial counts had been reduced to one-sixtieth of that in the influent.[54]

In the late nineteenth century, sanitary engineers knew that urban surface water supplies, particularly if impounded, were at risk of inadvertent contamination with human and animal wastes. In 1893, sanitary engineers carried out successful experiments with ozonation to purify the drinking water supply at Oudshoorn in the Netherlands, and thereafter a number of ozonation plants were built in the northern hemisphere, including in France, Germany, Russia, the United States, and Spain.[55]

A second approach to the disinfection of water was chemical treatment with chlorine. The first significant use was in 1897, when sanitary engineers used chlorine to quell a typhoid epidemic in Maidstone, England, that struck 5 percent of the town's population and killed 150 people. Five years later, in 1902, in Middelkirke, Belgium, engineers began the first continuous application of chlorine (chloride of lime) to a town's water supply. In 1904–5, a typhoid epidemic broke out in Lincoln, England, and it too was suppressed by chlorine.[56]

The acceptance of chlorine advanced slowly. In the United States, there was resistance to the idea of using a chemical to purify drinking water – perhaps in part due to the unregulated use of chemical additives in milk, meat, and other foods to make adulterated and spoiled foods palatable. There was also the apparent illogic of using what were known to be poisonous chemicals such as chloride of lime, copper, or oxalic acid to produce "clean" water.[57]

In Jersey City, New Jersey, water engineers became convinced that the use of chloride of lime or chlorine gas could disinfect the city's water supplies. They worked in secret to develop the protocols. In 1908, they dosed the Boonton Reservoir that supplied water to Jersey City with chlorine. It was the first large-scale municipal water supply to be so treated, and shortly thereafter at least another twenty-seven cities adopted the practice without informing their customers. The disinfection of the

---

[54] McGuire, *Chlorine Revolution*, 1–6.
[55] Bruno Langlais, David A. Reckhow, and Deborah R. Brink (eds.), *Ozone in Water Treatment: Application and Engineering* (Boca Raton, FL: CRC Press, 1991), 2–3.
[56] George A. Johnson, "Hypochlorite Treatment of Public Water Supplies: Its Adaptability and Limitations," *American Journal of Public Health*, vol. 1, no. 8 (1911), 562–74; McGuire, *Chlorine Revolution*, 72–75.
[57] McGuire, *Chlorine Revolution*, 86–89.

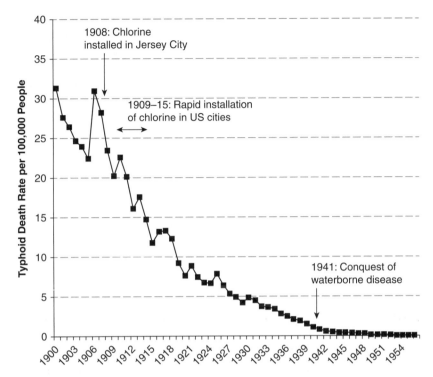

FIGURE 4.4 Typhoid fever rate in the United States, 1900–1956.
Source: Michael J. McGuire, *The Chlorine Revolution: Water Disinfection and the Fight to Save Lives* (Denver, CO: American Water Works Association, 2013), Figure 12-5

water supply was picking up speed.[58] Thereafter, engineers also began to experiment with the application of chlorine to sewage.[59]

In the United States, the success of chlorine was remarkable. Elsewhere its progress was neither rapid nor extensive, and as a result some urban populations were struck by typhoid fever epidemics. In 1926, an outbreak of typhoid fever struck Hanover, Germany. There were 2,423 cases and 545 deaths – a case fatality rate of 22 percent. In 1927, Montreal had

[58] McGuire, *Chlorine Revolution*, 246.
[59] Engineers had experimented on a small scale with the use of chlorine to disinfect sewage – that is, to kill the pathogenic bacteria but not to fully sterilize the sewage (which was practically impossible) – as early as 1892, but the application of chlorine to sewage was not extensively practiced until the second decade of the twentieth century – after chlorine had first been used in the Boonton Reservoir in New Jersey. McGuire, *Chlorine Revolution*, 96–97.

a typhoid fever outbreak that killed 488 of the 5,014 who fell ill (a case fatality rate of almost 10 percent) as a result of milk contaminated by typhoid carriers who worked in milk plants. Between late November 1928 and the end of January 1929, there were about 3,000 cases of typhoid fever in the Lyons Suburban District, with about 300 deaths.[60] The weak links in the water systems were the use of untreated surface supplies, contaminated groundwater supplies, inadequate purification, and contamination in the water collection and distribution systems. Calls rang out for government action that echoed those earlier in the twentieth century against animal diseases and unsanitary meatpacking practices.[61]

In the broader North Atlantic region, the quality of the urban water supplies improved greatly. The typhoid fever death rate in the United States and Canada declined steeply after 1900.[62] This was in good measure a result of the methods of water filtration and water purification with chlorine and ozone.

In the early nineteenth century, the problems of human and animal excrement disposal in rapidly growing urban areas loomed large. In London, engineers designed an underground sewer system to carry waterborne human waste that became the prototype of modern sewerage. Improved feces disposal, however, did little to lower the appalling toll of death exacted by infectious intestinal diseases. The breakthrough came after years of dumping raw sewage into nearby bodies of water and using sewage to fertilize agricultural fields. The combined filtration and purification of drinking water achieved lasting success in reducing the transmission of fecal–oral pathogens.

[60] Abel Wolman and A. E. Gorman, *The Significance of Waterborne Typhoid Fever Outbreaks 1920–1931* (Baltimore: Williams and Wilkins, 1931), 2, 45–46; H. D. Pease, "Public Health Engineering: An Investigation of the Montreal Typhoid Epidemic of 1927," *American Journal of Public Health and the Nations Health*, vol. 22, no.6 (1932), 654–56.
[61] Alan L. Olmstead and Paul W. Rhode, *Arresting Contagion: Science, Policy, and Conflicts over Animal Disease Control* (Cambridge, MA: Harvard University Press, 2015).
[62] Wolman and Gorman, *Waterborne Typhoid Fever Outbreaks*, 49.

# 5

# Adoptions and Adaptations

All growing cities confronted growing sanitation problems. As urban populations bulged from in-migration, municipal governments in the North Atlantic region made efforts to filter their water supplies and reduce the stench of human waste and thereby the limit outbreaks of miasmatic disease. Most early programs were partial and influenced by class interests. As they rang up successes, improved water supplies and sewerage became emblematic of an emerging sanitary modernity in which the reduction of stench was synonymous with progress.

Some governments, even before the adoption of the flush toilet, made extensive and visionary sanitary investments. Better storm water sewers alone, for example, could reduce urban flooding and pollution from overflowing cesspools. In Hamburg, after much of the city burned to the ground in 1842, the city authorities decided to construct an underground storm water sewer system as the city was rebuilt. Mid-nineteenth-century Paris underwent a massive urban renovation program that incorporated modern sanitation in stages. Storm sewer construction began in 1850; house connections for human waste were added from the 1880s into the 1910s; and an integrated system was completed in 1930.[1] In some European cities, epidemic cholera provided the impetus to make improvements. Most German cities committed to

[1] Lionel Kesztenbaum and Jean-Laurent Rosenthal, "Sewers' Diffusion and the Decline of Mortality: The Case of Paris, 1880–1914," *Journal of Urban Economics*, vol. 98 (2017), 178–86.

build sewerage systems to handle human waste in the wake of the cholera epidemics of the 1860s.[2]

Other industrializing cities made slower progress. Vienna had had an advanced storm sewer system as early as 1830, and some 80 percent of houses that were taxed had sewer connections. In the first half of the nineteenth century, most human waste was dumped into the sewers that led to the tributaries that fed the main sewage canal through the city and eventually made its way to the Danube River. Only in the 1860s did Vienna's authorities begin to finance an integrated sewer system to handle piped, waterborne sewage. It advanced in stages during an era in which the main sewer canal alternately experienced a low flow and produced a choking stench or a high flow and sent backed-up sewage flowing into the city streets, cellars, and houses.[3]

Some cities outside of the industrializing regions lagged behind. In the second half of the nineteenth century, Lisbon, for example, opted for an improvement in its water supply, without a sewer system to handle human waste. Planning for "modern" sewerage began only when the water system was completed in 1880, although its expansion was hampered by the fact that many city residents did not have piped water to their houses. The municipality advocated for linking the cesspits and privy vaults by pipes to the sewers; but this was imprudent when there was little or no water to flush the pipes. As a consequence, sewerage in Lisbon advanced fitfully. Only 60 percent of Lisbon's residents had piped household water in 1900.[4]

## WATER AND SANITATION IN LATIN AMERICA

In Latin America, modernizing elites sought to emulate the public health advances made in Europe. The leader in Latin America was Brazil. In the mid-nineteenth century, the municipal authorities in Rio di Janeiro contracted with a British firm to install plumbing fixtures in the city.

---

[2] Hendrik Seeger, "The History of German Waste Water Treatment," *European Water Management*, vol. 2 (1999), 51.

[3] Sylvia Gierlinger, Gertrud Haidvogl, Simone Gingrich, and Fridolin Krausmann, "Feeding and Cleaning the City: The Role of the Urban Waterscape in Provision and Disposal in Vienna during the Industrial Transformation," *Water History*, vol. 5, no. 2 (2013), 230–33.

[4] Luísa Schmidt, Tiago Saraiva, and João Pato, "In Search of the (Hidden) Portuguese Urban Water Conflicts: The Lisbon Water Story (1856–2006)," in Bernard O. Barraqué (ed.), *Urban Water Conflicts* (Boca Raton, FL: CRC Press, 2011), 76.

The engineers designed a system to direct the flow of mountain streams into Rio. Six hundred and seventy spigots sprouted in the urban center and the two thousand houses gained direct water pipes. There was no system of sewerage. The inhabitants of Rio used cesspits, and contractors sporadically removed the human waste from the city.[5] Elsewhere in Brazil, there was neither the capital nor motivation to undertake such public waterworks. Town dwellers and villagers drew their water from wells and local streams, rivers, and lakes. Sanitary conditions in the countryside and on plantations remained primitive.

Following the abolition of Brazilian slavery in 1888, many of the newly freed fled the plantations for the cities. With the new constitution of 1889, the provincial governments, autonomous in their sanitation policies, opted to allow private water companies to provide services to those who could afford to pay. In Brazilian cities, the impoverished ex-slaves were excluded from water services, and in popular protests against their conditions of life, they targeted the water companies as symbols of class and racial inequality. In the early twentieth century, water services were nationalized, but their reach advanced slowly. The systems were expensive; they served the core government buildings and elite neighborhoods.

In Argentina, where recent southern European migrants made up most of the population, a similar process unfolded, without the legacy of slavery. There, the water sector evolved as a hybrid, with government providing water services in the capital Buenos Aires, and private companies in other urban centers.[6] There was no modern sewerage, and private companies charged to clean out cesspits. In Buenos Aires, as in Rio di Janeiro, the mid-nineteenth-century system of cart haulage of human waste replicated that in mainland Spain and elsewhere in southern Europe.[7] Eventually the wealthy, who aspired to sanitary modernity, invested in water closets or earth closets inside their homes. As in much of Europe, the slow and incomplete adoption of modern sanitation in

[5] Christopher Abel, "Health, Hygiene and Sanitation in Latin America, c. 1870 to c. 1950," University of London, Institute for Latin American Studies, Research Paper no. 42 (1996), 29–30.

[6] José Esteban Castro and Leo Heller, "The Historical Development of Water and Sanitation in Brazil and Argentina," in Petri S. Juuti, Tapio S. Katko, and Heikki S. Vuorinen (eds.), *Environmental History of Water* (London: IWA, 2007), 434–35.

[7] Ángel Ó. Prignano, *El Inodoro y Sus Conexiones: La Indiscreta Historia del Lugar de Necesidad Que, Por Común, Excusado Es Nombrarlo* (Buenos Aires: Editorial Biblos, 2007).

Latin America reflected the limited financial means and lack of political will to undertake expensive public works.

Well into the twentieth century, in much of Latin America, the issue of race, in addition to that of social class, had a determinative influence. Piped water was the perquisite first of the wealthy and later the burgeoning middle classes, most of whom laid claim to European heritage. Throughout the continent, people of African or Native American descent continued to rely upon untreated surface and well water. Even as late as 1970 in Brazil, fewer than a third of households had piped water. Fewer than a fifth in urban areas had sewerage services.[8] Infectious intestinal disease remained one of the top killers throughout Latin America into the late twentieth century, principally because of the contamination of drinking water. Most deaths went unregistered.

## EUROPEAN COLONIAL MILITARY SANITATION

In the nineteenth century, European states acquired new overseas colonies in the tropics, where the disease threats were daunting. Mosquito-borne diseases such as yellow fever and malaria could be lethal, particularly for Europeans who had had no previous exposure to them.[9] The most dangerous health threats, however, were from infectious intestinal diseases, with typhoid fever (also known as enteric or camp fever) at the top of the list.[10]

Military hygiene specialists worked to reduce the troops' exposure to the stench that caused miasmas. They had three basic models of feces disposal to choose from – water flush, dry earth, and pit latrine. In the wake of the Indian Mutiny of 1857–58, as responsibility for the governance of India devolved from the British East India Company to the British Crown, sanitary improvements took on increased urgency: more British troops would have to be stationed in the colony even as investigations revealed that the Indian troops under British command were healthier

---

[8] Jairnilson Paim, Claudia Travassos, Celia Almeida, Ligia Bahia, and James Macinko, "The Brazilian Health System: History, Advances, and Challenges," *Lancet*, vol. 377, no. 9779 (2011), 4, Table 2.

[9] On malaria in tropical Africa, see James L. A. Webb Jr., *The Long Struggle against Malaria in Tropical Africa* (New York: Cambridge University Press, 2014).

[10] On the importance of infectious intestinal diseases for European troops sent to the tropics, see Philip D. Curtin, *Death by Migration: Europe's Encounter with the Tropical World in the Nineteenth Century* (New York: Cambridge University Press, 1989), 145–54.

than the British troops.[11] The British military recommended flush toilets in 1866 for all permanent military establishments, but this was not always feasible. In the Madras Presidency of India, for example, the military adopted the dry earth system.[12] The dry earth option, however, only made sense in environments in which the manure could be put to use as fertilizer. In the British hill stations, atop mountains with slopes unsuitable for cultivation, the military incinerated the excreta.[13]

By contrast, the French neither recommended nor provided flush toilets for their overseas troops, and they depended on either fixed pit latrines or one or another variation on the dry earth system. By the 1870s, the French had adopted a variant of the tub-and-pail system known as the "Goux system," named after a French landowner. Its core innovation lay in the idea of conveying tubs of excrement that had been lined with an absorptive layer of woolen shoddy or other textile waste to a "treatment center," where the urine and other liquids were allowed to drain off before the finished product was taken to the fields.[14]

## WATER AND SANITATION IN EAST ASIA

In the aftermath of the Opium Wars (1839–42, 1856–60), Britain and then other European industrial powers (and even later, the United States and Japan) gained political control over Qing Dynasty "treaty ports." Here the British and other European imperial powers imposed sanitary rules, treating night soil and animal waste removal as a matter of public health. By the 1870s, observers noted a contrast between the foul smells and filthy environments of other Chinese cities and those of the "sanitized" treaty ports.[15] By the turn of the twentieth century, in Tianjin, the most commercially important treaty port, Chinese entrepreneurs had begun to introduce urban public toilets whose contents were transported into the surrounding countryside. By the 1940s, in Tianjin there were nearly 500 public toilets available for public use. This was, however,

[11] Michael Zeheter, *Epidemics, Empire, and Environments: Cholera in Madras and Quebec City, 1818–1910* (Pittsburgh: University of Pittsburgh Press, 2015), 163–65.

[12] Curtin, *Death by Migration,* 56–60; on French and British efforts to provide pure water to their troops, 116–25; see also Zeheter, *Epidemics, Empire, and Environments,* 185.

[13] R. J. Blackham, "The Goux System and Its Application to India," *Journal of the Royal Army Medical Corps,* vol. 6 (1906), 662–27.

[14] Curtin, *Death by Migration,* 112–14.

[15] Xinzhong, "Night Soil and Waste in Modern China," 62–63; Ruth Rogaski, *Hygienic Modernity: Meanings of Health and Disease in Treaty-Port China* (Berkeley: University of California Press, 2014).

FIGURE 5.1  Night soil boats in Hankou, China, 1911.
Source: Franklin H. King, *Farmers of Forty Centuries; or, Permanent Agriculture in China, Korea, and Japan* (Madison, WI: Mrs. F. H. King, 1911)

a transitional moment. By the late 1940s, many residents were flushing their wastes into septic tanks.[16]

During the early decades of the Meiji Restoration (1868–1912), in Tokyo (formerly Edo), one of the most densely populated cities in the world, the residents conserved their human waste in receptacles that were transported to rural areas. Although there was no discharge of shit or urine into the streets or sewers, leaky toilets contaminated some water supplies. The Japanese suffered major cholera epidemics in the 1850s, 1870s, 1880s, and early 1890s. Only after the cholera epidemic of 1895, did the Meiji government institute a Cholera Prevention and Disinfection Law and a Cleanliness Law, apparently to good effect.[17]

In the late nineteenth century the Meiji government began modern waterworks for Tokyo that were completed in 1911.[18] Interestingly, the Japanese officials had little interest in modern sewerage. As late as the

[16] Interestingly, the urine from Tianjin was not valued and did not enter the distribution system. Cao Mu, "The Public Lavatory of Tianjin: A Change in Urban Faeces Disposal in the Process of Modernization," *Global Environment*, vol. 9 (2016), 200, 202, 213.

[17] William Johnston, "The Shifting Epistemological Foundations of Cholera Control in Japan (1822–1900)," *Extrême-Orient Extrême-Occident*, no. 37 (2014), 181–86.

[18] Yurina Otaki, "Case of Tokyo, Japan," in Petri S. Juuti, Tapio S. Katko, and Heikki S. Vuorinen (eds.), *Environmental History of Water* (London: IWA, 2007), 463–73.

1940s, most urban Japanese continued to husband their night soil for export to the farms.[19] During World War II, night soil removal from the capital was interrupted, and in the aftermath of the war, under the US occupation (1945–52), the city government attempted to revive the night soil system. Farmers, however, had begun to use chemical fertilizers, and the market for night soil shrank. In the early 1960s, Tokyo undertook the construction of a modern sewerage system.[20]

The city of Singapore broadly followed a trajectory similar to that of Tokyo, with an initial investment in waterworks and a lagging sewage sector. The public health outcomes in Singapore, however, have been judged better than those in Japan. This may have been the result of different methods of removing night soil from residences. The Singaporeans used the pail system of their British colonizers; the Japanese moved night soil by ladle, apparently with more spillage.[21]

For Europeans in the East Asian colonies, piped water was one of the principal markers of sanitary modernity. The early years of piped water, however, were a double-edged sanitary sword. Piped water encouraged better personal hygiene and reduced the labor of hauling water for cooking, cleaning, and washing clothes. Yet, when the pipes became contaminated, they could spread disease far and wide. As an early twentieth-century author put it: "Public water supplies and modern systems of sewerage were unknown in oriental cities until the Europeans arrived, hence, although endemic or sporadic cases occurred and took the nature of 'house-infections' amongst the natives before then, there could be no general outbreak from a common source."[22]

---

[19] Hanley, "Urban Sanitation in Preindustrial Japan," 2, 14.

[20] Paul Kreitman, "Attacked by Excrement: The Political Ecology of Shit in Wartime and Postwar Tokyo," *Environmental History*, vol. 23 (2018), 342–66.

[21] Yurina Otaki, Masahiro Otaki, and Osamu Sakura, "Water Systems and Urban Sanitation: A Historical Comparison of Tokyo and Singapore," in *Journal of Water and Health*, vol. 5, no. 2 (2007), 259–65.

[22] Anonymous, "Enteric or Typhoid Fever in the Hot Climates," *Journal of Tropical Medicine*, January 15, 1904, 27–28. The East Asian cultural practice of boiling water to make tea and using boiled rice water for drinking seems to have reduced the transmission of infectious intestinal disease. Canton compared very favorably with Hong Kong which was populated principally by Europeans who suffered fevers, diarrhea, and dysentery at all seasons. Ernest Norfleet, "Conservation of Filth in Chinese Cities and the Fruits Thereof," *The Sanitarian*, no. 270 (1892), 434–35; Edward S. Morse, "Latrines of the East," *American Architect and Building News*, vol. 39, no. 899 (1893), 171; Robert Coltman, *The Chinese, Their Present and Future: Medical, Political, and Social* (Philadelphia: F. A. Davis, 1891), 132, 144–45.

## WATER AND SANITATION IN TROPICAL AFRICA

In the European colonies of tropical Africa, the options to pursue sanitary modernity were limited. In most, the colonial governments had a small revenue base and were generally required to be self-sufficient. Some modest investments were made to improve water supplies in colonial West African towns when the local topography was favorable. In the French colony of Guinée, the colonizers piped water to Conakry from hills some forty-one kilometers away. In the British colony of Sierra Leone, the colonizers piped in water to Freetown from hills nearby.[23]

Other coastal West African towns, however, were low-lying with high water tables and solutions to the sanitary challenges were difficult to find. Most people drew their water from shallow wells or rivers that could be easily contaminated with human and animal waste. One of the worst was the town of Bathurst in the Gambia. There, in the early twentieth century, the British colonial government attempted to reduce the pollution of subsurface waters by reclaiming the headlands of two swamps that intersected the town and which were used as latrines. This effort produced a modest improvement, but the colonizers found that they could not eliminate their colonial subjects' use of tub latrines set in the ground and the practice of open defecation. Lagos in Southern Nigeria – with a population ten times that of Bathurst, was similarly low-lying, with nearby swamps. Ground water lay just below the surface, but it was polluted by cesspools that were frequently situated in close proximity to the shallow wells. By 1915, the British pumped poor-quality river water to the town, as the best available option.

In polluted environments, the Europeans and Africans alike frequently depended upon rainwater harvested from roofs and eaves. In Lagos, the Europeans stored the rainwater runoff in tanks, and then boiled and filtered it. There was, however, not enough rainwater for all domestic purposes, and the British used well water for washing and sometimes for cooking. They attempted to protect the subsurface waters from pollution by using a "self-sinking concrete well." As the population of Lagos increased, the British pumped runoff from catchment fields outside the town to a service reservoir in the town itself.[24] In the Gold Coast, the

---

[23] R. Boyce, A. Evans, and H. H. Clarke, *Report on the Sanitation and Anti-Malarial Measures in Practice in Bathurst, Conakry, and Freetown* (London: University Press of Liverpool, 1905), 26–28.

[24] Boyce et al., *Report on the Sanitation and Anti-Malarial Measures*, 26–28; Henry Reeve, "Water Supply of West African Towns," *Journal of the Royal Sanitary Institute*, vol. 24 (1904), 1057–67, esp. 1064.

British distributed metal tanks to the Europeans to collect rainwater and built a "reservoir" for the Africans that soon became too contaminated to use for domestic purposes.[25]

The revolution in chlorination and ozonation that provided "pure" water in the northern hemisphere was slow to reach into Africa. So were sewerage systems. In many towns in eastern, southern, and central Africa, the colonizers pumped river water without treatment.[26] The construction of surface sewers lagged behind the water supplies, with predictable results.[27] In rural Africa, the conditions could be dire. In the mid-1940s, for example, the Government of Southern Rhodesia reported that in the rural areas, on farms and even at government stations, the residents got their water from muddy waterholes or ponds infested with snails that carried schistosomiasis.[28]

Feces disposal was no less problematic. The Europeans brought with them their knowledge of earth closets and trenching and considered their practices sanitary.[29] They had mixed success in reforming their colonial subjects' defecation habits. In Bathurst, for example, the British discovered that some of the town's inhabitants relieved themselves in receptacles and dumped the night soil into the ocean and tidal river waters. Others used a modified cesspit with a tub placed in the ground or pit privies, and yet others defecated on the beaches, river flats, swamp edges, and town perimeters. The British recommended that the Africans adopt the use of

---

[25] The adoption of water tank storage of rainwater was an outcome of the interest in malaria Sir William McGregor, Governor of Southern Nigeria. Reeve, "Water Supply of West African Towns," 1058.

[26] In Livingstone, Southern Rhodesia, for example, the town's water was drawn direct from the Zambezi River. National Archives of the United Kingdom (hereafter NAUK), CO 795/41/1. Dr. de Boer, Report, May 21, 1931, 4–5.

[27] On Kampala, Uganda, see David Nilsson, "A Heritage of Unsustainability? Reviewing the Origin of the Large-Scale Water and Sanitation System in Kampala, Uganda," *Environment and Urbanization*, vol. 18, no. 2 (2006), 373. On the seaport of Tanga in Tanganyka, see NAUK, CO 691/107/9. P. E. Mitchell, Governor's Deputy to Sir Philip Cunliffe-Lister, Secretary of State for the Colonies, September 6, 1934.

[28] NAUK, CO 64/48. Sessional Papers of Southern Rhodesia, 1945. Report of the National Health Services Inquiry Commission 1945, 37.

[29] The general advice for British living in the tropics was to build a commode or an earth closet detached from the house or accessible from a separate verandah. After use, the commode could be emptied and disinfected and the contents put into a closed receptacle that would then be emptied by the authorities or buried in the garden, with care taken so that the ground surface was leveled and puddles could not form. William J. R. Simpson, *The Maintenance of Health in the Tropics*, 2nd ed. (London: Bale & Danielsson, 1917), 41–42. In West Africa, a trenching pit was recommended. J. Charles Ryan, *Health Preservation in West Africa* (London: John Bale, Sons & Danielssons, 1914), 65–66.

sanitary pails.[30] The pail or bucket system, in line with contemporary practices in many regions of Britain itself, seemed the best option to be had, but into the 1930s British exhortations had not had much effect.[31]

The sanitary challenges in Bathurst were common to most of coastal West Africa, where the water table was high and the local groundwater pollution was extensive. Animals scavenged the fecal deposits in the yards, along the roads, and on the beaches, but this did not prevent the contamination of local ponds.[32] In coastal West Africa, the major colonial success at sanitary reform was in Conakry. There, the French imposed a bucket-and-pail system on Europeans and Africans alike.[33]

In southern and central Africa, the general pattern was for both Europeans and Africans in cities and towns to adopt the bucket system and allow for disposal according to local circumstances. Even in the diamond mining town of Kimberley (now in South Africa), the first city in the southern hemisphere to have electric lighting, the European residents made do with a rudimentary system that employed prisoners to remove night soil pans and empty the pails into a 600-gallon tank mounted on wheels that was pulled by donkeys or oxen. The excrement was buried in trenches about three miles outside the town. In Livingstone, the capital of the colony of Northern Rhodesia (now Zambia), African workers picked up the buckets at night, carried them on poles to one of the entrenching grounds situated about one mile from the center of the town,

---

[30] Boyce et al., *Report on the Sanitation and Anti-Malarial Measures*, 3.
[31] The problem remained unresolved for decades. As the Governor of the Gambia complained in 1935: "The medical experts with complete unanimity say that the condition of Bathurst is a blot on the British name. The Health Authority is engaged in a labour of Sisyphus unless the engineering problem is attacked with equal and simultaneous vigor. I understand that the difficulty is almost entirely financial and therefore I plead for Imperial assistance. It seems to me a matter of some Imperial concern that the oldest British colony in Africa, although it is small and unimportant commercially, should present this spectacle to its neighbors." NAUK, CO 87/240/8. Governor A. R. Richards to Philip Cunliffe-Lister, Secretary of State for the Colonies, March 21, 1935, 14.
   The bucket system remained the basis of the sewage system of Bathurst even into the post–World War II years. NAUK, CO 87/258/12. Gov. Sir Hilary Blood to G. H. Hall, Secretary of State for the Colonies, May 14, 1946; Mr. Miles Cleffad, commentary on the proposal for a water-borne sewerage scheme for Bathurst, May 21, 1946.
[32] Henry Reeve, "Water Supply of West African Towns," *Journal of the Royal Sanitary Institute*, vol. 24 (1904), 1058. By 1900, the British colonists in the Gold Coast mounted a modest reform effort, sending out scavenging teams to clean the streets, and they built some public latrines. Thomas S. Gale, "The Struggle against Disease in the Gold Coast: Early Attempts at Urban Sanitary Reform," *Transactions of the Historical Society of Ghana*, vol. 16, no. 2 (1995), 185–203.
[33] Boyce et al., *Report on the Sanitation and Anti-Malarial Measures*, 14.

dumped the contents into pits five feet deep, and covered them with a thin layer of earth.[34] The bucket system reduced soil pollution and helminthic infections, but it could exacerbate the problem of fly-borne transmission. In Bechuanaland (now Botswana), it was judged possibly worse than allowing the feces to desiccate in the direct sun.[35]

In eastern Africa, the British in Kenya adopted the bucket system in urban areas, townships, and labor camps, and proselytized for pit latrines in the African "reserves" where they met with mixed successes. From 1929 to 1939, the British launched a public health campaign to improve feces disposal practices. Some communities were receptive; others were not, interpreting the campaign as officious interference. Neither the bucket nor the pit latrine system was without problems. The bucket system was expensive, because administrative oversight was needed, the transport of excreta involved inevitable spillage, and a large number of bucket latrines was required to service a dispersed population. Pit latrines bred flies and ran the risk of polluting the underground waters. Pit latrines could cave in during heavy rainfalls, and in some areas white ants ate away the wooden supports in the pit latrines, endangering the user's life. In other areas, rock strata made pit latrines impossible to dig.[36]

Before World War II, in tropical Africa colonial investments in sanitation were scant. There was no single model of sanitation that could be adopted across the diverse environments. The overall thrust of colonial sanitation was simply to reduce fecal pollution, where possible. There was no effort to compost or recycle human waste for fertilizer.[37]

## WATER AND SANITATION IN INDIA

In comparison to tropical Africa, the challenges in India were of a different order of magnitude. There were many large towns and cities, and following the transfer of governmental authority from the British East India Company to the British Crown in 1858, the first sanitation challenge for the British was to build storm sewers in the large cities of administrative

[34] NAUK, CO 795/41/1. Dr. de Boer, Report, May 21, 1931, 4–5.
[35] World Health Organization Archives (hereafter, WHO), AFR/EH/3. H. G. Baity, "Report on a Visit to Bechuanaland, 23 August to 4 September 1956," 20.
[36] Ezekial Nyangeri and Kenneth S. Ombongi, "History of Water Supply and Sanitation in Kenya, 1895–2002," in Petri S. Juuti, Tapio S. Katko, and Heikki S. Vuorinen (eds.), *Environmental History of Water* (London: IWA, 2007), 302–3.
[37] James S. Dunn, "The Borough of Kimberley," *Journal of the Sanitary Institute*, vol. 23 (1902), 369.

importance. The timing was roughly coincident with similar developments in Europe. In Calcutta (now Kolkata), the British had deliberated about the construction of storm sewers since the early nineteenth century and finally approved their construction in the 1850s. The sewer system was completed in the mid-1880s and extended by some 177 kilometers by 1890.[38]

Piped river water was provided to the colonial and wealthier Indian neighborhoods and gradually flush toilets made their debut in the same neighborhoods. A dual system developed. A core of colonial British and wealthy Indian domiciles, with access both to piped house water and protected wells, was surrounded by expanding communities of poor Indians who had access to water through street pumps and who used pit toilets or defecated in the streets.[39]

In India, the provision of piped water had uncertain epidemiological effects. When the pipes became contaminated with pathogens, in the era before water purification, the new water systems could become efficient vehicles for the dissemination of disease. Some observers thought that piped water was responsible for wider outbreaks of typhoid fever than had previously occurred.[40] Others held that following the installation of water systems the urban death rates had increased as a result of an increase in standing water that extended the malarial season.[41] Yet others came to entirely contrary conclusions. As of the First All-India Sanitary Conference in 1911, in the twelve towns in the Madras Presidency that had piped water for more than five years, the death rate attributed to water pollution had declined from 9.8 to 5.8 percent of total mortality. Deaths from "fevers" also decreased markedly from 25 to 16.5 percent.[42]

---

[38] Nilangshu Bhusan Basu, Ayanangshu Dey, and P. G. D. B. M. Duke Ghosh, "Kolkata's Brick Sewer Renewal: History, Challenges and Benefits," *Proceedings of the Institution of Civil Engineers*, vol. 166, no. 2 (2013), 74–81.

[39] Kuntala Lahiri-Dutt, "Researching World Class Watering in Metropolitan Calcutta," *ACME: An International Journal for Critical Geographies*, vol. 14, no. 3 (2015), 700–720.

[40] Anonymous, "Enteric or Typhoid Fever in the Hot Climates," *Journal of Tropical Medicine*, January 15, 1904, 27–28.

[41] Lieut. Colonel Giles, *General Sanitation and Anti-Malarial Measures in Sekondi: The Goldfields and Kumassi* (London: Williams & Norgate for the University Press of Liverpool, 1905), 6.

[42] On this selective evidence, the Madras Presidency adopted a de facto policy of approving the introduction of piped water prior to the introduction of a drainage scheme. In 1911, there were only two modern sewerage or drainage systems in all of the Madras Presidency – one in the city of Madras (now Chennai) and one at the hill station of Ootacamund, although others – including a large project for the town of Madura – were

Urban waterworks, however, reached a small percentage of the total Indian population, and the incidence of cholera in India remained high. Medical specialists thought the overall toll had increased from the late nineteenth century into the early twentieth century. Data were not comprehensive, but even so, reported deaths ran into the hundreds of thousands every year, and in some successive years reached more than a half million per annum.[43] Some could be directly attributed to colonial irrigation policy. In the vast irrigated tracts of the Madras Presidency, for example, sanitary conditions were abominable. The irrigation schemes had been engineered with the goal of increasing revenue through the cultivation of wet crops in order to address the problems of famine that had shaken India during the 1876–78 drought. The irrigated zones were entirely flooded during the rainy seasons. The Indian communities huddled in highly densely populated islands with one human being per two square yards in small houses, with no accommodations for latrines and no sources of drinking water that were not fouled. It was truly a nightmarish result of imperial choices in political economy.[44]

The overall evolution in urban feces disposal practices in India reflected advances in sanitary engineering and patterns of caste and racial privilege. The flush toilet made some headway in elite families, and septic tanks were installed in some of the British urban enclaves. But the major urban sanitation problem for the administrators of British India remained the disposal of a large volume of human shit. (Much of the cattle dung was collected, dried, and burned for fuel.) One solution was to build public latrines that would funnel their contents into septic tanks from which a less objectionable effluent could be discharged into streams and rivers. The solid materials could be removed from the septic tanks and taken to the countryside. Another urban solution was to construct a skeletal sewer

---

in the works. In the city of Madras, the sewage drained by gravity to pump wells, from which it was forced through a rising cast iron main nine miles in length to be spread on a sewage farm. *The Proceedings of the First All-India Sanitary Conference Held at Bombay on 13th and 14th November 1911* (Calcutta: Superintendent Government Printing, 1912), Appendix 8: W. Hutton Superintending Engineer, "Water-Supply and Drainage Works in the Madras Presidency," 84–96.

[43] *The Proceedings of the Second All-India Sanitary Conference Held at Madras, November 11th to 16th, 1912* (Simla: Government Central Branch Press, 1913), vol. 3 Research. Captain C. W. Ross, "The Epidemiology of Cholera," 152–53.

[44] *The Proceedings of the Third All-India Sanitary Conference Held at Lucknow, January 19th to 27th, 1914* (Calcutta: Thacker, Spink, 1914), vol. 2, Papers. Rao Bahadur M. Ramachandra Rao, "Drainage and Sanitation in Rural Areas of the Madras Presidency," 75–84.

without house connections, connect the sewers with public latrines, and to install dumping depots for the waste. The arguments in favor of septic tanks and skeletal sewers were twofold. The sanitary works would reduce the dependence on the caste of Dalits, who occasionally carried out strikes which threatened public health, and reduce costs.[45]

Factories and government institutions posed special sanitation challenges because of the concentration of large numbers of people. Private owners of mills and the directors of government institutions such as railway workshops and asylums were enjoined to adopt the use of industrial-sized septic tanks. These tanks worked well for institutions in which the latrines would have between one and four thousand uses per day, but they were not suitable for small towns, where they would be underutilized.[46]

A less expensive option was shallow trenching. This would not work in all environments, but when the soils were loamy or alluvial, the night soil could be buried. In many cases, the night soil decomposed in six months, and it could then be dug out and sold to cultivators. In some areas, trenches could be planted over in vegetables, tobacco, or other soil-depleting crops, and then retrenched the following year. There was considerable variation. At Lucknow in northern India, the cultivators made arrangements to have the town's excreta brought to the fields, where it was buried for three months. In some of the western districts of India, workers hauled the excreta to dump into large pits from which it was sometimes sold raw to cultivators. One of the major challenges was to ensure that liquid feces did not rise to the surface. When this happened, the results could be spectacular. By one calculation, for example, a 2.3-acre mismanaged trenching ground in Allahabad produced 24 million flies.[47]

In Bangalore in southern India, the British attempted to produce a fully dried and powdered human manure, known as *poudrette*, much as the French had done outside Paris. As Ronald Ross (winner of the 1902 Nobel Prize in Physiology or Medicine) reported in 1896, night soil was collected, layered with ash, and allowed to desiccate in the sun. The product

---

[45] William Wesley Clemesha, *Sewage Disposal in the Tropics* (London: Thacker, Spink, 1910), 4–6.

[46] *The Proceedings of the First All-India Sanitary Conference Held at Bombay on 13th and 14th November 1911* (Calcutta: Superintendent Government Printing, 1912), Appendix 7: W. W. Clemesha, "Uses and Limitations of Small Models of Septic Tanks," 8.

[47] William Wesley Clemesha, *Sewage Disposal in the Tropics* (London: Thacker, Spink, 1910), 2–4; *The Proceedings of the Second All-India Sanitary Conference Held at Madras, November 11th to 16th, 1912* (Simla: Government Central Branch Press, 1913), vol. 2, Hygiene. Major S. A. Harriss, "Night Soil Disposal and Associated Fly Breeding," 393–99.

was found to be particularly useful for some "wet crops" such as sugar-cane, pearl millet, and wheat. Local farmers preferred raw human excrement for other crops such as commercial grasses, paddy rice, and maize.[48]

Sanitary practices in rural India resisted change. In 1911, at the First All-India Sanitary Conference, the sanitary specialists judged that the rural programs of the past half-century had accomplished next to nothing. As of 1910, a mere 595 of the 48,852 towns in the Madras Presidency had any program for improved human waste disposal. One proposal was to concentrate sanitary efforts only on villages with a heavy death toll from cholera. This was despite the fact that rural death rates had been reduced by 20–30 percent when "proper sanitary regulations" had been implemented.[49]

### SANITATION AT MID-TWENTIETH CENTURY

World War II wreaked havoc throughout Europe and East Asia. The number of dead from military violence, genocide, starvation, and population displacements can only be estimated, and no one has even tried to guess at the death toll from infectious intestinal disease. Bombing destroyed urban sanitation systems, and the pollution of water supplies that followed took a large toll in human life. Large numbers died in concentration camps from typhoid fever and cholera, as did large numbers of refugees and those who suffered in city sieges. One of the central tasks of European reconstruction was to rebuild the sanitation infrastructure.

In the aftermath of the war, the western bloc of nations steeled itself for the hostilities known as the Cold War. Neoclassical economists and development planners were confident that economic development and capitalism would counter the political appeal of socialism to poor people. In this context, the economic costs of infectious intestinal disease attracted intense political interest. Development experts estimated that the economic losses from infectious intestinal disease in some countries were so high that the expense of improving rural water supplies and building latrines, including labor, materials, and equipment, could be amortized

---

[48] London School of Hygiene and Ttropical Medicine, Ross Archives, GB0809 Ross/30/01. Surgeon-Major Ronald Ross, *Report on Cholera, General Sanitation, and the Sanitary Department and Regulations in the C. & M. Station of Bangalore* (1896), 63–64.

[49] *The Proceedings of the Second All-India Sanitary Conference Held at Madras, November 11th to 16th, 1912* (Simla: Government Central Branch Press, 1913), vol. 4. Engineering. Chas. N. Mandy, "Note on Sanitation in India," 48.

in two to five years.[50] The US government took advantage of its postwar economic boom to extend water services to most of its urban and rural populations, in contrast to the nation-states to its south.[51]

Latin America states, with the exception of Paraguay, in the era before World War II had piped water supply systems in the capital cities that serviced many of the urban residents. During the war, the United States was fearful of Axis intervention in Latin America and established the Institute for Inter-American Affairs (IIAA) to promote trade within the Americas and to off-set the loss of trade with a Europe at war. The IIAA developed, through the aegis of the Rockefeller Foundation, a program to improve health and sanitation in Latin America, and one of its first projects was to build a public water supply in Asunción, the capital of Paraguay.[52] Health and sanitation projects, launched in all the participating countries, absorbed most of the IIAA resources. The largest projects were in Brazil, the country considered to be most vital to the Allied War effort. The IIAA launched programs in eight countries almost immediately, and by 1950 the IIAA had provided technical assistance to all eighteen member-states. Some cities got sewerage systems and a more secure water supply, including chlorination.[53]

Beyond the urban areas, however, there was little progress. In 1954, sixteen countries in the Americas reported the major causes of death among their national populations. "Diarrheal diseases" were first in importance in nine countries and second in three others. The most important public health challenge in the Americas was determined to be the

[50] The expenses could be reduced considerably if the householders participated directly in the program, supplying labor and local materials. WHO/Env.San./56. C. H. Atkins, "Some Economic Aspects of Sanitation Programmes in Rural Areas and Small Communities" (1953).

[51] John C. Belcher, "Sanitation Norms in Rural Areas: A Cross-Cultural Comparison," *Bulletin of the Pan American Health Organization*, vol. 12, no. 1 (1978), 34; Abel Wolman, "Environmental Sanitation in Urban and Rural Areas: Its Importance in the Control of Enteric Infections," *Bulletin of the Pan American Health Organization*, vol. 9, no. 2 (1975), 157–59.

[52] Claude C. Erb, "Prelude to Point Four: The Institute of Inter-American Affairs," *Diplomatic History*, vol. 9, no. 3 (1985), 256–57. The IIAA program also included the construction of sewers in some parts of the city, an antihookworm program, and other targeted interventions. According to Erb's Table 4.1, "Aid Funds Pledged for Food Supply and Health and Sanitation by the Institute of Inter-American Affairs, to 1945," 88 percent of the IIAA funds went to "Health and Sanitation" projects.

[53] George C. Dunham, "The Coöperative Health Program of the American Republics," *American Journal of Public Health and the Nation's Health*, vol. 34, no. 8 (1944), 817–27; Henry Van Zile Hyde, "Sanitation in the International Health Field," *American Journal of Public Health*, vol. 41, no. 1 (1951), 3.

prevention of infectious intestinal disease transmission. But it proved difficult to mobilize the elites to take it on. Death in childhood was numbingly commonplace, and most deaths took place in the infant (0–1 year) and young child (1–4 year) rural age cohorts of people of Native American or African descent.[54]

In postwar Africa, in the years immediately following World War II, Britain and France increased their financial assistance to their colonies in an effort to speed development and bolster political support for empire.[55] Most of this aid went toward infrastructure projects to improve the economic integration of the colonies with the metropoles.

A modest stream of colonial funds became available for investments in sanitation. Some African towns and cities with a significant European presence acquired flush toilets and septic tanks. The improved accommodations, built with African labor, were typically restricted to government offices and hospitals and the European neighborhoods, although in the late 1950s and early 1960s some urban Africans received improved services.[56] Many urban residents, however, saw no improvements. In Bathurst, for example, with the exception of government buildings and few private residences, the urban population was still served by one hundred water taps in the streets and the bucket-and-pail system.[57] In Burundi, the water supply at the capital Usumbura (now Bujumbura), drawn from the Ntahangwa River, a local source, and two wells, was insecure, with inadequate testing and the immediate danger of contamination from leaking septic systems. The system for cleaning out the urban cesspits barely worked.[58] Those who lived in the burgeoning shantytowns

---

[54] Albert V. Hardy, "Diarrheal Diseases of Man: A Historical Review and Global Appraisal," *Annals of the New York Academy of Sciences*, vol. 66, no. 1 (1956), 5–13.

[55] In 1945, the British passed a Colonial Welfare and Development Act, and in 1946, the French in 1946 passed similar legislation, the Fonds d'Investissement pour le Développement Economique et Social (Investment Fund for Economic and Social Development: FIDES).

[56] Ambe J. Njoh, "Colonization and Sanitation in Urban Africa: A Logistics Analysis of the Availability of Central Sewage Systems as a Function of Colonialism," *Habitat International*, vol. 38 (2013), 207–13.

[57] Some waste was dumped into the storm drains or just left about elsewhere in the city. Earlier in the 1950s, the effluents from the communal latrines and soakaways had been composted with peanut shells and given away free of charge to farmers. But the costs of this system had been deemed prohibitive and the program had ended by the late 1950s. WHO AFR/EH/7. L. A. Orihuela, "Report on a Visit to Gambia, 14 October–24 October 1958," 1–7.

[58] WHO AFR/EH/29. Alain Thys, "Situation générale de l'hygiène du milieu au Royaume du Burundi," June 1963, 5–9.

that encircled the urban centers continued to suffer with inadequate and polluted water sources and rudimentary feces disposal. The peri-urban sanitation problems festered.[59] Typically, there was no plan at all for improving the water supplies and sanitation in rural Africa.

The achievement of Indian national independence in 1947 was quickly followed by a massive loss of life in the chaotic partition of the former British India into the states of India, East Pakistan (now Bangladesh), and West Pakistan (now Pakistan). In a time of acute political crisis, little effort was devoted to improve sanitation. There was a general acceptance of the apparent inevitability of pollution from human waste, and in South Asia, as in much of the world, the deaths from infectious intestinal diseases went uncounted and unremarked upon. Among specialists, the numbers were known to be high, but there were few hard data. The informed estimates of the time have the ability to shock today. In the decade of the 1940s, for example, an estimated 27,438,000 Indians lost their lives to infectious intestinal disease.[60] At the time, the toll excited little general interest.

The transfer of "modern sanitation" to the wider world was sharply limited by financial constraints. Most sanitation efforts focused on the simple removal of human waste from cities and towns. Into the mid-twentieth century, the flush toilet and the disposal of human waste via water carriage made little impact on the overall problem of excreta disposal, and even the provision of piped water was generally limited to the cities and large towns in which Europeans, local elites of European ancestry, and/or non-European elites had an authoritative presence.

---

[59] In Uganda, for example, sewage treatment plants served many urban centers, and on the eve of decolonization in 1960 another eleven were under construction in large towns. The Ministry of Health of the Uganda Protectorate noted, however, that there was still waste water flowing into the streets, insanitary night soil collection, foul open drains, and other urban nuisances, but expressed the hope that these should soon disappear. *Annual Report of the Ministry of Health, Uganda Protectorate, for the Year from 1st July, 1959 to 30th June, 1960*, 19–20; *Annual Report of the Ministry of Health, Uganda Protectorate, for the Year from 1st July, 1960 to 30th June, 1961*, 19–20.

[60] E. G. Wagner and J. Lanoix, *Excreta Disposal for Rural Areas and Small Countries*, WHO Monograph Series no. 39 (Geneva: World Health Organization, 1958), 13.

# 6

## The Struggle against Hookworm Disease

During the late nineteenth century, as cities in the North Atlantic were coping with massive fecal pollution, medical researchers in Europe discovered hookworm disease. It was a widespread intestinal infection that caused anemia and could be fatal, and it was spread through skin contact with soils polluted with infected human shit. In the early twentieth century, the oil magnate John D. Rockefeller launched a campaign to control hookworm infections in the US South and then extended the efforts abroad. The struggle to understand and treat hookworm disease marks the beginning of modern global health interventions.

### EARLY CONTROL PROGRAMS

In the 1870s, workers carving out the Saint Gotthard tunnel in the Alps between Switzerland and Italy came down with severe anemia. Some died. The symptoms were similar to those of "miner's disease," common in Europe. In 1880, in the course of an autopsy, the Italian parasitologist Edoardo Perroncito counted 1,500 hookworm *Ancylostoma duodenale* attached to the small intestine of a dead tunnel worker. Other investigators discovered hookworm eggs in the feces of sick tunnel workers. The mystery of the disease began to unravel.[1] Physicians found hookworm

---

[1] Although hookworms had been present in the eastern hemisphere for millennia, they had occasioned little notice. In the eleventh century CE, the Persian physician Ibn Sena (Avicenna) may have identified hookworm through post-mortem examination, and in 1838, the Italian physician Angelo Dubini, again through autopsy, identified it

eggs in miners' feces in France, Hungary, Germany, Sardinia, Italy, Russia, Austria, Belgium, England, Wales, South Africa, and California.[2] Investigators farther afield found hookworm eggs in the feces of anemic plantation and farm workers in Egypt, Brazil, northern South America, Central America, and the Caribbean.[3] The further one looked, the more one found.[4]

Healers reached into the herbal medical cabinet for remedies. Perroncito used extracts of male fern (*Dryopteris filix-mas*) that proved effective against roundworm and tapeworm.[5] Camillo Bozzolo, the Italian physician who had discovered hookworm eggs in workers' feces, advocated for the use of thymol, one of the principal constituents of the essential oil of thyme (*Thymus vulgaris*), because of its antiseptic powers.[6] Male fern became the most widely

anew. M. Khalil, "An Early Contribution to Medical Helminthology, Translated from the Writings of the Arabian Physician Ibn Sina (Avicenna) with a Short Biography," *Journal of Tropical Medicine and Hygiene*, vol. 25 (1922), 65–67; Angelo Dubini, "Nuovo Verme Intestinal Umano (Agchylostoma duodenale) Constituente un Sesto Genere dei Nematoidea Propri dell'Uomo," *Annali Universali de Medicina*, vol. 106 (1843), 5–13.

    Some authors credit the ancient Egyptians with knowledge of hookworm, citing Cyril P. Bryan (translator from the German version), *Ancient Egyptian Medicine: The Papyrus Ebers* (Chicago: Ares, 1974). The references to helminths in this translation, however, are to roundworm and tapeworm. A mention is also made of "stercoral masses in the body," which presumably refer either to fecalomas or (less probably) to agglomerations of round-worms. Bryan, *The Papyrus Ebers*, 55–57, 46.

[2] Ralph W. Nauss, "Hookworm in California Gold Mines," *American Journal of Public Health*, vol. 11, no. 5 (1921), 439–51; James Mathias, "An Epidemic of Ankylostomiasis," *South African Medical Journal*, vol. 6 (1898), 108–11.

[3] Steven Palmer, *Launching Global Health: The Caribbean Odyssey of the Rockefeller Foundation* (Ann Arbor: University of Michigan Press, 2010), 22–54.

[4] Some of the findings were surprising indeed. In Portuguese East Africa (now Mozambique), a British physician examined 200 individuals (mostly male) and dis-covered that 97 percent were infected with hookworm but that none had infections heavy enough to produce any symptoms. The group examined also hosted other intestinal helminths (64 percent with roundworm; 14.5 percent with whipworm; 5 percent with tapeworm). The asymptomatism was taken to reflect the relatively light population densities in the district as well as the practice of open defecation that allowed for irregular exposure to reinfection. R. M. Macfarlane, "Sanitation of a Small European Settlement in Portuguese East Africa; with Notes on Some of the Diseases Prevalent in the District," *Transactions of the Society of Tropical Medicine and Hygiene*, vol. 9 (1916), 140–44.

[5] R. Peduzzi and J. C. Piffaretti, "*Ancylostoma duodenale* and the Saint Gothard Anaemia," *British Medical Journal*, vol. 287, December 24–31, 1983, 1944.

[6] Thymol is present in *Thymus vulgaris* (common thyme), as well as several other plant species. The thymol remedy for hookworm anemia had been used in Europe, at least since the late 1870s. Camillo Bozzolo, the director of the Medical Clinic at the Royal

used chemical therapy in Europe, because physicians believed that it was less toxic than thymol. Thymol became the most widely adopted anti-hookworm therapy in the Americas, because physicians believed that it was more effective.[7]

The first programs for miners were rolled out in Germany in the late 1890s in response to disease outbreaks. The German programs provided sanitary buckets for the miners' use underground and treatment for the sick and incapacitated. Anemia among the miners continued to spread. In 1903, the Germans adopted a comprehensive approach that screened the feces of all miners for hookworm eggs and then treated those who tested positive. This proved effective, but the screening-and-treatment programs were expensive and not widely adopted.[8]

Early in the twentieth century, physicians in the Americas, newly sensitized to the widespread prevalence of anemia, launched hookworm surveys in agricultural communities. They discovered that hookworm infections were remarkably common. The magnitude of the hookworm problem was astonishing. In Puerto Rico, an estimated 80 percent of the population (800,000 of 1 million) was infected with hookworm, and an estimated 70 percent of those who tested positive for hookworm had symptoms of infection, principally anemia. In 1904, the US Department of the Army launched a campaign against hookworm in Puerto Rico, and in 1906, the Puerto Rican physicians assumed control. It rang up a major success.

University in Turin, had used thymol since 1879 and was convinced of its safety, at least in men of middle age with vigorous constitutions, which was the age group generally treated. Drug safety, however, was far from absolute. He admitted the possibility that one woman's death might have occurred from the administration of thymol and that his earliest treatment regimen of 6mg of thymol administered 6 hours apart might not have been fully prudent. Camillo Bozzolo, "Notes on the Treatment of Ankylostoma Anemia (Uncinariasis, Hookworm Disease) with Thymol," *Journal of the American Medical Association*, vol. 58, no. 23 (1912), 1744–46.

Thymol could also act as an abortifacient. H. H. Howard, *The Control of Hookworm Disease by the Intensive Method* (New York: Rockefeller Foundation, International Health Board, 1919), 83–84.

[7] Bailey K. Ashford and Pedro Gutierrez Igaravidez, *Uncinariasis (Hookworm Disease) in Porto Rico: A Medical and Economic Problem* (Washington, DC: Government Printing Office, 1911), 136–43.

[8] The less comprehensive programs produced uneven results. In the Austrian mines, anemia remained a common affliction. In British and French mines, there was a high degree of disease control. Ralph W. Nauss, "Hookworm in California Gold Mines," *American Journal of Public Health*, vol. 11, no. 5 (1921), 439.

*Statement of Deaths from Anemia from 1900 to 1908*

| | |
|---|---|
| 1900–1901 | 11,875 |
| 1901–1902 | 6,284 |
| 1902–1903 | 6,830 |
| 1903–1904 | 6,179 |
| 1904–1905 | 4,963 |
| 1905–1906 | 3,769 |
| 1906–1907 | 1,134 |
| 1907–1908 | 1,785 |

*Source:* Bailey K. Ashford and Pedro Gutierrez Igaravidez,
*Uncinariasis (Hookworm Disease) in Porto Rico: A Medical and
Economic Problem* (Washington, DC: Government Printing
Office, 1911), 226.

In the course of the campaign, the physicians won an important insight
into hookworm epidemiology. Over the course of a few years, they noted
a dramatic decline in the prevalence and severity of hookworm infections
among the soldiers of the Puerto Rican regiment. The soldiers, almost all
of whom were infected at the time of their first enlistment, had been
compelled to wear shoes and had been fed well. The improvement in
their health status was evidence of the "natural cure."[9]

The thymol treatment program, too, enjoyed good success. The American
and Puerto Rican directors of the campaign noted that although some hookworm sufferers did not self-medicate properly and a few did not take their
medicine, most of those who suffered from anemia would make great personal sacrifices to travel to get medicine and would return multiple times.[10]

In short order, hookworm prevention and treatment programs began
to appear in other regions of the globe. In 1907, Costa Rica embarked on
the world's first national hookworm treatment program guided by local

[9] B. K. Ashford and W. W. King, "Observations on the Campaign Against Uncinariasis in
Porto Rico," *Boston Medical and Surgical Journal*, vol. 156, no. 14 (1907), 416.
[10] Ashford and Gutierrez Igaravidez, *Uncinariasis (Hookworm Disease) in Porto Rico*, 137.
The thymol treatment protocol, however, was not without risk. In Puerto Rico, for example,
the hookworm sufferers were given purgatives and thymol, asked to self-administer the drugs
at home, and warned against the use of alcohol during treatment. (Alcohol facilitated the
absorption of the thymol and could produce toxic reactions and even death.) The authorities
in Puerto Rico reported a death rate of 0.49 percent (27 deaths from 5,490 case treatments) in
the two municipalities of Bayamón and Utuado. These deaths included those of a number of
individuals who did not receive thymol. The other deaths were attributed either to complications from severe hookworm infections (uncinariasis) or other infections. Ashford and
Gutierrez Igaravidez, *Uncinariasis (Hookworm Disease) in Porto Rico*, 143–44, 148–49.

medical research. Other programs that were launched in Brazil, Colombia, El Salvador, and Guatemala were less ambitious in scale, but paralleled the one in Costa Rica.[11] In 1907, the US authorities in the colonial Philippines began a hookworm program. In 1908, the British created a Colonial Office Hookworm Committee, and the state board of health in Florida initiated a control campaign.[12]

The call to arms against hookworm disease reverberated throughout the British Empire. The indentured "coolie" (Tamil: wage) workers of India were of particular concern to their British overlords because the wage laborers were in demand in British colonies throughout the tropics. As early as 1903, when early apprehensions in the Americas were given voice, the British Guiana government recommended that all laborers departing from Calcutta (now Kolkata) for British Guiana should be examined for hookworm infection and treated. The British estimated that 75 percent of the coolies were infected, although many appeared to be in good health. In the event, the proposal for mass drug treatment in the Calcutta depot was deemed impracticable.[13]

Medical officers also voiced concern from Malaya and the Straits Settlements (a British Crown colony in Southeast Asia comprising Singapore, Malacca, Penang, Labuan, and some small islands) where Tamil workers from the Madras Presidency made up the principal labor supply. They discovered cases of hookworm disease and high rates of hookworm infection among them. This encouraged some officers to attribute a broad spectrum of disease symptoms to hookworm. In 1908, it led W. L. Brandon, State Surgeon on Negri Sembilan in the Straits Settlements, to an alarmist view: "I would affirm that, with the rarest exceptions, nearly every one of the cases of great anaemia or of severe dropsy [edema] occurring among the Tamils is attributable to infection with hookworm and to no other cause. *The disease is, when left untreated,*

---

[11] Palmer, *Launching Global Health*, 9–10.

[12] Palmer, *Launching Global Health*, 38–39.

[13] The grounds were that the coolies' numbers were too great and that treatment with thymol would cause desertions and that those who were suffering from the side-effects of thymol such as gastric pain, nausea, vomiting, and central hyperactivity (talkativeness) would be less able to bear the rigors of the voyage. The proposal was raised again in 1905, and again was rejected. CO 885/18/7. Miscellaneous No. 204. Further Correspondence (June 22, 1906 to December 31, 1907). No. 127. "Ankylostomiasis in the West Indies," 170. Thymol could occasionally cause more serious complications such as convulsions, coma, cardiac and respiratory collapse. See https://toxnet.nlm.nih.gov/cgi-bin/sis/search/a?dbs+hsdb:@term+@DOCNO+866.

*almost uniformly fatal, and this issue is reached usually in a few months* [emphasis original]."[14]

Medical officers knew little about the extent of hookworm disease in tropical Africa. Many researchers assumed that the low population density in parts of rural Africa meant that hookworm could not be a substantial problem there.[15] The reigning idea was that significant hookworm disease could occur only where large numbers of people were concentrated without adequate feces disposal. This seemed to be borne out by the experiences of plantation laborers elsewhere in the tropics. The scant early evidence from Africa seemed broadly supportive. A European physician reported that hookworm infections in the Angolan highlands were common but light.[16] Another reported that hookworm infections in Saint-Louis du Sénégal were relatively uncommon.[17]

### THE ROCKEFELLER SANITARY COMMISSION FOR THE ERADICATION OF HOOKWORM DISEASE

The science of hookworm developed briskly. In 1902, the redoubtable parasitologist Charles W. Stiles discovered a second human hookworm species, *Uncinaria americana*, that he later renamed *Necator americanus* ("American murderer"). Stiles was convinced, due to the presence of hookworms in animals in the United States, that human hookworm would be "more or less common" in the South, and he journeyed from Washington, DC to Florida, visiting penitentiaries, mines, farms, asylums,

[14] CO 885/20/10. Miscellaneous No. 238. Further Correspondence Relating to [1909]. III. Ankylostomiasis. Report by Dr. W. L. Braddon, State Surgeon, Negri Sembilan, September 26, 1909 [Straits Settlements], 100.

[15] See, for example, R. M. Macfarlane, "Sanitation of a Small European Settlement in Portuguese East Africa; with Notes on Some of the Diseases Prevalent in the District," *Transactions of the Society of Tropical Medicine and Hygiene*, vol. 9 (1916), 144: "In the present condition of the country, where villages and houses are so scattered, the influence of ankylostomiasis upon the general health of the population is probably not great. The disease, however, would be very liable to assume some economic importance, were the country to be opened up to civilisation, and agricultural or other industries to develop, which would cause the collection of large numbers of the population as labour into restricted areas without adequate sanitary provision. All the conditions for massive as well as constant infection would then be present. Such has been the history of ankylostomiasis in Porto Rico and other West Indian islands."

[16] F. C. Wellman, "Notes on the Tropical Diseases of the Angola Highlands," *New York Medical Journal*, vol. 82 (1905), 375.

[17] Dr. Bourret, "Recherches sur le parasitisme, la dysenterie, et la maladie du sommeil à Saint-Louis (Sénégal)," *Annales d'hygiène et de médecine coloniales*, vol. 16 (1913), 283–84.

schools, and factories. He concluded that hookworm infection was "one of the most important factors in the inferior mental, physical, and financial condition of the poor classes of the white population of the rural sand and piney wood districts ... This sounds like an extreme statement, but it is based upon extreme facts."[18]

Stiles felt the urgent need for a broad hookworm control program to reach the southern US populations. In 1909, the oil magnate John D. Rockefeller, concerned to build a philanthropic legacy that would eclipse a reputation clouded by accusations of unethical business practices, donated $1 million to create the Rockefeller Sanitary Commission for the Eradication of Hookworm Disease, and Stiles signed on as chief scientific officer.[19]

Stiles was the most influential scientist in the United States involved with hookworm. He posited three levels of hookworm infection – light, medium, and heavy – and made the case that no hookworm infection was too light to ignore because each adult female worm laid eggs that had the potential to increase the burden of disease. Many southern physicians, however, held the view that light infections did not produce disease symptoms and thus were unnecessary to treat.[20]

The purpose of the Rockefeller Sanitary Commission for the Eradication of Hookworm Disease (RSC) was twofold: to treat those who suffered from hookworm infections and to reduce disease transmission. Its major thrust was for improved sanitation. In the rural US South, this meant convincing poor, laboring people to build and regularly use sanitary privies ("outhouses") and to forgo open defecation. (There was no campaign emphasis on shoe-wearing, because the cost of shoes was beyond the means of most of the rural poor.) The RSC campaigns, like those in the Caribbean and South America, leveraged the effectiveness of treatment in order to promote sanitation. Treatment with thymol and purgative Epsom salts could clear or reduce infection; improved feces disposal prevented reinfection. The balance of effort was strongly tilted toward sanitation. As Stiles noted: "This was frequently expressed in the

---

[18] Charles Wardell Stiles, *Report upon the Prevalence and Geographic Distribution of Hookworm Disease (Uncinariasis or Anchylostomiasis) in the United States*, no. 10 (Washington, DC: US Government Printing Office, 1903), 9, 97.

[19] John Ettling, *The Germ of Laziness: Rockefeller Philanthropy and Public Health in the New South* (Cambridge, MA: Harvard University Press, 1981), 100–102.

[20] Stiles, *Report upon the Prevalence and Geographic Distribution of Hookworm Disease*, 93.

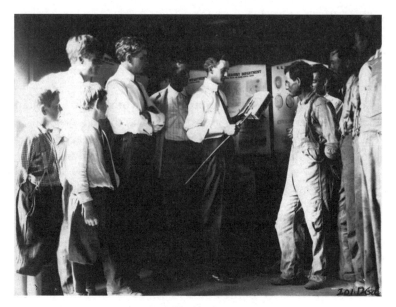

FIGURE 6.1 Dispensary scene: teaching by lecture and demonstration.
Source: Rockefeller Foundation Digital Archives

field as '80 to 90 per cent sanitary privy, 20 to 10 percent thymol and epsom salts.'"[21]

The strategy of the RSC campaign was to set up free clinics to diagnose hookworm disease, provide chemical treatment, and demonstrate the sanitary privy. The RSC campaign ran from 1909 to 1914. Its track record was mixed.

It some states, the clinical outreach encountered resistance. As the historian William A. Link wrote of the North Carolina campaign:

The ways of rural North Carolinians, and their seemingly uncaring attitudes about health, presented reformers with a major, almost insurmountable, obstacle. Dispensaries might work in one community one week and then fail in another community for apparently fickle reasons. And reformers, as outsiders, always

[21] C. W. Stiles, "Decrease of Hookworm Disease in the United States," *Public Health Reports* (1896–1970), vol. 45, no. 1 (1930), 1767. In a later essay, Stiles would recall that "one favorite expression was to the effect that the eradication of hookworm disease should be based upon 20 per cent. thymol and epsom salts [treatment] combined with 80 per cent. sanitation." Charles Wardell Stiles, "Early History, in Part Esoteric, of the Hookworm (Uncinariasis) Campaign in Our Southern United States," *Journal of Parasitology*, vol. 25, no. 4 (1939), 296–97.

FIGURE 6.2 Hookworm treatment dispensary, Robertson County, Tennessee, 1914.
Source: Rockefeller Foundation Digital Archives

faced suspicion and reserve: as a result, sanitarians often noted that popular interest coincided with reluctance to participate in treatment. In a northwestern county, a field director wrote in August 1914 that his dispensaries attracted large crowds but failed to "persuade them in any way to be examined." Even those once agreeing to treatment had "lost all interest in the work"; by the conclusion of the dispensary there was "absolutely no interest anywhere."[22]

In Louisiana, by contrast, the RSC hookworm campaign had a broad success in jumpstarting a sanitary revolution. The RSC developed an enormous public educational effort to convince the populace that hookworm was spread through skin contact with feces-polluted soils. Over time, a wide array of new sanitation practices including the construction of septic systems on farms, sewer lines in rural towns, better sanitation in the schools, and more wearing of shoes had a profound impact on the prevalence of hookworm infections. Only about 5 percent of Louisiana's population was ever treated with chemical therapy for hookworm infection.[23]

[22] William A. Link, "'The Harvest Is Ripe, but the Laborers Are Few': The Hookworm Crusade in North Carolina, 1909–1915," *North Carolina Historical Review*, vol. 67, no. 1 (1990), 10, 17, 22.

[23] Thomas Waisley, "Public Health Programs in Early Twentieth-Century Louisiana," *Louisiana History: The Journal of the Louisiana Historical Association*, vol. 41, no. 1 (2000), 41, 67–68.

The initial surveys by the RSC estimated that hookworm had infected 39.5 percent of school-age children in the US South, and in some counties the infection rates were between 70 and 90 percent. In some schools, hookworm infections were universal among both pupils and teachers.[24] The epidemiologists of the RSC determined that the rural school was the principal site of transmission. When schools adopted a program of on-site sanitation, the rates could be driven down, and the schools transformed into centers of sanitation evangelism.[25]

The overall number of people treated by the RSC campaigns in the US South cannot be known. The RSC record keeping was incomplete, and to the great confusion of the historical record, the annual reports used the nomenclature "Number of Cases Treated" to refer to the number of people to whom medicine was given with instructions on how to administer it at home. Stiles suggested that the RSC modify the nomenclature to the more accurate "Number of Persons to Whom Medicine Was Dispensed," but his suggestion was ignored. As early as 1912 he had reported: "The more I go around the country where clinics have been held the less importance I am able to attach to the statistics of the clinics. I have seen family after family where they tell me they have visited the clinics, had been told that they had hookworm disease, had taken the medicine home, but were afraid to take it." Stiles stated that if more than half the people given the medicine had actually swallowed it, he would be surprised.[26]

The long-term impact of the RSC campaigns in the US South was to spur the creation of state public health systems that encouraged the use of sanitary privies and discouraged "promiscuous defecation." The work advanced slowly. By the early 1930s, many regions still lacked privies, and many agricultural workers still responded to the call of nature outdoors, where their feces were exposed to the elements. As Stiles put it: "The final problem is to change the daily habits of hundreds of thousands of whites,

---

[24] C. W. Stiles, "Decrease of Hookworm Disease in the United States," *Public Health Reports* (1896–1970), vol. 45, no. 1 (1930), 1763; John Atkinson Ferrell, *The Rural School and Hookworm Disease*, US Bureau of Education Bulletin no. 20 (Washington, DC, 1914), 10.

[25] Ferrell, *The Rural School and Hookworm Disease*, 14. The RF surveys also turned up evidence of the prevalence of tainted drinking water and unsanitary methods of drinking. The hookworm campaign activated and synergized a regional movement against the common drinking cup and impure water in the schools. William A. Link, "Privies, Progressivism, and Public Schools: Health Reform and Education in the Rural South, 1909–1920," *Journal of Southern History*, vol. 54, no. 4 (1988), 632.

[26] Ettling, *Germ of Laziness*, 165–66.

Indians, and negroes (who are living under a system of 'dog sanitation') to the Mosaic system of 'cat sanitation.' This will take at least three generations longer of educational health work."[27]

During the 1930s, the rural sanitation initiative accelerated. The US government hired 15,000 workers into the Civil Works Administration who dug 3,000,000 privies throughout rural America. The Community Sanitation Program and the Farm Security Administration also got involved. The workers constructed the largest numbers of privies in West Virginia, Tennessee, North Carolina, and Mississippi. The 1940 census, however, estimated that although there were about 6.3 million privies serving rural homes, at least another 4 million were needed.[28]

## THE ROCKEFELLER FOUNDATION'S INTERNATIONAL PROGRAMS

In 1911, the newly formed Rockefeller Foundation undertook an overseas survey of hookworm infections through correspondence with American representatives abroad and determined that hookworm disease in the tropics and subtropics constituted a heavy economic burden.[29] The survey was marred by a basic error: it attributed the prevalence of anemia only to hookworm infection. Malaria, which also produces anemia, was extremely common in the same regions among the impoverished populations infected with hookworm.

In 1913, the Rockefeller Foundation created an International Health Commission to extend its hookworm campaigns to British Guyana, the English-speaking islands in the Caribbean, Mexico, Brazil, Egypt, India, Ceylon, the Malay States, and beyond.[30] The Rockefeller Foundation goals were similar to those in the US South – to use hookworm treatment to catalyze public interest in improved sanitation. The campaigners

---

[27] Charles Wardell Stiles, "Some Practical Considerations in Regard to Control of Hookworm Disease in the United States Under Present Conditions," *Journal of Parasitology*, vol. 18, no. 3 (1932), 172.

[28] E. S. Tisdale and C. H. Atkins, "The Sanitary Privy and Its Relation to Public Health," *American Journal of Public Health*, vol. 33 (1943), 1319–22.

[29] Rockefeller Sanitary Commission for the Eradication of Hookworm Disease, *Hookworm Infection in Foreign Countries* (Washington, DC: Offices of the Commission, 1911).

[30] The use of the term *international health board* is a convenience. The Rockefeller Foundation established its International Health Commission in 1916 and then changed its name to the International Health Board (1916–27) and to the International Health Division (1927–51).

determined to work with local authorities toward public health. The means were flexible.[31]

The International Health Commission sought partnerships across the British Empire to fight hookworm. It saw its role as establishing models for curing and preventing hookworm disease in select areas at low cost to the colonial governments, with the intention of withdrawing when local agencies were capable of taking over the work.[32] As its Director-General wrote in the First Annual Report:

The International Health Commission has not undertaken to eradicate uncinariasis [hookworm disease] in any country. The accomplishment of this work will require the operation of permanent agencies working over long periods of time. The attitude assumed by the International Health Commission towards this work is that assumed by the Rockefeller Sanitary Commission in the Southern States, namely, that the bringing of this disease under control in any country is a work which no outside agency, working independently, could do if it would, and one which no outside agency should do if it could; that if the infection is to be stamped out in any area the country in which it exists must assume the responsibility; and that the Commission may be of service in so far as it may co-operate in the relief and control of this disease.[33]

In the summer of 1914, the First World War erupted in Europe and almost immediately derailed one of the first overseas hookworm efforts. Early in 1915, the authorities in Egypt closed all of the hospitals set up to treat hookworm and seconded the personnel and equipment to the war hospitals. The hookworm campaign was suspended.[34]

### THE INTERNATIONAL HEALTH BOARD (1916–27)

In 1916, the officers and physicians of the Rockefeller Foundation's now renamed International Health Board attempted to push forward with

---

[31] Palmer, *Launching Global Health*, 4.
[32] James E. Ackert, "Some Influences of the American Hookworm," *American Midland Naturalist*, vol. 47, no. 3 (1952), 756.
[33] Cited in CO 321/294/13. Miscellaneous No. 320 Further Correspondence (July 1915–June 1916) Relating to Ankylostomiasis. Enclosure in No. 26. Grenada, International Health Commission. October 1, 1915. Angus MacDonald, Medical Officer in Charge, 44–45.
[34] Little was done until 1926, when the British in Egypt oversaw the administration of 1 million free doses of deworming drugs in the hospitals. But the critical part of the campaign – to reduce open defecation and thereby to reduce transmission – collapsed. The hookworm treatment program operated on its own, without an effort to improve rural sanitation. WHO EM/RC9A/Tech.Disc/7. Ismail Saleh Himly, "A History of the Discovery of the Human Hookworm," August 24, 1959, 5–6.

hookworm control in areas beyond the war zones. They discovered that the hookworm programs had to face the challenges of local environmental conditions, and that solutions were elusive. On some of the plantations in the Straits Settlements, for example, the water table was high, and after the recommended latrines had been built, they flooded and bred mosquitoes. The plantation owners provided latrine buckets for use near the coolie housing "lines," and the workers continued to relieve themselves in the plantation fields.

Nor could the treatment protocols be straightforward. Local epidemiology proved paramount. In the flatlands and hilly estates of Malaya, for example, those with anemia were treated with a deworming drug. In the flatlands, hookworm was the principal cause of anemia, but the benefits from treatment were generally undone by rapid reinfection. In the hills, malaria was the principal cause; the deworming drugs reduced the severity of the hookworm infections, but the workers remained anemic. Crucially, there was no way to distinguish between anemia caused by hookworm and malaria, and many workers were infected by both.[35]

From 1916 to 1923, in Negapatam in the Madras Presidency of India (now Nagapattinam, Tamil Nadu) the British estimated the prevalence of hookworm infection among townspeople and villagers of different social classes, carried out hemoglobin studies to determine the extent of anemia, and tried to improve feces disposal practices. Negapatam was of particular interest because it was the principal depot for shipping coolie laborers to Malaya, and in the British economic calculus, sick coolies made unproductive plantation workers. The investigators found that the degree of infection among the coolies was sky high at 98.6 percent. The town dwellers themselves had an infection level of 91 percent. The British sanitary education program met with considerable hostility and achieved little. The idea that upper-caste as well as lower-caste Hindus became infected with hookworm as a result of dermal exposure to feces insulted the upper castes' pretensions to purity.[36]

As hookworm campaigners in the Madras Presidency ran afoul of Hindu cultural norms, research epidemiologists made revolutionary

[35] S. T. Darling, M. A. Barber, and H. P. Hacker, *Hookworm and Malaria Research in Malaya, Java, and the Fiji Islands. Report of Uncinariasis Commission to the Orient, 1915–1917* (New York: Rockefeller Foundation, International Health Board, 1920), 12, 19–20.

[36] K. S. Mhaskar, "Report of the Ankylostomiasis Inquiry in Madras," *Indian Medical Research Memoirs*, Memoir no. 1 (1924), 13, 21–22.

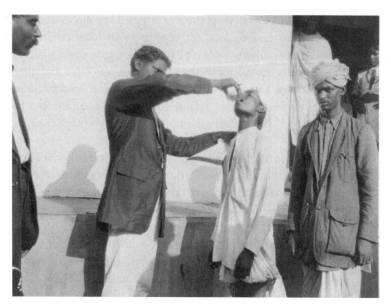

FIGURE 6.3  Administering hookworm treatment in Karapa, Madras Presidency.
Source: Rockefeller Foundation Digital Archives

discoveries. They found that most individuals with hookworm infections enjoyed apparent good health, even when they also had roundworm (as did 60 percent) and whipworm (37 percent) infections. The
researchers rarely encountered anemia and emaciation. Ground itch
(an inflammation of the sensitive areas between the toes) and derma-
titis – which had been signal indicators of hookworm infection in the
US South – were "invariably absent" in the Madras Presidency.
Moreover, the scores on the hemoglobin indexes that determined
anemia did not match up with the extent of hookworm infection,
and thus there seemed to be no justification for the classifications of
light, mild, and heavy infection based on the degree of anemia.[37] At
one fell swoop, the very diagnosis of hookworm disease itself was
thrown into confusion. So was the matter of cure. The researchers

[37] Mhaskar, "Ankylostomiasis Inquiry," 88–91. The relationship between the intensity
of hookworm infection and hookworm disease is not linear. Severe anemia occurs
when there are thousands of worms, but a few hundred worms can cause a clinically
important degree of anemia. The host's iron status is critically important.
D. A. P. Bundy, A. Hall, G. F. Medley, and L. Savioli, "Evaluating Measures to
Control Intestinal Parasitic Infections," *World Health Statistics Quarterly*, vol. 45,
no. 2–3 (1992), 173.

found that "mere improvements in sanitary conditions without the help of any specific treatment is sufficient to bring down the intensity of hookworm infection."[38]

The findings presented the International Health Board with a conundrum. The International Health Board's stated goal was to improve feces disposal and reduce hookworm disease, and its therapeutic approach in South Asia now seemed to be largely ineffective. The "demonstration effect" that had been moderately effective in the southern United States was largely ineffective in southern India.

The International Health Board turned the evidence aside and forged ahead. Consider first the case of Ceylon. The annual outflow and return of Tamil workers from southern India to the highland tea plantations in Ceylon supported the island's most profitable export sector. The International Health Board invested in hookworm treatment in Ceylon, all the while recognizing that it could not be successful without improved sanitation. It lobbied the British Colonial Office, colonial government authorities in Colombo, and the planters' association in the highlands of Ceylon to champion improved sanitation to no avail. None could see a direct economic benefit from improved sanitation and would not act. At the end of the Ceylon campaign, the International Health Board had accomplished little.[39] The levels of hookworm infection among the Tamil plantation workers and the Singhalese villagers nearby remained high. As in Malaya and the Straits Settlements and in the Madras Presidency, most hookworm infections did not produce telltale disease symptoms.

In the Caribbean and South and Central America, hard experience taught other epidemiological lessons. In Antigua in the Leeward Islands, for example, during the 1915–17 campaign, the treatment plan was rolled out before the latrine-building component. The chemical therapy enjoyed some initial success, although the rates of reinfection threatened to undo the good work. The lesson was clear: "It is evident that no treatment work should be started in an area which has not been previously sanitated ... An organization competent to maintain unrelaxed public health education, sanitation and

---

[38] K. S. Mhaskar, "Hookworm Infection and Sanitation," *Indian Journal of Medical Research*, vol. 8 (1920), 398.

[39] Soma Hewa, "The Hookworm Epidemic on the Plantations in Colonial Sri Lanka," *Medical History*, vol. 38, no. 1 (1994), 73–90.

treatment is essential to the maintenance of the results of hookworm-disease prophylaxis."[40]

On other Caribbean islands, after the hookworm campaigns, International Health Board epidemiologists likewise found high rates of reinfection. A survey in two different areas of Puerto Rico – one "unsanitated" and the other in which latrines were constructed at all the houses therein and surrounding territory – found that one year after hookworm treatment, the population treated in the unsanitated area had been nearly all reinfected, with an intensity that had been reduced by half. The sanitated area had an infection rate of close to 50 percent, but the intensity was only 12 percent of that before treatment.[41] This, too, argued for latrine construction before chemical therapy.[42]

Yet, in some other areas, the epidemiological evidence could tell a different story. In Brazil, for example, researchers found that a single standard treatment (or two, in the case of heavily infected individuals) would reduce the worm burden to a low level. They considered this an "economic cure" and deemed it unnecessary to require the infected individual to submit to further treatment.[43] They also found hookworm to be principally a disease of adults, rather than children. In Brazil, hookworm was mostly an occupational disease.[44]

[40] Dwight L. Sisco, "Incidence of Hookworm Disease among Persons Who Were Cured Five Years Ago," *Journal of the American Medical Association*, vol. 80, no. 7 (1923), 452, 454.

[41] Rolla B. Hill, "Hookworm Reinfestation in Sanitated and Unsanitated Areas," *Southern Medical Journal*, vol. 18 (1925), 667.

[42] There was some experimentation with dosages. In British Guyana, for example, the campaigners experimented with a new treatment regimen that required the daily ingestion of small quantities of thymol over a period of three or four months. As H. H. Howard noted, the daily method was a failure, largely because the process of cure was so gradual that the improvements could not be discerned by the patient, and any illness experienced during the course of treatment was attributed to the thymol. NAUK CO/885/24/6. Miscellaneous No. 310. Further Correspondence Relating to Ankylostomiasis (July 3, 1914–July 2, 1915), Enclosure 1 in No. 26, Letter from H. H. Howard, July 15, 1914, 24–26.

[43] The researchers arrived at these understandings by a difficult route. They had carried out a four-year program of hookworm treatment and latrine building, and the initially disappointing results showed a decrease of roughly 2 percent in the percentage of the population infected with the helminth. A full 69 percent of the population was still infected at the end of four years. Further investigations revealed, however, that hookworm disease had all but disappeared, appearing only in new immigrants. The intensity of infection in the population was very low, averaging 14 worms per case. Wilson G. Smillie, "The Results of Hookworm Disease Prophylaxis in Brazil," *American Journal of Epidemiology*, vol. 2, no. 1 (1922), 77–95.

[44] S. T. Darling and W. G. Smillie, "Studies on Hookworm Infection in Brazil. First Paper," *Monograph of the Rockefeller Institute for Medical Research*, no. 14 (1921), 15.

## ANEMIA AS DIAGNOSTIC CONUNDRUM

As it became clear that both hookworm and malaria caused anemia, the imperative for hookworm treatment became less certain. In areas of malaria transmission, it was not possible to determine the cause of anemia in a given individual without expensive testing. Another approach was needed.

One option was mass treatment without testing. Mass treatment, however, was expensive (because many who did not have hookworm infections would have to be treated), and its efficacy unmeasurable, if the cause and extent of the anemia were undetermined. This quandary was acute in tropical Africa. Colonial medical budgets were tight, and hookworm and malaria (which in the early twentieth century was considered principally a medical vulnerability of Europeans) made the largest claims.[45] Moreover, studies in West Africa found that there was a lack of correlation between higher worm burdens and lower hemoglobin levels and no correlation between worm burdens and standards of physical fitness, health, or mental status. The West African evidence thus seemed to be a paradigm breaker. The epidemiologist R. M. Gordon sounded the alarm: "It therefore follows from these conclusions that before treatment, and especially before the so-called Mass treatment, of ankylostomiasis [hookworm disease], is applied to any native race, careful investigation should be made whether ankylostomiasis has any definite pathogenic effect on that race, and if pathogenic effects are noted, with what degree of infection they are associated."[46]

## THE UNMET CHALLENGES OF HUMAN FECES DISPOSAL

The core challenge of how to safely dispose of human feces varied enormously by topography and ecological zone. Consider, for example, the Caribbean islands. On small islands, the populations relieved themselves on the beaches, and tidal flushes carried their deposits out to sea twice a day. On larger, low-lying islands, where much of the population lived at a distance from the beaches, there seemed to be no good solution. The water tables were

---

[45] R. M. Gordon, "The Effect of Ancylostome, Ascaris, and Trichuris Infections on the Health of the West African Native," *Annals of Tropical Medicine and Parasitology*, vol. 19 (1925), 430; on malaria, James L. A. Webb Jr., *The Long Struggle against Malaria in Tropical Africa* (New York: Cambridge University Press, 2014).

[46] Gordon, "The Effect of Ancylostome, Ascaris, and Trichuris Infections on the Health of the West African Native," 457.

high and thus in-ground latrines were impractical, and there could be insufficient elevation for sewers that depended upon gravity. Professional opinion diverged. Some experts advocated a "dry system" of open latrines even though it promoted the transmission of pathogens by flies. Others advocated a "wet system" of dumping the raw excreta into the rivers or sea. Neither approach met the needs of agricultural laborers who relieved themselves in the fields, where their exposure to infection varied by crop, season, and soil type. When sugar soils were allowed to dry out, for example, the hookworm larvae died off. When crops such as cocoa replaced sugar, the prevalence of hookworm infections increased.[47]

During the 1920s, the International Health Board began to investigate hookworm and sanitation in China. The researchers realized in short order that the use of night soil was central to Chinese agriculture and that the reform of Chinese sanitary practices would have profound economic consequences. The only prospect to reduce hookworm transmission was through mass deworming campaigns, and these were deemed impractical.[48] There was no system of public health through which to distribute a deworming drug, and the cost would have been prohibitive. Reinfection would have occurred almost immediately. For the parasitologist Norman Stoll, the Chinese experience called into question the gospel of sanitation. As he put it, "Public health practice, in the control of any disease related to human feces, must therefore reexamine the precepts upon which it stands, rather than dogmatically attempt to combat a thrifty Chinese practice with wasteful Western custom."[49]

By the 1930s, epidemiological studies in China had shed light on the overall distribution of intestinal worm infections. In northern China, hookworm was completely absent, and whipworm and roundworm were rare. In southern China, where farmers used raw human feces on wet rice fields, roundworm racked up an infection rate of 81 percent.[50] In

---

[47] NAUK CO 885/19/14. No. 224. Further Correspondence [1908] IV. Ankylostomiasis. No. 63, 130–31.

[48] Samuel T. Darling, "The Hookworm Index and Mass Treatment," *American Journal of Tropical Medicine*, vol. 2, no. 5 (1922), 443.

[49] Norman R. Stoll, "On the Economic Value of Nightsoil in China," in W. W. Cort, J. B. Grant, and N. R. Stoll (eds.), *Researches on Hookworm in China: Embodying the Results of the Work of the China Hookworm Commission, June, 1923 to November, 1924*, Monographic Series no. 7 (Baltimore: The American Journal of Hygiene, 1926), 263.

[50] G. F. Winfield, "On the Use of *Ascaris lumbricoides* as a Public Health Standard in the Study of Problems of Rural Sanitation," *Transactions of the Ninth Congress of the Far Eastern Association of Tropical Medicine of Nanking*, vol. 2 (1934), 791–97.

the vegetable-growing sector of cities such as Suzhou and Nanjing, hookworm infection was a problem. A higher incidence of serious infections was found in Kwangtung Province laborers who worked in the mulberry groves where, after the first picking of leaves, they broke up the soil underneath the trees and applied night soil to force new growth. The China Hookworm Commission determined that a hookworm campaign, if mounted, should work to modify night soil practices, not eliminate them.[51] The lessons learned in China did not seem widely applicable.

The International Health Board became disillusioned. What had worked in the US South – to dispense chemical therapy in order to spur the construction of latrines and the creation of public health systems – did not work elsewhere. Latrines had to be in place and in use before hookworm could be controlled.[52] At length, the International Health Board pivoted to other disease targets and abandoned the hookworm crusade.[53]

### ASSESSMENTS OF THE HOOKWORM CAMPAIGNS

The assessments of the Rockefeller Sanitary Commission and International Health Board hookworm campaigns have varied greatly, particularly between the official annual reports and the epidemiologists' retrospective studies. The official pronouncements were particularly unrealistic. The Fifth Report of the Rockefeller Sanitary Commission stunned its hookworm workers by declaring that its campaign in the US South was a success and would close up operations at the end of 1914.[54] Stiles did not believe a word of this touted success and, four years later, shortly before his retirement from the Public Health Service, he made another tour of the US South. He visited schools, inspected children, and, in the sites that he visited, determined that the rate of hookworm infection varied between 26 and 49 percent.[55] Twelve years later, the

---

[51] The areas with severe hookworm problems were in relatively inaccessible regions. W. W. Cort, J. B. Grant, and N. R. Stoll, "General Summary of Results," in W. W. Cort, J. B. Grant, and N. R. Stoll (eds.), *Researches on Hookworm in China: Embodying the Results of the Work of the China Hookworm Commission, June, 1923 to November, 1924*, Monographic Series no. 7 (Baltimore: The American Journal of Hygiene, 1926), 393–98.

[52] John Farley, *To Cast Out Disease: A History of the International Health Division of the Rockefeller Foundation (1913–1951)* (New York: Oxford University Press, 2004), 70–71.

[53] The directorship briefly entertained the notion that the eradication of hookworm itself might be taken as their major goal. Farley, *Cast Out Disease*, 72.

[54] Ettling, *Germ of Laziness*, 177.   [55] Ettling, *Germ of Laziness*, 209.

Rockefeller Foundation sounded another false note, when it announced that hookworm had almost disappeared from the United States.[56] Alas, this was far from the case.

In the late 1920s, the epidemiologist Austin Kerr undertook an investigation of the prevalence and intensity of hookworm infestation in Florida. He discovered a massive public health problem. Hookworm infection was widespread. Regional rates ranged from 26.5 to 97 percent, with most regions having more than half the population infected. In western Florida, 100 percent of the children in some rural schools had hookworm.[57] A later hookworm study in 1937–38, found that Florida remained a hot spot. More than a third of school children aged five to nine years were infected, and the prevalence increased in older age cohorts.[58]

During the 1930s, epidemiologists conducted hookworm surveys elsewhere in the US South. The evidence was not all of a piece, and two decades after the ending of the RSC campaigns, with ongoing progress in sanitation in many areas, it was difficult to interpret the results. In North Carolina, hookworm prevalence had dropped by two-thirds.[59] In South Carolina, the prevalence had dropped by only one-third, and there was still a hookworm problem of major proportions. The average worm burden in both men and women was high enough to produce clinical morbidity.[60] In Kentucky, hookworm incidence dropped by about three-fourths. Sanitation there had apparently played little role, because the prevalence rate for roundworm infection was about one in three.[61] In Tennessee, hookworm infections had also declined by three-fourths. Tennessee soils were not conducive to hookworm propagation; the initial intensities of infection during the RSC campaign years were presumed

[56] One economist has taken this announcement at face value and calculated the economic benefits of the illusory eradication. Hoyt Bleakley, "Disease and Development: Evidence from Hookworm Eradication in the American South," *Quarterly Journal of Economics*, vol. 122, no. 1 (2007), 73–117.

[57] J. Austin Kerr, "The Incidence and Intensity of Hookworm Infestation in the State of Florida," *Bulletin of the International Health Board*, vol. 7 (1927), 193, 210.

[58] W. S. Leathers, A. E. Keller, and W. A. McPhaul, "An Investigation Concerning the Status of Hookworm in Florida," *American Journal of Hygiene*, vol. 29, section D (1939), 8–9.

[59] A. E. Keller, W. S. Leathers, and J. C. Knox, "The Present Status of Hookworm Infestation in North Carolina," *American Journal of Hygiene*, vol. 26 (1937), 440, 450.

[60] W. S. Leathers, A. E. Keller, and B. F. Wyman, "A State-Wide Investigation of Hookworm in South Carolina," *American Journal of Epidemiology*, vol. 23, no. 3 (1936), 602–3, 612–14.

[61] A. E. Keller, W. S. Leathers, and M. H. Jensen, "An Investigation of Hookworm Infestation in Thirty-Six Counties of Kentucky," *American Journal of Hygiene*, vol. 23 (1936), 36, 44–45.

low; and routine deworming treatment, given by parents to their children, had also played a role.[62] In Mississippi, hookworm prevalence had declined by two-thirds in southern Mississippi where soils were conducive to hookworm propagation and about four-fifths in northern Mississippi where soils were not.[63]

The big picture was that by the 1930s in most regions of the southern US hookworm disease was on the wane. Many people still had hookworm infections, and of those, one-quarter had hookworm infections severe enough to produce clinical symptoms.[64] The researchers' view was that sanitation and education would eventually lead toward the disappearance of hookworm disease.[65]

The hookworm campaigns of the early twentieth century mark the beginnings of global health programs. The experience in the US South was not replicated in the wider world. The spatial extent of hookworm began to shrink in modernizing states principally as a result of improved sanitation, rather than medical interventions. In the Global South, where the levels of economic development were low and the infrastructure for feces disposal primitive, intestinal worm infections remained rife.

[62] A. E. Keller, "A State-Wide Study of the Human Intestinal Helminths in Tennessee," *Journal of Preventive Medicine*, vol. 6 (1932), 167–70.

[63] A. E. Keller, W. S. Leathers, and H. C. Ricks, "An Investigation of the Incidence and Intensity of Infestation of Hookworm in Mississippi," *American Journal of Hygiene*, vol. 19 (1934), 629–56.

[64] N. R. Stoll, "This Wormy World," *Journal of Parasitology*, vol. 33, no. 1 (1947), 8. It is clear that the hookworm problem was not confined to the US South. A survey of National Guard soldiers from Texas and Oklahoma in 1921 found that 12.3 percent were infected with hookworm, although most infections were light. Overall, those with hookworm infections were found to suffer more illness and require more hospital admissions. See Charles A. Kofoid and John P. Tucker, "On the Relationship of Infection by Hookworm to the Incidence of Morbidity and Mortality in 22,842 Men of the United States Army," *American Journal of Hygiene*, vol. 1, no. 1 (1921), 79–117.

[65] W. G. Smillie and D. L. Augustine, "Hookworm Infestation: The Effect of Varying Intensities on the Physical Condition of School Children," *American Journal of Diseases of Children*, vol. 31, no. 2 (1926), 166.

# 7

# An Era of Optimism

In the late nineteenth and early twentieth centuries, an increasing number of "modern" people in the North Atlantic region learned to defecate indoors in "water closets," outfitted with U-shaped traps that blocked sewer gases, and use toilet paper.[1] The process was gradual. In 1880, 20 percent of urban residents in the United States had indoor facilities, and masses of urban poor still deposited their excrement in cesspits, privy vaults, or tub latrines, from which it was hauled away by municipal scavengers.[2] By the early decades of the twentieth century, a large percentage of the North Atlantic urban population had acquired modern sanitary conveniences and embraced the regular use of soap for hand cleansing. By the mid-twentieth century, the urban flush toilet had become nearly universal.

The revolution of sanitary modernity extended beyond the indoor toilet. Urban populations in the North Atlantic region adopted iceboxes and then electric refrigerators to avoid food spoilage and screened their

---

[1] The first reference to the use of paper to wipe the anus and/or perineal area appears in a sixth-century Chinese text, and the practice was also noted by an Arab traveler in ninth-century China. Several fourteenth-century texts indicate that toilet paper was produced on a considerable scale to serve the needs of the imperial court and other Chinese elite. Joseph Needham and Tsien Tsuen-Hsuin, *Science and Civilisation in China*, vol. 5, *Chemistry and Chemical Engineering, Part I, Paper and Printing* (Cambridge: Cambridge University Press, 1985), 123.

In 1857 in the United States, Joseph C. Gayetty "invented" a toilet paper made from Manilla hemp and softened with aloe that he sold as a "medicated paper for the water closet." "Gayetty's Medicated Paper [advertisement]," *New York Daily Tribune*, February 3, 1859.

[2] Joel A. Tarr, James McCurley III, Francis C. McMichael, and Terry Yosie, "Water and Wastes: A Retrospective Assessment of Wastewater Technology in the United States, 1900–1932," *Technology and Culture*, vol. 25, no. 2 (1984), 231.

ARE THERE ANY LEAKS IN YOUR DAM?

FIGURE 7.1 "Are there any leaks in your dam?"
Source: "Typhoid Fever and Its Prevention in Town and Country," *Virginia Health Bulletin*, vol. 3, no. 6 (1911)

windows and doors to block flies. Scientists scored breakthroughs with poliovirus vaccines and oral rehydration therapy that reached distant populations. For those within the orbit of sanitary modernity, it was an era of optimism.

### SANITARY PRACTICES: SOAP, REFRIGERATION, AND SCREENS

In the North Atlantic region, the popularization of new scientific understandings of the role of "germs" in disease transmission facilitated the adoption of sanitary behaviors.[3] Three were core: handwashing to reduce the contamination of food stuffs; refrigeration to slow the growth of bacteria on food; and window and door screening to block flies from flitting between excrement and prepared foodstuffs. All improved upon prior practice. All were initially adopted by the wealthy and eventually trickled down to the lower socio-economic classes.

---

[3] For a general cultural history of cleanliness in Europe, see Virginia Smith, *Clean: A History of Personal Hygiene and Purity* (Oxford: Oxford University Press, 2007).

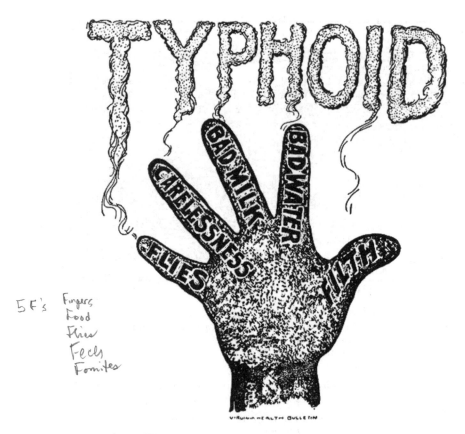

5 F's  Fingers
      Food
      Flies
      Feces
      Fomites

**Beware The Black Hand**

FIGURE 7.2 "Typhoid: Beware the black hand."
Source: *Virginia Health Bulletin*, vol. 15, no. 9 (1923)

Soap making with lye and animal fats was an ancient art, and in early nineteenth-century Europe, as piped water became available, the use of new perfumed "toilet" soaps became an object of consumption by the urban bourgeoisie.[4] By the late nineteenth century, personal hygiene soaps had become a mass-market phenomenon. European merchants supplied peanut

---

[4] The earliest textual reference to making solutions of lye – by leaching wood or vegetable ashes – dates from Babylon in the third millennium BCE. See John A. Hunt, "A Short History of Soap," *Pharmaceutical Journal*, vol. 263 (1999), 985. The lye solutions were too harsh for direct application to human skin, and they were likely used for other purposes, such as washing clothes or cleaning utensils.

oil, palm oil, and palm kernel oil from Africa and Asia to the new European soap industries, and the growing middle class lathered up. Their higher standards of cleanliness signaled their cultural ascent.[5]

In the European tropical colonies, a diverse set of cultural forces helped to shape a growing market for soap.[6] For the colonizers, regular bathing with soap was a sign of moral virtue, and they interpreted the adoption of soap use among the colonized as an important milestone on a pilgrimage from the primitive toward the modern. African and Asian peoples, of course, had their own standards of beauty and hygiene, and they often put the personal hygienic goods to different uses than those envisioned by their manufacturers – such as oiling the body with cosmetic creams, rather than cleansing the skin or masking skin imperfections.[7]

Refrigeration advanced along a similar timeline. In the era before electrification, wealthier families in the North Atlantic region purchased ice cut from northern ponds, lakes, and rivers in order to reduce food spoilage from bacterial growth and protect the foods in the "ice box" from contamination by flies. During the late nineteenth-century burgeoning of the urban middle class, the demand for cold storage increased apace.[8] Manufactured ice had a brief heyday.[9] But by the 1920s the electric refrigerator had begun to win over consumers, and by the late

[5] On the meanings of cleanliness in nineteenth- and early twentieth-century Britain, see Victoria Kelley, *Soap and Water: Cleanliness, Dirt and the Working Classes in Victorian and Edwardian Britain* (London: I. B. Taurus, 2010).

[6] The market for "modern" soap varied markedly by cultural region. West Africa, for example, was a model market for the European exporter. By 1910, the UK exported 9,369 tons of household and fancy soap to West Africa, compared to 13,560 tons to India, Burma, and Ceylon combined, with their immensely larger combined population. The difference in demand between the British West African colonies and East African colonies was likewise great. David K. Fieldhouse, *Unilever Overseas: The Anatomy of a Multinational, 1895–1965* (London: Croom Helm, 1978), 341, 392, 400, 411.

[7] Timothy Burke, *Lifebuoy Men, Lux Women: Commodification, Consumption, and Cleanliness in Modern Zimbabwe* (Durham, NC: Duke University Press, 1996). Some tropical oils were produced on colonial plantations under European control. On some of plantations, workers were subject to abuse. Lord Leverhulme, the leading capitalist producer of soap, and other soap-producing firms established copra plantations in the Solomon Islands on which workers were flogged and even killed, in an effort to force more productivity. In 1913–14, an epidemic of dysentery during which five percent of the workers died further exacerbated the abysmal conditions. Brian Lewis, *"So Clean": Lord Leverhulme, Soap and Civilization* (Manchester: Manchester University Press, 2008), 161–62.

[8] Jonathan Rees, *Refrigeration Nation: A History of Ice, Appliances, and Refrigeration in America* (Baltimore: Johns Hopkins University Press, 2013), 136–37.

[9] An early twentieth-century outbreak of typhoid fever in New York State turned purchasers toward safer "manufactured ice." Previously, freezing temperatures were thought to kill all the bacteria in polluted water. Rees, *Refrigeration Nation*, 62.

1930s the end of the ice age was in sight.[10] The electric refrigerator achieved near universality by the 1950s and has been uncontested since.

The third sanitary practice developed from health concerns about the role of flies in spreading filth. Metal mesh screens became commercially available in the second half of the nineteenth century, although their use was initially confined to those with substantial incomes. In the first half of the twentieth century, they spread more broadly into rural and urban settings. They could effectively prevent flies from entering a domicile via windows and doors, although when flies made their way inside, the screens blocked their escape. Annoyed residents made use of flyswatters – newly available in the early twentieth century and a marked improvement over whisks and fans – to kill flies that alighted, but flies were notoriously difficult to locate late in the evening. Commercially available flypaper addressed this problem. Long strips of paper, laced with a chemical attractant and sticky adhesive, could be hung from the ceiling, light fixtures, or door frames to trap flies at any hour.

Beyond the home, flies continued to breed outside in human and animal feces, rotting vegetable matter, animal carcasses, and the like. Cleaning up this putrid matter ("environmental sanitation") was an option, but the scale and range of the problem was daunting. Public health specialists, in the aftermath of the Second World War, hoped for a major breakthrough with DDT to reduce the incidence of acute diarrhea. In southern Texas where the first experiments against flies took place, researchers concluded that, although DDT was somewhat effective, environmental sanitation was the better approach.[11]

## VACCINES AGAINST POLIOMYELITIS

During the first half of the twentieth century, as modern sanitation spread throughout the North Atlantic region, illnesses and deaths declined precipitously. Most successes were owing to the purification of the water supplies; some were owing to improved feces disposal; and some were owing to the more frequent washing of hands with soap after defecation or handling baby diapers and before preparing or eating meals. As these

[10] Rees, *Refrigeration Nation*, 164, citing Neil H. Borden, *The Economic Effects of Advertising* (Chicago: Richard D. Irwin, 1947), 398.

[11] James Watt and Dale R. Lindsay, "Diarrheal Disease Control Studies. I. Effect of Fly Control in a High Morbidity Area," *Public Health Reports*, vol. 63, no. 41 (1948), 1319–49.

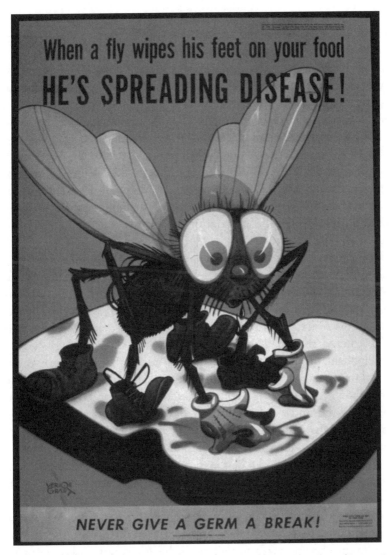

FIGURE 7.3 "When a fly wipes his feet on your food, he's spreading disease!"
Source: US War Department, 1944

public health gains were rung up, clusters of muscular paralysis caused by poliovirus appeared. The cases were not numerous, but they were terrifying because their cause was unknown.

Poliovirus has probably infected hominins since our earliest speciations, and it may (or may not) have been all but ubiquitous in a world without basic sanitation. Evidence is sparse, but many specialists believe that in earlier eras poliovirus had only rarely produced its signature paralysis. Seen through the lens of the "hygiene hypothesis," most human beings, infected with poliovirus in their early years of life, had asymptomatic and benign infections that produced a durable immune response that protected against disease. Children exposed to poliovirus for the first time in their middle childhood years or later risked serious although far-from-common complications. About one in a thousand children infected between the ages of five and twelve acquired serious complications, although in older age ranges the incidence increased sharply. One in seventy-five nonimmune adults who became infected experienced some degree of muscular paralysis, ranging from a compromised limb to death by asphyxiation as a result of atrophied breathing muscles.

In the first decade of the twentieth century, Swedish researchers found that poliovirus could be spread by asymptomatic, apparently healthy individuals. The route of transmission was thought to be via nasal mucosa. This view was significantly revised in 1941, when the American researchers Albert Sabin and Robert Ward showed definitively that poliovirus entered the small intestine and that the small intestine was the principal site of localization.[12] They determined that the principal route of transmission was fecal–oral: the small intestine disseminated the virus through expelled feces that contaminated fingers, foods, eating utensils, and drinking fluids such as milk and water. The virus could also be transmitted via airborne droplets from the pharynx, as was the case with chicken pox, diphtheria, measles, and rubella.

Until the Second World War, experts thought that poliomyelitis was a disease of the temperate latitudes. During the war, however, some Allied troops stationed in the tropics and subtropics were stricken with paralysis. An outbreak among US Army troops in the Philippines from 1944 to 1946 erupted in the midst of Filipinos among whom the disease seemed to be rare. In the early postwar period, public health experts discovered a high prevalence of polio among native populations in many regions of the tropics and subtropics, including Hawaii, Puerto Rico, Panama, Venezuela, Ecuador, El Salvador, the islands of Malta, Mauritius, and

---

[12] The definitive work of Sabin and Ward on the natural history of poliomyelitis confirmed the 1912 hypothesis of Swedish researchers that had been ignored for decades. Hans J. Eggers, "Milestones in Early Poliomyelitis Research (1840 to 1949)," *Journal of Virology*, vol. 73, no. 6 (1999), 4533–35.

Singapore. This led to a partial reassessment of the epidemiology of the disease.[13]

It soon became clear that there were three different polioviruses and many strains of each, and thus it was possible for populations that had been exposed to one poliovirus and acquired an immunity to be vulnerable to novel infections. For this reason, epidemics could occur in the midst of endemic infections. This was apparently what had happened, for example, during an epidemic in Kenya in 1953–55 that struck Europeans, Asians, and Africans at markedly different rates and with concentrations in different age ranges.[14]

What seemed clear was that sporadic cases led to small outbreaks and then to epidemics. The evidence from Central and South American states seemed to fit this pattern.[15] There seemed to be a broadening disease incidence on all the inhabited continents that eclipsed the late nineteenth- and early twentieth-century patterns of geographically isolated outbreaks. Some experts thought (and some still do), in line with the hygiene hypothesis, that the human costs of this global "emerging" disease were heaviest in the regions that had made the greatest advances in sanitary engineering.[16]

In the early to mid-1950s, research scientists in the United States made revolutionary breakthroughs in poliovirus vaccines. In 1952, Jonas Salk created a vaccine from a killed virus, and in 1955 the US government decided to roll out the Salk vaccine at the end of the summer "polio season." This produced a public health nightmare. Cutter Laboratories and Wyeth Laboratories had imperfect vaccine production controls, and they released contaminated batches that caused dozens of cases of persistent polio paralysis and some deaths. The defective batches were withdrawn, and the campaign continued.[17]

---

[13] M. Smallman-Raynor, A. D. Cliff, B. Trevelyan, C. Nettleton, and S. Sneddon, *Poliomyelitis: Emergence to Eradication* (Oxford: Oxford University Press, 2006), 221–31.

[14] Smallman-Raynor et al., *Poliomyelitis*, 233–39. See also N. R. E. Fendall, "Poliomyelitis in Kenya: A Review of the Present Position," *East African Medical Journal*, vol. 37, no. 2 (1960), 89–103.

[15] John R. Paul, "Endemic and Epidemic Trends of Poliomyelitis in Central and South America," *Bulletin of the World Health Organization*, vol. 19 (1958), 747–58.

[16] Barry Trevelyan, Matthew Smallman-Raynor, and Andrew D. Cliff, "The Spatial Dynamics of Poliomyelitis in the United States: From Epidemic Emergence to Vaccine-Induced Retreat, 1910–1971," *Annals of the Association of American Geographers*, vol. 95, no. 2 (2005), 269–93.

[17] Arthur Allen, *Vaccine: The Controversial Story of Medicine's Greatest Lifesaver* (New York: W. W. Norton, 2007), 197–205.

By 1956, Albert Sabin's vaccine that used a live, attenuated virus was ready to be tested in a mass trial. This could not be done in the United States, because the widespread administration of the Salk vaccine meant that many children had levels of antibodies too high for a different vaccine to be tested. Sabin reached out to the Soviets and convinced them to undertake a massive testing of his vaccine.[18] Soviet public health physicians administered both the Salk vaccine and the Sabin vaccine on a limited basis in 1958–59, and in 1960 the Soviets decided to vaccinate the entire Soviet population.[19] They selected the Sabin vaccine because it was comparatively inexpensive to produce and could be administered orally. The Soviets began to mass produce the Sabin vaccine to protect their own populations and to have a supply of polio vaccine to express Soviet power and influence abroad. The Americans, once convinced that the Sabin vaccine was safe, also adopted it. In the 1960s, the Sabin vaccine was used extensively in the United States, Soviet Union, parts of Eastern Europe, Mexico, Singapore, and the Netherlands. It became the most widely used polio vaccine throughout the 1960s and 1970s. (Its reach did not extend to mainland China where, following the Sino-Soviet split in 1961, the door to international health initiatives had been bolted shut.)

In the European tropical colonies, the efforts at polio vaccination were modest in scope and met with major obstacles. The roll-outs were problematic, because of inadequate road infrastructure and the difficulties of maintaining the continuous refrigeration necessary to protect the potency of the vaccines. In some regions, colonial medical officials advised against vaccination. In Katanga Province in the Belgian Congo, for example, health officials in opposed the use of attenuated live vaccine. In some other regions of the Belgian Congo, however, the experimental vaccination campaign with attenuated live virus reached large numbers of people.[20] Elsewhere, in the waning years of colonial rule in Africa, the colonialists tried experimental polio vaccines on African subjects, with mixed success.[21]

[18]  Stuart S. Blume, "Lock-In, the State and Vaccine Development: Lessons from the History of the Polio Vaccines," *Research Policy*, vol. 34 (2005), 163.

[19]  Smallman-Raynor et al., *Poliomyelitis*, 489–92.

[20]  Stanley A. Plotkin, "CHAT Oral Polio Vaccine Was Not the Source of Human Immunodeficiency Virus Type 1 Group M for Humans," *Clinical Infectious Diseases*, vol. 32 (2001), 1077.

[21]  Edward T. Hooper, *The River: A Journey to the Source of HIV and AIDS* (Boston: Little, Brown, 1999). The book's speculative thesis about the dispersal of HIV has been debunked, but its evidence on polio trials in Africa is soundly researched.

FIGURE 7.4 Centers for Disease Control polio oral vaccine poster, 1963.
Source: public domain

The net result of the polio vaccination campaigns from the mid-1950s through the 1970s was a precipitous decline in paralytic polio among immunized populations whose protection through herd immunity extended to neighbors who had not received the vaccine. Sabin in 1987 estimated that worldwide the vaccine had prevented 5 million cases of persistent paralysis and 500,000 deaths. In the United States the public health victory was nearly total. The transmission of polio ceased in 1979, with the last domestic cases occurring in religious communities that had refused vaccination. From 1976 until 1988, the numbers of paralytic cases had dropped so low that the rare cases of vaccine-associated paralytic poliomyelitis had become the predominant form. Eighty-three cases were recorded in this period. In the 1980s, a handful of new cases of paralytic polio were contracted abroad and imported to the United States.[22]

Until the 1970s, the hygiene hypothesis, which seemed to explain the emergence of epidemic polio in the temperate countries, was assumed to hold in other areas of the world. The general consensus was that poliomyelitis was a benign infection in tropical Africa, for the simple reason that improved sanitation had not been widely implemented there. Children were assumed to have been exposed to poliovirus early in life and to be partially protected by maternal antibodies. They were thought to be at insignificant risk for paralysis because of immunity acquired through subclinical infections.

This anodyne view was not unchallenged. It ran counter to the experience of some physicians with extensive global careers. Franz E. Parebo, for example, a physician with sixteen years of service as a pediatrician with the WHO, noted in 1970 that he had seen paralytic poliomyelitis in every developing country in Asia and Africa in which he had served. He drew together the clinical evidence in Abidjan, Ivory Coast, and described paralytic poliomyelitis in developing countries as a "silent disease" that ran its course in the backyards of the poor.[23]

Beginning in 1974, approximately one hundred surveys were carried out in developing countries to determine the prevalence of lameness due to poliomyelitis. The results varied from less than one case to 25 cases per 1,000 children. The surveys altered the global outlook among international health experts: Polio could no longer be considered an insignificant problem.[24] The surveys also found high levels of rural paralytic poliomyelitis and, in some regions, epidemic poliomyelitis. The two were apparently not discrete. Later in the 1970s, an epidemiological study of paralytic poliomyelitis in rural Ghana showed clearly that the complication was not rare. In fact, when those who had died or recovered completely from a paralytic attack were included, the prevalence was higher in rural Ghana than in the United States during the 1945–54 era, when the worst of the national epidemics had struck.[25] The notion that paralytic

[22] Smallman-Raynor et al., *Poliomyelitis*, 462–68.

[23] Franz E. Perabo, "Poliomyelitis in the Ivory Coast," *Lancet*, October 31, 1970, 927–28.

[24] Roger H. Bernier, "Observations on Poliomyelitis Lameness Surveys," *Reviews of Infectious Diseases*, vol. 6, Suppl. 2 (1984), S371–75.

[25] David D. Nicholas, James H. Kratzer, Samuel Ofosu-Amaah, and Donald W. Belcher, "Is Poliomyelitis a Serious Problem in Developing Countries? The Danfa Experience," *British Medical Journal*, 1, no. 6067 (1977), 1009–12.

polio was necessarily rare in areas with unimproved sanitation was swept away. This did not invalidate the hygiene hypothesis as a whole, but at a minimum it suggested that the transmission of the polioviruses in the tropics had different dynamics if not a different etiology.[26]

Before the 1970s, the underestimation of paralytic poliomyelitis in the developing world meant that international health officials had not seen a need for global vaccination. A generation of young children was exposed to potential paralysis as a result. Yet even when the necessity became apparent, it proved difficult to act. The Salk vaccine was stable but too expensive to be used in most regions of the developing world. The Sabin vaccine was unstable and deteriorated quickly without a well-functioning system of handling, storage, and distribution. Continuous refrigeration – a "cold chain" – was the sine qua non of a successful vaccination campaign.

Beginning in the 1970s poliomyelitis vaccination initiatives were finally extended to the developing world. In 1974, the World Health Organization created its Expanded Program on Immunization (EPI), and in 1977 the World Health Assembly formulated the EPI policies. This ignited a momentous undertaking in global health. Previously there had been no global system, and vaccination in the developing world had been quite modest in extent. Indeed, experts estimated that perhaps only 10 percent of the population in developing countries had received the benefits of childhood vaccines. As the Expanded Program on Immunization advanced, the best guesses about prior coverage were scaled back by half.[27]

### THE REVOLUTION OF ORAL REHYDRATION THERAPY

Cholera, unlike poliomyelitis, was a highly lethal disease. Treatment with intravenous fluids dramatically improved one's chances of survival, but outside of hospitals and clinics, the case fatality rates were about 50–60 percent. Cholera was endemic in southern Asia, where it flared up seasonally in smaller or larger outbreaks, depending on the local rains that flushed fecal matter into wells, ponds, streams, or rivers from which people drew water for drinking and food preparation.

---

[26] Albert B. Sabin, "Role of My Cooperation with Soviet Scientists in the Elimination of Polio: Possible Lessons for Relations between the USA and the USSR," *Perspectives in Biology and Medicine*, vol. 31, no. 1 (1987), 57, 58.

[27] Smallman-Raynor et al., *Poliomyelitis*, 472.

As early as 1953, the physician Hemendra Nath Chatterjee had pioneered a way to rehydrate patients with mild to moderately severe
cholera using an oral glucose-sodium electrolyte solution, and he had
published his results in *Lancet*. But Chatterjee had not used meaningful
controls nor provided careful balance sheets to show the volume of fluids
introduced by an oral route and the loss of fluids through cholera
evacuations, and his research had little impact. Most physicians doubted
that an oral therapy could be effective. In addition, the fact that
Chatterjee was an Indian working in Calcutta (now Kolkata) may have
predisposed Western physicians against taking seriously his revolutionary findings. In 1966, in Baghdad, Qais Al-Awqati, an Iraqi physician,
likewise used an oral rehydration therapy during an outbreak of cholera
to great success. His work with two other doctors was also published in
*Lancet*, although the editors of the journal rewrote the article, empha-
sizing the public health success and barely mentioning the role of oral
rehydration therapy.[28] The findings of Chatterjee and Al-Awqati ran
counter to the reigning cholera treatment paradigm of the gradual intravenous administration of electrolyte solutions, blood transfusions, fast-
ing, and then the gradual resumption of feeding at the end of a
"starvation" period.

In the late 1960s, a group of US scientists in South Asia investigating the
transport of electrolyte solutions across the intestinal membranes found
that sufferers with cholera or other diarrheal diseases could be treated
with an oral solution of salt, sugar, and water – in practical terms, the
findings of Chatterjee and Al-Awqati. Yet even with the endorsement of
Western physicians, oral rehydration therapy faced stiff resistance,
because it could be successfully administered by a caregiver without
medical training outside of a clinical setting. Oral rehydration therapy
(ORT) was tragically slow to influence global health practice.[29] Many
hundreds of thousands died in the interim.

By the late 1970s, the medical establishment's endorsement of ORT
finally opened up new possibilities for the control of diarrheal disease. It
was now acceptable to intervene directly, inexpensively, and effectively.
The revolutionary importance of ORT can hardly be overstated. In Egypt,
a national awareness program to promote its use brought about a dramatic decline in the infant diarrheal death rate. Between 1981 and 1990,

---

[28] Joshua Nalibow Ruxin, "Magic Bullet: The History of Oral Rehydration Therapy,"
  *Medical History*, vol. 38 (1994), 394–95.
[29] Ruxin lucidly explores the Western researchers' path to ORT in "Magic Bullet," 366–94.

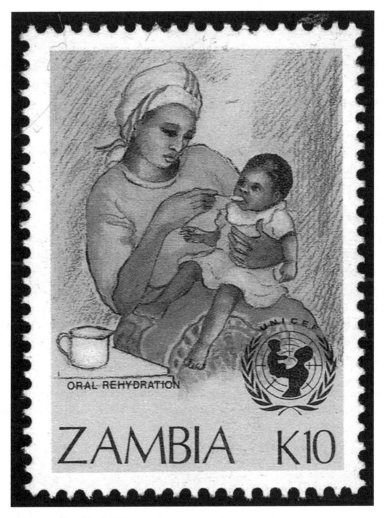

FIGURE 7.5 Zambia ORT postage stamp.
Source: public domain

the infant death rate dropped from 35.7 to 9.3 per 1,000 livebirths – a reduction of 74 percent.[30]

The global impact of oral rehydration therapy was profound. Fewer children in absolute numbers were dying from diarrhea and far fewer as a

[30] Mathuram Santosham, Aruna Chandran, Sean Fitzwater, Christa Fischer-Walker, Abdullah H. Baqui, and Robert Black, "Progress and Barriers for the Control of Diarrhoeal Disease," *Lancet*, vol. 376 (2010), 63.

percentage of world population. Diarrheal deaths per annum from dehydration fell from 4.2 million in 1960 to fewer than 2.5 million by the end of the twentieth century, a period during which human populations more than doubled. This large public health success unveiled a related and disconcerting public health problem. Childhood morbidity from diarrhea diseases rose during the same era in which childhood deaths fell.[31] In unsanitary conditions the humble ORT interventions could save lives but not prevent recurrent infections.

In the mid-1990s, the movement to increase the availability and use of oral rehydration solutions stagnated. Funding shifted toward programs focused on the integrated management of childhood diseases, to the disadvantage of the programs focused on diarrhea control. Moreover, advocates for control of other diseases such as malaria, tuberculosis, and HIV/AIDS were highly successful in garnering resources, and diarrheal diseases got demoted to a lower priority, despite the fact that these diseases were, when considered together with the health complications of malnutrition, the largest killer of children.[32] The loss of momentum in ORT advocacy was tragic. It was owing in part to a greater confidence in biomedical drugs and a preference for using them, in spite of evidence that ORT was far more effective, as well as a failure to get out the word about the public health miracle of oral rehydration solutions.[33]

Oral rehydration therapy had come into practice during the middle stages of the seventh global cholera pandemic.[34] The number of deaths was low compared with earlier pandemics when oral rehydration

[31] Richard L. Guerrant, Margaret Kosek, Sean Moore, Breyette Lorntz, Richard Brantley, and Aldo A. M. Lima, "Magnitude and Impact of Diarrheal Diseases," *Archives of Medical Research*, vol. 33 (2002), 351–55.

[32] Santosham et al, "Progress and Barriers," 65.

[33] Birger Carl Forsberg, Max G. Petzold, Göran Tomson, and Peter Allebeck, "Diarrhoea Case Management in Low- and Middle-Income Countries: An Unfinished Agenda," *Bulletin of the World Health* Organization, vol. 85, no. 1 (2007), 42–48; Pavani Kalluri Ram, Misun Choi, Lauren S. Blum, Annah W. Wamae, Eric D. Mintz, and Alfred V. Bartlett, "Declines in Case Management of Diarrhoea among Children Less than Five Years Old," *Bulletin of the World Health Organization*, vol. 86, no. 3 (2008), E–F.

For a study of caregiver knowledge about and attitudes toward oral rehydration solution, see Lauren S. Blum, Prisca A. Oria, Christine K. Olson, Robert F. Breiman, and Pavani K. Ram, "Examining the Use of Oral Rehydration Salts and Other Oral Rehydration Therapy for Childhood Diarrhea in Kenya," *American Journal of Tropical Medicine and Hygiene*, vol. 85, no. 6 (2011), 1126–33.

[34] For phylogenetic analysis of the different strains and their movements over space and time, see Ankur Mutreja, Dong Wook Kim, Nicholas R. Thomson, Thomas R. Connor, Je Hee Lee, Samuel Kariuki, Nicholas J. Croucher et al., "Evidence for Several Waves of

therapies had been unknown. When a relatively less virulent strain of cholera known as El Tor began to spread and reach epidemic intensity in East Africa after 1970, large numbers of people were affected – an estimated 150,000 came down with cholera, and there were at least 20,000 deaths. It was clear that ORT had not been widely used to counter the outbreak. The contamination of some lakes was extensive, and the El Tor strain of cholera adapted to the lacustrine environments and became endemic.[35]

## THE WORLD HEALTH ORGANIZATION AND SANITATION INITIATIVES

During the first half of the twentieth century, in the most developed states the sanitation revolution had made good progress. Even many smaller cities and towns had installed sewerage systems and water treatment plants, and many rural regions had improved their systems of feces disposal. Beyond the North Atlantic and urban Japan, however, progress toward safer water and better sanitation was slow. In part, this was a result of the global economic crisis of the 1930s and the chaos of the Second World War that had precluded major capital investments.

In the immediate postwar era, with capital resources still in short supply, colonial development schemes focused on building transportation infrastructure. In most colonies and in many independent developing states, the local tax bases were inadequate to finance sanitation schemes and there was scant internal political pressure to do so.[36] For many international health specialists, however, water and sanitation systems were still of the first order of importance, and slowly these specialists made some inroads into development thinking.

During the 1950s and 1960s, the World Health Organization (WHO) explored the prospects for improving sewerage and water systems in the developing world. The major justification for doing so was to assess the prospects for reducing the burden of morbidity. As the public health

Global Transmission in the Seventh Cholera Pandemic," *Nature*, vol. 477, no. 7365 (2011), 462–65.

[35] Myron Echenberg, *Africa in the Time of Cholera: A History of Pandemics from 1817 to the Present* (New York: Cambridge University Press, 2011), 109–24.

[36] For reflections on the East African case, see David Nilsson and Arne Kaijser, "Discrimination by Default: The Post-Colonial Heritage of Urban Water Provision in East Africa," in José Esteban Castro and Léo Heller (eds.), *Water and Sanitation Services: Public Policy and Management* (New York: Earthscan, 2012), 275–91.

specialist Henry Van Zile Hyde put it, "The major health problem of the
world today is not death ... It is chronic and repeated infection and
infestation which converts man from a productive unit of society to a
liability to society."[37] With fewer bouts of illness, the working population
would be more productive. This was the same development discourse that
had underwritten the Rockefeller hookworm campaigns of the first half of
the twentieth century and was being used to bolster the contemporaneous
WHO global malaria eradication program (1955–69). Labor was the
motor of economic development, and it was not running at speed.

In the mid-1950s, the WHO formed expert committees and undertook
surveys to determine the extent of worm infections and status of treatments.[38] There was no doubt that bacterial, viral, and protozoal intestinal
infections were also widespread. The bacterial pathogens that caused cholera
and typhoid killed large numbers of adults and children outright. In some
regions, protozoal infections by themselves seemed to constitute a public
health crisis. In rural areas of North China, for example, experts estimated
that 76 percent of the population suffered from amoebic dysentery (bloody
diarrhea) caused by *Entamoeba histolytica*, which was often accompanied
by other severe health consequences. The global toll was immense.[39]

Infectious intestinal diseases that caused loose stools were frequently
grouped together under the rubric of "diarrheal diseases." This was short-
hand. Most sufferers of diarrheal diseases did not receive a medical
diagnosis, and the terminology – such as diarrhea and enteritis, or dysentery, or gastroenteritis and colitis – varied by country and even by province. The diarrheal diseases rubric was useful in pointing up the scale of
the problem. For example, of the sixteen countries in Central and South
America that reported causes of death in 1952, diarrheal diseases were the
major cause of death in nine. Indeed, they were the major public health
problem in most of the Americas in the mid-twentieth century.[40]

[37] Henry Van Zile Hyde, "Sanitation in the International Health Field," *American Journal of Public Health*, vol. 41, no. 1 (1951), 2.
[38] New understandings were won. One significant finding was that in the tropics deworming drugs needed be supplemented with iron therapy. Patients who had been treated for hookworm without iron supplements presented with gross anemia; those taking iron but not deworming drugs had heavy worm loads but no anemia. See Henry Foy and Athena Kondi, "Hookworms in the Aetiology of Tropical Anaemia," *Transactions of the Royal Society of Tropical Medicine and Hygiene*, vol. 54, no. 5 (1960), 419–33.
[39] E. G. Wagner and J. Lanoix, *Excreta Disposal for Rural Areas and Small Countries*, WHO Monograph Series no. 39 (Geneva: World Health Organization, 1958), 13.
[40] Albert V. Hardy, "Diarrheal Diseases of Man: A Historical Review and Global Appraisal," *Annals of the New York Academy of Sciences*, vol. 66, no. 1 (1956), 8.

Diarrheal diseases killed mostly infants and children. In 1954, in Egypt, almost 18 percent of all children died by the end of their first year, and more than half of these deaths (54.7 percent) were attributed to diarrhea and enteritis (a nonspecific inflammation of the small intestine). By contrast, in Sweden, where the water supply was purified, 1.9 percent of children did not survive to their first birthdays, and a mere 1 percent of those deaths were from diarrhea and enteritis.[41] The gulf between Western Europe, North America, and Japan and the rest of the world was wide.

Momentum for addressing these disparities was slow to build. One reason was misdiagnosis. Many specialists believed that the major cause of diarrheal deaths of children was poor nutrition that could be addressed through greater attention to infant feeding. Another reason was deeply fixed in the human experience. The entire run of human history had been marked by high rates of infant and childhood death, and, in virtually all cultures, parents accepted childhood deaths as natural.[42]

There was, however, light on the horizon. In the 1950s, the general prospects for human health in many regions beyond the North Atlantic and Japan brightened. The reasons were many. The economic strictures of the Second World War years were fading. An increase in world trade and declining transport costs made it feasible to move foodstuffs to some areas stricken by famine. The postwar economic boom distributed material benefits more widely than in the past. New antibiotics (sulfa drugs, and then penicillin, streptomycin, and chloroquine) in combination with new vaccines (measles, mumps, rubella, and poliovirus) made the prospects for defeating diseases tangible and real. Taken together, these medical advances laid the material foundation for the radical ethical position that all human lives had the same value, regardless of age. This vision accompanied the largest, most rapid wave of human population expansion in world history. Over the course of the twentieth century, the number of people on the planet roughly quadrupled. The most rapid increase occurred during the second half of the century and continued at a somewhat lower rate into the first half of the twenty-first century. We are still riding its crest.

During this era of rapid growth, the base of the age pyramid of the human population broadened. In most world regions, a higher percentage

---

[41] Wagner and Lanoix, *Excreta Disposal*, Table I, "Infant Mortality and Mortality from Diarrhea and Enteritis for the Year 1954," 10.
[42] Hardy, "Diarrheal Diseases," 12–13.

of children survived the onslaughts of childhood killing diseases, particularly because of the availability of chloroquine for malaria and oral rehydration therapy for diarrheal diseases.[43] And broader, fundamental economic forces continued their work. The thickening of the global webs of communication and transport meant that the possibilities for trade and internal migration were better than ever before.

## THE FIRST AND SECOND UNITED NATIONS DEVELOPMENT DECADES (1960S–70S)

The United Nations' commitment to address "development" issues began in 1960 with the first United Nations Development Decade; a second Development Decade followed in 1970. Water and sanitation services were one of the general development goals, but they had to compete with claims that other investments in infrastructure would produce rapid economic growth.

Within the Global South, there were stark disparities between the sanitation conditions in urban and rural environments. For example, by the beginning of the 1960s in the Latin American and Caribbean countries, roughly the same number of people lived in urban areas (102 million) as in rural areas (107 million). Yet some 59 percent of urban residents had access to potable water, as compared with 8 percent of rural residents. Some 28 percent of those in urban areas had modern sewerage; virtually no one in the rural areas did. Broad gains were made during the 1970s, although the gulf between urban and rural persisted: In urban areas, 80 percent of the population had gained access to potable water either through house connections or a standpipe nearby, and in rural areas, only 34 percent. In urban environments, sewerage had been extended to 43 percent of the population, and in the rural areas, to only 3 percent.[44] In successive decades, in Latin America and the Caribbean, the predominant pattern continued to be the gradual extension of improved water and sanitation in urban areas, with a lagged response in the countryside.

In tropical Africa, the pattern differed considerably. Virtually all of tropical Africa had come under European rule, and Europeans in the African tropics suffered higher rates of mortality than their age cohorts in Europe or

---

[43] For the impact on tropical Africa, see Webb, *Long Struggle against Malaria*, 101–5.
[44] David Donaldson, "Overview of Rural Water and Sanitation Programs for Latin America," *Journal of the American Water Works Association*, vol. 75, no. 5 (1983), 225–26.

those posted to other parts of tropical empire.[45] In Africa, Europeans generally participated in schemes of racial segregation, and most of the investments in water and sanitation focused on protecting their own health.[46] Before the great independence movements that liberated Africans from colonial rule during the late 1950s into the mid-1970s (with later independence movements in southern Africa), rural Africans benefited little from colonial investments in improved water and sanitation. Consider, for example, a rather typical case – that of Burundi, a state that gained its political independence from Belgium in 1962. A 1963 WHO report described the infrastructure in the capital. The water supply was barely adequate in volume, with water shut off approximately fifteen times per month for at least six hours; it was at risk from contamination from cesspits, and there were inadequate personnel with inadequate authority to protect the water supply; the two sewer networks were not connected, and most of the inhabitants used cesspits that were not regularly cleaned out. There was no overall plan to improve sanitation in rural areas.[47] A decade later, little had changed in Africa.[48]

Experts agreed that something needed to be done to improve childhood survival rates, but they disagreed on what. Indeed, as early as the mid-1960s some specialists held that entirely too much emphasis had been placed on public health infrastructural interventions, and that individual households needed to make commitments to better hygiene.[49] Moreover,

[45] Philip D. Curtin, *Death by Migration: Europe's Encounter with the Tropical World in the Nineteenth Century* (New York: Cambridge University Press, 1989), see esp. tabular annexes.

[46] Not all practices worked as intended. As the author of a 1956 WHO report put it: "It is unfortunate, in my opinion, that the bucket latrine has been introduced so widely in Africa, especially in the British areas of influence. While this device offers fairly good protection against soil pollution, and will undoubtedly offer considerable protection against helminth transmissions, it offers no barrier to fly transmission of infection. Actually, it may be worse in this connection than having the faeces deposited in the open where it is quickly dried by the sun. Moreover, the collection, transportation and disposal of the nightsoil is a troublesome and messy business and usually involves considerable nuisance and sanitary hazard. This type of latrine does provide privacy and, if properly maintained, prevents local insect breeding, but the pit type of latrine has so many advantages in places where soil conditions have made its use possible as to make it much more preferable." WHO AFR/EH/3. H. G. Baity, "Report on a Visit to Bechuanaland, 23 August to 4 September 1956," 20.

[47] WHO AFR/EH/29. Alain Thys, "Situation générale de l'hygiène du milieu au Royaume du Burundi," June 1963, 5, 8–9.

[48] WHO/AFRO, "Environmental Health Activities in the Context of an Integrated Concept of Public Health Services," AFRO Technical Papers no. 5 (Brazzaville: WHO, 1973), 9–10.

[49] John E. Gordon, Moisés Béhar, and Nevin S. Scrimshaw, "Acute Diarrhoeal Disease in Less Developed Countries: 3. Methods for Prevention and Control," *Bulletin of the World Health Organization*, vol. 31, no. 1 (1964), 27.

in an era of booming population growth, some ecologists and economists in the Global North argued that the future of the planet depended upon reductions in the unprecedentedly rapid increase in human numbers. They made dire predictions of famine and disease. Birth control was one obvious check to population growth, and a movement formed to export birth control to the developing world.[50]

To many, the causal links between unpurified water and unimproved sanitation and sickness and death seemed obvious. There were, however, vital disputes about whether and to what extent investments in water and sanitation would improve health outcomes. During the 1970s, researchers had struggled to demonstrate direct causal relationships between improved water and sanitation services and health and in the main had not succeeded. Indeed, in 1976 a World Bank expert panel advised against further attempts to do so.[51]

## THE INTERNATIONAL DRINKING WATER AND SANITATION DECADE (1980s)

Public health experts felt certain nonetheless that the provision of basic water and sanitation infrastructure was critically important, even if researchers couldn't calculate the health benefits, and for the 1980s the WHO launched a new initiative known as the International Drinking Water and Sanitation Decade. Its rationale was that the major constraints to progress in health were inadequate investment and a lack of appropriate technology.[52]

In urban areas, donors and government agencies built major water and sanitation systems that they hoped would shine as symbols of development. This approach proved to be fraught. The infrastructure was expensive, and typically there were few funds left over for operation and maintenance. Projects fell into disrepair. In rural areas, public health experts rolled out community-level water and sanitation programs based on successes in the Global North. In the Global South, many of these programs were not

---

[50] Matthew Connelly, *Fatal Misconception: The Struggle to Control World Population* (Cambridge, MA: Harvard University Press, 2008).

[51] Dennis B. Warner and Louis Laugeri, "Health for All: The Legacy of the Water Decade," *Water International*, vol. 16, no. 3 (1991), 136.

[52] In an insightful article published before the International Drinking Water and Sanitation Decade kicked off, R. G. Feacham, who would become dean of the London School of Hygiene and Tropical Medicine, forecast difficulties with poor management, inadequate institutions, and the scarcity of skilled manpower. R. G. Feacham, "Community Participation in Appropriate Water Supply and Sanitation Technologies: The Mythology for the Decade," *Proceedings of the Royal Society of London, Section B*, vol. 209 (1980), 15–29.

embraced by their intended beneficiaries. Nonetheless, the experts claimed success. As two participants in the International Drinking Water and Sanitation Decade observed, "The expansion of coverage became a numbers game ... Little attention was paid to whether the systems functioned as designed or, indeed, whether people actually used them."[53]

The principal metric of success was how many people were "covered" by improved services. Yet, there was little agreement on what the term meant, let alone how to measure it. For example, should a public standpipe be considered an "improved" technology, if it brought untreated river water to city neighborhoods? Did it depend on the water quantity or the water quality available from the standpipe? Or both? Should a simple pit latrine be considered an improved technology? In what respects was it superior to a bucket latrine? There were also the issues of whether or not the improved services were actually used, how often, and by whom. This could only be known with certainty through detailed studies, and these were generally not undertaken because of cost and social difficulty. Few people wanted their defecation habits monitored. Self-reported behavioral data were known to be inaccurate, although there was little agreement on the degree of inaccuracy and whether this changed over time. In brief, evaluation was (and remained) a quagmire.[54]

The WHO tried to put the best spin possible on what some began to refer to as the "lost decade."[55] The Director-General of the WHO

---

[53] Warner and Laugeri, "Health for All," 137.

[54] When researchers invoked different methodologies, definitions, and assumptions, they achieved very different analytical results. Consider, for example, the large disparities in the water and sanitation coverage data from Ghana and Uganda in 1990 reported by government agencies and the Joint Monitoring Programme of the World Health Organization:

*Comparison of Coverage Data for Ghana and Uganda in 1990*

|  | Coverage in 1990 | Urban san. | Rural san. | Urban water | Rural water |
|---|---|---|---|---|---|
| Ghana | Govt. reported | 63% | 60% | 63% | not reported |
|  | Household sur. (JMP) | 23% | 10% | 86% | 37% |
| Uganda | Govt. reported | 32% | 60% | 60% | 30% |
|  | Household sur. (JMP) | 54% | 41% | 80% | 40% |

*Source:* Andrew Cotton and Jamie Bartram, "Sanitation: On- or Off-Track? Issues of Monitoring Sanitation and the Role of the Joint Monitoring Programme," *Waterlines*, vol. 27, no. 1 (2008), 18, Table 1

[55] Warner and Laugeri, "Health for All," 139.

estimated that 1.5 billion people had gained access to potable water and 427 million had secured an adequate means of excreta disposal.[56] Yet some of the national claims upon which the WHO estimates were based, however, were later determined to have been gross misrepresentations. The People's Republic of China, for example, had reported immense improvements, with nearly 600 million gaining access to improved water supplies and almost the entire population found to have improved sanitation. A 1994 World Bank report that followed a few years later, however, made a starkly different assessment: 40 percent of urban China had no sewers and only 4.5 percent of municipal wastewater received any treatment.[57]

Sub-Saharan African nations had benefited less than expected from large-scale investments and lagged far behind. In 1992, researchers estimated that in Kenya, for example, only 20 percent of the rural areas and 40 percent of the urban areas had improved sanitation.[58] Moreover, the rapid rates of population growth in sub-Saharan Africa imperiled the gains that had been made, and some evidence suggested that ground was being lost. The massive gap between expectations and realized programs in Africa pushed public health professionals back to the drawing board.[59]

Some researchers discovered that decreases in childhood mortality from diarrheal diseases were a function of the *quantity* of water available. Access to piped water alone promoted better hygiene, and this in turn reduced the transmission of pathogens.[60] It did not seem to matter a great

---

[56] WHO/EB89, "Evaluation of the International Drinking Water Supply and Sanitation Decade, 1981–1990. Report by the Director General. 21 November 1991," 4–5.

[57] World Bank, *China,* Urban Environmental Service Management Report no. 13073-CHA (1994), x.

[58] Ezekial Nyangeri and Kenneth S. Ombongi, "History of Water Supply and Sanitation in Kenya, 1895–2002," in Petri S. Juuti, Tapio S. Katko, and Heikki S. Vuorinen (eds.), *Environmental History of Water* (London: IWA, 2007), 310.

[59] The reassessment of water and sanitation prospects in Africa exposed an historical irony. In Africa, the sanitary engineers had been trained using European syllabi. Few had any idea about the design features of pit latrines, composting toilets, bucket latrines, or any other systems in use in rural areas. K. O. Iwugo, "Factors Affecting the Implementation of Improved Sanitation in Africa," *Journal of the Royal Society for the Promotion of Health,* vol. 99, no. 1 (1979), 28–30.

[60] In one sense, their findings echoed those of the first epidemiological studies of diarrheal disease in Great Britain early in the twentieth century that had concluded that modern sewerage in and of itself conveyed scant health benefits. It had made little difference if the inhabitants of a dwelling used a cesspit or had water-borne human waste flushed from a toilet to an underground sewer. O. H. Peters, *Observations upon the Natural History of Epidemic Diarrhoea* (Cambridge: Cambridge University Press, 1911), 58.

deal, if the water had been rendered safe to drink or not.[61] This new appreciation of piped water heralded a new era of smaller-scale, community-level interventions to improve rural health. It would engage a massive infusion of NGO money and technical assistance.

Societies in the North Atlantic region were the first to embrace sanitary modernity. Major advances in poliovirus vaccines and in oral rehydration therapy reduced the global damage caused by infectious intestinal diseases. Major disparities between the Global North and the Global South, however, remained, even as advances were made in some regions. Yet, by the late twentieth century, the model of centralized water purification and the water carriage of human waste was no longer taken to be universal. The paths forward would be forged by trial and error.

---

[61] As the authors of a study on piped water in Brazil noted: "Contrary to most studies on under-fives' mortality due to all causes, we found no evidence that those in homes with flush toilets were at reduced risk of dying from diarrhea, after adjusting for the effects of other variables. Furthermore, infants receiving untreated water were not at significantly higher risk that those receiving treated water. These findings suggest that the beneficial effects of piped water may relate to the easy availability of water rather than to its quality, which is in agreement with previous research on child mortality due to all causes." César G. Victora, Peter G. Smith, J. Patrick Vaughan, Leticia C. Nobre, C. Lombard, Ana Maria B. Teixeira, Sandra Costa Fuchs, L. B. Moreira, L. P. Gigante, and Fernando C. Barros, "Water Supply, Sanitation and Housing in Relation to the Risk of Infant Mortality from Diarrhoea," *International Journal of Epidemiology*, vol. 17, no. 3 (1988), 654.

# 8

# Global Health and Infectious Intestinal Disease

Beginning in the 1970s, new sets of actors took up the crusade against diarrheal diseases. Physicians and activists organized in response to a spike in infant deaths in the Global South linked to bottle-feeding, in order to bring political pressure to bear on manufacturers of infant formula. Nongovernmental agencies and national politicians encouraged behavioral change to end open defecation. Biomedical scientists developed additional vaccines against poliovirus and rotavirus. Epidemiologists threw new light on the global prevalence of diarrheal diseases and regional disparities in childhood survival rates.

Physicians, laboratory scientists, activists, and global health experts collectively achieved major reductions in childhood mortality in the Global South. The new focus on biomedical interventions and programs of community- or national-level behavioral change constituted a new era in the control of infectious intestinal disease. No longer were high rates of infant and childhood mortality considered natural and inevitable.

## THE INFANT FORMULA CONTROVERSY

Infant formulas based on cow's milk with additives were developed in Western Europe in the second half of the nineteenth century.[1] They had gained wide acceptance in the United States as early as the first decades of the twentieth century. Indeed, the scant historical evidence suggests that most

[1] Frank R. Greer and Rima D. Apple, "Physicians, Formula Companies, and Advertising: A Historical Perspective," *American Journal of Diseases of Children*, vol. 145, no. 3 (1991), 282–86.

urban children in the early twentieth-century United States were nourished both by the breast and bottle. There was, however, a fundamental difference in the Western European and US practices. Western Europeans routinely used boiled milk to prepare infant formula, whereas the Americans used raw milk, believing that it protected against scurvy. The illusion was costly. In the early twentieth century, the United States suffered an urban childhood mortality crisis caused in good measure by the contamination of milk. The crisis abated after 1912, when cleaner milk was stored in the icebox.

From the 1930s to the 1970s, breastfeeding decreased in popularity in the Western world. Some mothers did not breastfeed, and others stopped suckling their infants at an earlier age. Indeed, this transition away from lengthy breastfeeding promoted the baby bottle – with its rubber nipple and transparent glass (and later plastic) bottle – to prominence as a powerful symbol of gendered modernity. The model of bottle-feeding with formula would be exported to the wider world in the 1960s and 1970s, even as the return to breastfeeding in industrialized countries had begun.[2]

The baby bottle met an economic need. More lactating mothers were in the urban workforce, wet nurses were scarce, and many mothers found it impossible to return home to breastfeed during working hours or to bring their children to work. During the postwar decades, infant formula manufacturers sought to expand their markets, aggressively seeking new consumers in the regions of most promising growth – the developing world.

By the 1970s, the aggressive marketing strategies of some major infant formula manufacturers – notably, the Swiss multinational Nestlé – came under attack by health care professionals and activists who charged that Nestlé's strategies had killed babies in the developing world. The bases for the attack were threefold. Those with extensive health care experience in the developing world argued that the replacement of mother's milk with infant formula damaged babies by leaving them unprotected by the antibodies in mother's milk; that mothers either were ignorant of the need to use boiled water or could not afford to do so and prepared infant formula with contaminated water; and that mothers who could not afford to use the formula at full strength diluted the product and thereby deprived their children of needed nutrients.[3] The WHO estimated that approximately 5 million children died from diarrheal diseases and malnutrition each year

---

[2] Samuel J. Fomon, "Infant Feeding in the 20th Century: Formula and Beikost," *Journal of Nutrition*, vol. 131, no. 2 (2001), 409S–20S.

[3] Colin Boyd, "The Nestlé Infant Formula Controversy and a Strange Web of Subsequent Business Scandals," *Journal of Business Ethics*, vol. 106, no. 3 (2012), 285.

FIGURE 8.1  Boycott Nestlé poster.
Source: reproduced with the permission of the artist, Rachel Romero, San
Francisco Poster Brigade, 1978

and that 1 million of those deaths were attributable to contaminated infant
formula.[4] Activists organized a boycott of Nestlé products, the very first

[4] Stephen C. Joseph, "The Anatomy of the Infant Formula Controversy," *American Journal
of Diseases of Children*, vol. 135, no. 10 (1981), 889–92; for an opposing view, see Charles

international protest against a multinational corporation. The upshot was a heightened awareness of health professionals around the world about the desirability of breastfeeding as the best means to ensure infant nutrition.[5]

In the late 1980s, epidemiologists undertook studies in the developing world that confirmed the anecdotal evidence and assumptions that had undergirded the Nestlé boycott. The results were convincing. A first study of the use of infant formula and diarrheal deaths of infants in Brazil demonstrated a strong relationship. After allowance was made for confounding variables, infants who received powdered milk or cow's milk, in addition to breast milk, had greater than four times the risk of death from diarrhea compared with infants who did not receive artificial milk. The risk for infants who did not receive *any* breast milk was more than fourteen times higher. The authors found similar results when they compared infants who died from diarrhea with infants who died from diseases that were presumed to be due to noninfectious causes. It was clear that there was a strong protective effect from breastfeeding in developing countries.[6]

The infant formula industry surprisingly experienced an increase in sales, following the years of horrific publicity. Global sales in 1978 rang up at $1.5 billion, of which some $600 million were in developing countries. In 1983, global sales had boomed to $4 billion, with developing nations accounting for roughly half.[7]

### THE CHILD SURVIVAL REVOLUTION

By the mid-1970s, health experts at the WHO were beginning to articulate a new vision for international health that moved beyond a commitment to so-called vertical programs that targeted individual diseases such as polio, malaria, or tuberculosis. The primary health care movement prioritized basic health services for all the world's peoples on the principle that health was a human right.

---

D. May, "The 'Infant Formula Controversy': A Notorious Threat to Reason in Matters of Health," *Pediatrics*, vol. 68, no. 3 (1981), 428–30.

[5] James E. Post, "Assessing the Nestlé Boycott: Corporate Accountability and Human Rights," *California Management Review*, vol. 27, no. 2 (1985), 116–21.

[6] Cesar G. Victora, Peter G. Smith, J. Patrick Vaughan, Leticia C. Nobre, Cintia Lombardi, Ana Maria B. Teixeira, Sandra C. Fuchs, Leila B. Moreira, Luciana P. Gigante, and Fernando C. Barros, "Infant Feeding and Deaths due to Diarrhea: A Case-Control Study," *American Journal of Epidemiology*, vol. 129, no. 5 (1989), 1032–41.

[7] Post, "Assessing the Nestlé Boycott," 121.

Primary Health Care developed in part as a response to the broadening of political participation in the United Nations. The decolonization movements of the 1950s, 1960s, and 1970s gave birth to independent states that joined the United Nations and the World Health Organization. Some aligned with the US-led bloc of nonsocialist/noncommunist nations; others aligned with the USSR-led socialist/communist bloc; and others staked out neutral turf. During the Cold War (1947–91), the intense competition between the two blocs spilled into the arena of health. The United States had financially backed the WHO's global malaria eradication campaign (1955–69) which failed to reach its goal. In 1958, the Soviet Union had proposed the global eradication of smallpox, and in 1966, after years of delay the WHO launched a vaccination program (for which the Soviet Union provided 80 percent of the vaccines) that attained its goal in the late 1970s.[8] The Soviet Union had also proposed an investigation of the best methods to promote basic health services, and the study results were presented in 1973 to the World Health Assembly.[9] There were fundamental questions in play. What vision should guide the WHO? What approach to human health would best meet the needs of the world's peoples, most of whom were poor? The issues were debated at a meeting of the World Health Organization at Alma-Ata (now Almaty), in Kazakhstan, USSR in 1978. There, the World Health Assembly delegates voted to endorse an aspirational commitment to expanding primary health care for all the world's peoples.

Within a few years, some important steps were taken in the direction of primary health care that focused on children's health. In 1980, James Grant took over the leadership of UNICEF in 1980 and advocated a limited set of medical interventions that could reach all children – in line with the Alma-Ata principle of universal coverage. In 1982, health experts identified affordable and effective interventions against malnutrition, diarrhea, and vaccine-preventable diseases that were already available and could be scaled up cost effectively. A new acronym was coined – GOBI – that stood for the four pillars of the approach: growth monitoring, oral rehydration, breastfeeding, and immunization. It initiated what is known today as the child survival revolution.

[8] Donald Henderson, "Smallpox Eradication: A Cold War Victory," *World Health Forum*, vol. 19 (1998), 113–19.
[9] Theodore M. Brown, Marcos Cueto, and Elizabeth Fee, "The World Health Organization and the Transition from 'International' to 'Global' Public Health," *American Journal of Public Health*, vol. 96, no. 1 (2006), 66.

Oral rehydration and immunization were the most important of the four pillars because these interventions were predictable and trackable. In some Latin American countries, other interventions were added on the GOBI programs and eventually amounted to something close to comprehensive primary health care for children. Elsewhere, by the late 1980s, the major focus of child survival was pared down to a push for universal immunization against diphtheria, pertussis, and tetanus (DPT3) that was delivered through the Expanded Program on Immunization that had been in existence since 1974. (The Expanded Program on Immunization had initially focused on immunizations against diphtheria, whooping cough, tetanus, measles, poliomyelitis, and tuberculosis.)[10] This limited intervention was a resounding success: DPT3 global coverage rose from 20 percent in 1980 to 75 percent by 1990.[11]

Some critics decried the selectivity as an abandonment of the model of primary health care for all. The charge was that the targeted immunization programs undercut the prospects for national health care systems as well as failed to provide adequate primary health care. The allegation was not baseless, but even in retrospect it is difficult to imagine how the Alma-Ata goals might realistically have been achieved. Many newly independent states – such as those in tropical Africa – had prioritized investments in economic development over the development of their national health care systems, and in these environments, there was little doubt that selective primary health care – of which the Expanded Program on Immunization was a part – marked a major advance. It saved millions of young lives.

Infectious intestinal diseases went to the back burner. The evidence did not suggest that capital investments in improved water supply and feces disposal would pay large dividends in human health, and the improved infrastructure demanded maintenance and a highly trained workforce. The Expanded Program on Immunization package of vaccines did not cover any of the pathogens that caused diarrheal diseases, but the oral rehydration salts were highly effective and could be packaged for sale even in remote rural areas. In retrospect, it seems quite understandable how the attention of the global health community turned away from the problem. When the basic approach was to focus on the set of the most important

[10] www.who.int/immunization/programmes_systems/supply_chain/benefits_of_immuniza tion/en/.
[11] Joy E. Lawn, Jon Rohde, Susan Rifkin, Miriam Were, Vinod K. Paul, and Mickey Chopra, "Alma-Ata 30 Years On: Revolutionary, Relevant, and Time to Revitalise," *Lancet*, vol. 372, no. 9642 (2008), 920.

health problems for which solutions were available and cost-effective, infectious intestinal diseases could not compete. Childhood deaths from diarrheal diseases, however, remained shockingly high.

In 1984, USAID began a program to collect demographic health data in the developing world. Over time, these demographic health surveys were highly useful in many respects, and they allowed for an assessment of health trends in countries that participated in more than one survey. Eighty-five countries participated at least once, and fifty-seven did so more than once between 1984 and 2012. Most of the surveys depended upon self-reporting, and, from the point of view of diarrheal disease control, they asked important questions about oral rehydration therapy and the incidence of diarrhea in children.[12] They were not intended to elicit the health concerns of the populations who were surveyed and did not do so. They did succeed in developing a more accurate statistical picture of morbidity and mortality, and the high rates of under-five mortality came into sharper focus. This was important, in part, because time-tested, effective vaccines were being made newly available and new vaccines were being developed that promised large-scale improvements in child survival rates.

## A NEW CAMPAIGN TO ERADICATE POLIOMYELITIS

The campaigns against poliomyelitis enjoyed major victories in the era 1955–88, and the viral infection went into worldwide retreat. The campaigns succeeded in reducing the incidence of paralytic polio throughout the developed world to the point of eventual elimination, and in the developing world, the numbers plummeted in areas that the vaccination programs reached. In 1988, following on the unprecedented success of the World Health Organization's smallpox eradication program, the World Health Organization committed to the goal of polio eradication. Polio seemed a prime candidate for global eradication because, like smallpox, it was a viral disease with a human reservoir that did not infect other species. Its transmission was principally through a fecal–oral route, although transmission could also take place via an oral-oral route – for example, by breathing in tiny airborne droplets from someone infected with poliovirus. Despite the similarities, polio was far trickier to combat than

[12] Daniel J. Corsi, Melissa Neuman, Jocelyn E. Finlay, and S. V. Subramanian, "Demographic and Health Surveys: A Profile," *International Journal of Epidemiology*, vol. 41, no. 6 (2012), 1602–13.

smallpox because the vast majority who were infected with poliovirus were asymptomatic.

The WHO, Rotary International (which raised funds), the US Centers for Disease Control, and the United Nations Children's Fund polio eradication program joined forces in a global crusade.[13] Over the next thirty years (1988–2018), the polio eradication program made enormous strides, eliminating wild poliovirus paralysis from the Americas, most of Asia, and most of Africa. The remaining areas of wild poliovirus transmission today are in Nigeria, Pakistan, and Afghanistan, and there have been some recent cases of paralysis from contagious vaccine-derived poliomyelitis virus in the Lao People's Democratic Republic in 2015 and 2016 and in Syria in 2016 and 2017. The three wild polioviruses cause paralysis in roughly 1 in every 200 infections, and a much smaller proportion of those with paralysis have deadly complications. The Salk and Sabin polio vaccines are extremely safe, but they are not perfect. A very small number of those who are vaccinated develop polio paralysis. The incidence rate of vaccine-caused polio paralysis is roughly 1 case in every 2.7 million vaccinations, but it is, of course, a tragedy for those who contract it.[14]

In March 2017, a synchronized program of polio vaccination, engaging 190,000 vaccinators, administered the vaccine to 116 million African children in 13 countries (Benin, Cameroon, Central African Republic, Chad, Côte d'Ivoire, Democratic Republic of Congo, Guinea, Liberia, Mali, Mauritania, Niger, Nigeria, Sierra Leone), in an effort to finally sever polio's grip. This phase was launched in response to an outbreak in a conflict zone in northern Nigeria that resulted in four cases of paralytic polio.[15] It was a case study of how Rotary International, a philanthropic organization, was willing to invest enormous resources in an attempt to accomplish the endgame of eradication. The global campaign had dragged on for years past its projected completion date. Getting to zero cases was proving to be an enormously long slog, and on a per case basis it was fabulously expensive.[16]

It was projected that the vaccination campaign in western Africa would cause forty to forty-five cases of permanent paralysis. This was collateral

---

[13] Smallman-Raynor et al., *Poliomyelitis: Emergence to Eradication*, 571–73.

[14] http://polioeradication.org/polio-today/polio-prevention/the-vaccines/opv/.

[15] http://polioeradication.org/news-post/from-coast-to-coast-africa-unites-to-tackle-threat-of-polio/.

[16] The campaign had been temporarily crippled by resistance in some Muslim communities where suspicion of the vaccinators and mistrust of the state were rife. See Elisha P. Renne, *The Politics of Polio in Northern Nigeria* (Bloomington: Indiana University Press, 2010).

damage in an effort to prevent a wider outbreak. There was no guarantee of success. There was always the possibility of the reestablishment of transmission introduced by an asymptomatic carrier. Complicating the calculus was the remote prospect that a mutation in the oral polio vaccine could cause "circulating vaccine-derived poliovirus."[17]

### COMMUNITY-LED TOTAL SANITATION

Through the era of the global polio eradication initiative and the GOBI and Expanded Program on Immunization programs to improve child survival, diarrheal diseases continued as major killers of infants and small children in the Global South. In the late 1990s, nongovernmental organizations sprang up to address the problems of unimproved rural and urban sanitation. Some of them received international donor funding, in the hope that addressing sanitation practices at the community level might have a major impact on diarrheal disease transmission.

The approach that most radically departed from the top-down model of improved sanitation began in 1999. It was called Community-Led Total Sanitation (CLTS). It depended upon community mobilization, the dissemination of public health information, and community shaming. It focused principally on rural communities, although some urban communities also participated.[18] Unlike top-down government programs that paid contractors to build and install toilets in the hope that community members would use them, CLTS operated largely independently from national government control.

CLTS rang up many partial and full successes. Ironically, the absence of any direct government or NGO funding for latrines or toilets was among the conditions deemed propitious for success. The CLTS program prided itself on proselytizing about the health dangers of open defecation. This information then "triggered" community awareness, and many communities promoted local leaders to advance the program. Community engagement and focused social pressures were key. Those who were observed defecating in the open were shamed. Even children could be brought into the process, as in Bangladesh where groups known as

---

[17] Vaccine-associated paralytic polio occurs in approximately 1 of every 2.7 million doses vaccinated with oral polio vaccine, usually following the first dose. See http://polioeradi cation.org/wp-content/uploads/2016/07/GPEI-cVDPV-factsheet_March-2017.pdf.

[18] Robert Chambers, "Going to Scale with Community-Led Total Sanitation: Reflections on Experience, Issues and Ways Forward," *IDS Practice Papers*, no. 1 (2009), 10.

"armies of scorpions" blew whistles at individuals who were discovered defecating in the open.[19] It was a bottom-up program that fundamentally challenged the paradigm of development advocated by the World Bank and other large funders of development projects.

The CLTS model, however, did not catch on everywhere. Ecological conditions varied. When feces were deposited in areas near settlements and stank, it was one matter to convince the community that other means of feces disposal might be an improvement. It was a different matter altogether if the feces were eaten more or less immediately by animals. When free-ranging pigs in eastern Zambia, for example, cleaned up the immediate environment, villagers thought it fine to defecate even directly next to the homestead at night or during inclement weather. Another problematic variable was the rhythm of agricultural labor. During the agricultural season, many villagers worked in distant fields and defecated nearby. During these months, the latrines of the CLTS program were only partially useful.

In some areas, the CLTS latrines had to be built with expensive imported materials that were hard to come by, because there were no locally available materials that could serve. In these cases, the differences among the CLTS latrines became markers of socio-economic status and tended to undercut the message that open defecation affected everyone in the community equally. In some regions, local political authorities, rather than community members, decided whether a community would partici-pate in the CLTS program. In these cases, the fact that CLTS did not have surplus funds to dole out could work against their success. In eastern Zambia, for example, the chiefs were mostly concerned with the material benefits that flowed from participation in development projects, and there were relatively few who backed the CLTS program.[20]

OPEN DEFECATION AND THE STRUGGLE FOR MODERNITY

In the first half of the twentieth century, during the struggle for Indian independence, the nationalist leader Mohandas K. Gandhi famously said that India needed modern sanitation more than it needed independence.[21]

---

[19] Chambers, "Going to Scale," 27.

[20] Kevin Bardosh, "Achieving 'Total Sanitation' in Rural African Geographies: Poverty, Participation, and Pit Latrines in Eastern Zambia," *Geoforum*, vol. 66 (2015), 57–58.

[21] This saying is frequently cited by sanitation activists and politicians in India, but I have been unable to locate the original statement in the voluminous works of M. K. Gandhi, which as of this writing are available in digital format but are not keyword searchable.

Gandhi believed in the moral imperative to raise the status of the Dalits (often referred to as untouchables) whose tasks were to remove excreta from the streets, cesspits, fields, and latrines, and that the best way to do this was to embrace modern sanitation.[22]

In 1947, the nationalists achieved independence for India. Modern sanitation and social transformation proved more difficult to accomplish. A generation later, India had the highest percentage of its population still defecating out-of-doors of any national population in Eurasia, and the Dalits were still burdened with social stigma. As ever, the sanitary situation was worse in the cities than the countryside.[23] Tens of millions of slum dwellers lived without access to clean water or adequate means for excreta disposal. These conditions bred disease, and forward thinkers grappled for solutions.

In 1970, Bindeshwar Pathak founded an organization to address the problem of open defecation and to take up the challenge of liberating the Dalits from the humiliation of head-loading human waste. Sulabh International Social Service Organization developed Sulabh Complexes where the poor could have access to toilets, urinals, baths, and laundry facilities on a pay-to-use basis. The revenues paid for maintenance and the construction of new facilities. The human waste was repurposed to produce bio-gas and fertilizer. Sulabh International also built low-maintenance waste water treatment plants for institutions and industries and two-pit toilets that allowed rural families to compost their human waste, rendering it free of pathogens, before spreading it on their fields.[24] By the second decade of the twenty-first century, it was the largest non-governmental organization in India, drawing upon the assistance of some 50,000 volunteers.[25]

---

[22] For a collection of Gandhi's thoughts about sanitation, see Y. P. Anand, "Cleanliness-Sanitation: Gandhian Movement and Swachh Bharat Abhiyan," www.mkgandhi.org/articles/cleanliness-sanitation-gandhian-movement-swachh-bharat-abhiyan.html.
[23] Even the water supply of the capital city of Delhi was subject to catastrophic problems. In 1955–1956, an epidemic of infectious hepatitis sickened an estimated 1 million people. It was the largest outbreak of infectious hepatitis in history and the first well-documented epidemic of infectious hepatitis involved a treated water supply. Joseph M. Dennis and Abel Wolman, "1955–56 Infectious Hepatitis Epidemic in Delhi, India [with Discussion]," *Journal of the American Water Works Association*, vol. 51, no. 10 (1959), 1288–98.
[24] Bindeswar Pathak, *Road to Freedom: A Sociological Study on the Abolition of Scavenging in India* (New Delhi: Motilal Benarsidass, 2000); B. N. Srivastava, *Manual Scavenging in India: A Disgrace to the Country* (New Delhi: Concept, 1997), 46–52.
[25] www.sulabhinternational.org/meet-sulabh/.

The government of India also developed its own sanitation initiatives. In 2014, Prime Minister Narendra Modi launched the Swachh Bharat (Clean India) program. The political impetus was an aspiration for sanitary modernity, to allow India to join the group of nations whose citizens defecated indoors. Its programmatic goal was to build 8 million toilets.[26] Its premise was that simple access to toilets would eliminate the practice of open defecation, although a government program of toilet building had previously been tried in India with limited success.

Swachh Bharat ran into a predictable set of problems. Many villagers enjoyed open defecation and considered it healthier than using a latrine – just as had the inhabitants of the southern United States in the first half of the twentieth century. Few believed that open defecation was linked to the transmission of fecal–oral pathogens.[27] In villages, there was considerable concern over who could use the new toilets and what caste prohibitions were involved. In practice, some toilets were used only by women and children. Many toilets were converted to other uses. As the Swachh Bharat program advanced, it unveiled a mosaic of acceptance and rejection of modern sanitation in India that shared some similarities to rural tropical Africa.[28]

It was clear that there could be no universal answer to the global conundrum of how to end open defecation. The response at the level of the international health organizations was to push on. In 2000, the World Health Organization adopted its Millennial Development Goals, one of which was to cut in half by 2015 the proportion of people without safe drinking water and basic sanitation. This commitment was bolstered by another decade-length WHO commitment to Water for Life (2005–15). The goals were worthy, the rhetoric lofty. The successes were difficult to measure. Most states had no accurate data on who had access to adequate sanitation and thus no way to measure how sanitation usage and hygienic behaviors were changing.[29] Some researchers suspected that improved

---

[26] A video of Modi's 2014 speech at the launch of the Swachh Bharat mission is available online: www.youtube.com/watch?v=HmtxA_iXvbY.

[27] See, for example, Kalyan Banda, Rajiv Sarkar, Srila Gopal, Jeyanthi Govindarajan, Bhim Bahadur Harijan, Mary Benita Jeyakumar, Philip Mitta et al., "Water Handling, Sanitation and Defecation Practices in Rural Southern India: A Knowledge, Attitudes and Practices Study," *Transactions of the Royal Society of Tropical Medicine and Hygiene*, vol. 101, no. 11 (2007), 1124–30.

[28] The official website of the Swachh Bharat program, housed within the Ministry of Housing and Urban Affairs, is www.swachhbharaturban.in/sbm/home/ - /SBM.

[29] Kristof Bostoen and Barbara Evans, "Crossfire: Measures of Sanitation Coverage for the MDGs Are Unreliable, Only Raising a False Sense of Achievement," *Waterlines*, vol. 27, no. 1 (2008), 5–11, esp. Barbara Evans's initial statement on pp. 5–6.

communal rural water supplies might be an effective intervention, but a World Bank study turned up scant evidence that communal water infrastructure had much impact on diarrheal disease transmission.[30]

The official WHO figures suggested striking advances: in the quarter-century from 1990 to 2015, fully one-third of the world's population gained access to improved sanitation. This still left nearly a third of the world's population without improved toilets or latrines, however, and just under a billion people who defecated in the open.[31] Critics pointed out that this massively overestimated the success: many who had been accorded access to "improved sanitation" (usually a pit latrine) declined to use them because the latrines were filthy. By one estimate, the number of people without improved sanitation was on the order of 2.5 billion of which roughly 1.8 billion, mostly in rural areas, practiced open defecation.[32]

DEWORMING THE WORLD

During the International Drinking Water and Sanitation Decade, some public health specialists began to promote programs to combat soil-transmitted helminthic infections. In part, this was a result of new attention from the WHO that restarted a program of research and control of gastrointestinal helminthic infections.[33] Since the early Rockefeller Foundation era, there had been no concerted effort to reduce the global intestinal worm burden.[34]

One line of argument for new intestinal worm control programs was economic. For example, because intestinal worms lived from the nutrients drawn from the intestines, not only was the loss of blood important – so was the diversion of other nutrients from the human host to the worms. One scholar had estimated, for example, that in the Philippines round-worms alone might have consumed twenty-five metric tons of rice

[30] Alix Peterson Zwane and Michael Kremer, "What Works in Fighting Diarrheal Diseases in Developing Countries? A Critical Review," *The World Bank Research Observer*, vol. 22, no. 1 (2007), 16.
[31] www.who.int/mediacentre/factsheets/fs392/en/.
[32] Chambers, "Going to Scale," 10–11.
[33] D. A. P. Bundy and E. S. Cooper, "Trichuris and Trichuriasis in Humans," *Advances in Parasitology*, vol. 28 (1989), 108.
[34] Some owners of some commercial plantations had recognized an interest in keeping their workforces healthy. In Sri Lanka, for example, the tea plantation workers were required to participate in an annual mass hookworm treatment program. WHO7.0720. Fol. 179223. P. C. Beaver, "Visit to Colombo, Ceylon for Information on Intestinal Helminths and Filariasis, August 1962," 5.

per day.[35] There seemed to be a financial imperative to reduce the level of infection, even if it were not possible to interrupt transmission.

By the early 1990s, public health experts realized that it was difficult to quantify the economic and health impacts of intestinal worm infections, and as a result it was difficult to make the case that the infections were economically important. Many other diseases had higher profiles, and their advocates claimed the lion's share of financial resources. One core difficulty was the complexity of the relationships between infection and disability and between disability and reduced labor productivity.[36] This had been bedrock rhetoric of international public health since the earliest days of the Rockefeller Sanitary Commission. There was no doubt that high worm burdens produced anemia and worse. The problem was that the relationships were not reliably linear, and that the costs of determining the worm burden via microscopy were high.

Some proponents of deworming advocated for new programs of mass drug administration. They justified this approach, in part, by citing an economic analysis of the effects of chemical therapy in the US South during the years of the RSC. One economist had written that, at the end of the initial five-year program of thymol treatment, the RSC had all but eliminated hookworm, and he attempted to measure the benefits of the program forward in time. As we have seen in Chapter 6, however, this misstated the virtues of the hookworm program. The principal success of the RSC program was in creating a demand for latrines and public health departments. Chemical therapy had played a minor and indeterminate role. Indeed, even twenty-five years after the ending of the Rockefeller projects in the US South, there were hundreds of thousands of clinical infections.

In 2005, the World Health Organization defined seventeen core health conditions as neglected tropical diseases, and soil-transmitted helminthic infections were part of the mix. The WHO advocated for "preventive chemotherapy" to reduce the intestinal worm burden. School-age children would be given purgatives twice each year to expel the parasites. The medicines were so safe that they could be administered by teachers or

[35] A. Davis, "Ascariasis: Drugs and Drug Policy," in D. W. T. Crompton, M. C. Nesheim, and Z. S. Pawlowski (eds.), *Ascariasis and Its Public Health Significance* (London: Taylor and Francis, 1985), 239–40, citing B. D. Cabrera, "Reinfection and Infection Rates of Ascariasis in Relation to Seasonal Variation in the Philippines," *Southeast Asian Journal of Tropical Medicine and Public Health*, vol. 15, no. 3 (1984), 394–401.

[36] H. L. Guyatt and D. Evans, "Economic Considerations for Helminth Control," *Parasitology Today*, vol. 8, no. 12 (1992), 397–402.

others without special training. The mass drug administration programs ran parallel to the national health care systems. Their big advantage was that they were financed largely through drugs donated by the pharmaceutical behemoths GlaxoSmithKline and Johnson & Johnson. For advocates of this approach, the benefits were so substantial that it rendered moot the criticisms that the programs undercut the national health care systems.[37] The deworming programs, however, generally were not rigorously monitored or evaluated, and critics pushed for greater accountability.[38]

One problem was that mass drug administration could not produce sustainable reductions in the prevalence or intensity of helminthic infection. Without major improvements in sanitation, notably a drastic reduction in open defecation, students that got deworming medicines would simply get reinfected. One new rationale was that the infrastructure for the deworming of school children could be leveraged to facilitate the introduction of a new anthelminthic vaccine that might become available and might serve as a platform for interventions for the integrated control of coinfections with other neglected tropical diseases.[39] Another was that deworming would improve attendance at school and academic performance. A comprehensive 2007 study, however, found this not to be the case, concluding that "in mass treatment of all children in endemic areas, there is now substantial evidence that this does not improve average nutritional status, hemoglobin, cognition, school performance, or survival."[40]

The deworming programs thus were far from ideal for school-age children, and the programs missed entirely younger children, who were also subject to intestinal worm infections. This is significant because heavy roundworm infections cause stunting and it is difficult to reverse the effects, if children remain in the same environment. Growth deficits,

---

[37] David H. Molyneux and Mwele N. Malecela, "Neglected Tropical Diseases and the Millennium Development Goals – Why the 'Other Diseases' Matter: Reality versus Rhetoric," *Parasites and Vectors*, vol. 4, no. 234 (2011), 1–13.

[38] See, for example, Melissa Parker and Tim Allen, "De-Politicizing Parasites: Reflections on Attempts to Control the Control of Neglected Tropical Diseases," *Medical Anthropology: Cross-Cultural Studies in Health and Illness*, vol. 33, no. 3 (2014), 226–27.

[39] Jeffrey Bethony, Simon Brooker, Marco Albonico, Stefan M. Geiger, Alex Loukas, David Diemert, and Peter J. Hotez, "Soil-Transmitted Helminth Infections: Ascariasis, Trichuriasis, and Hookworm," *Lancet*, vol. 367 (2006), 1521–32.

[40] David C. Taylor-Robinson, Nicola Maayan, Karla Soares-Weiser, Sarah Donegan, and Paul Garner, "Deworming Drugs for Soil-Transmitted Intestinal Worms in Children: Effects on Nutritional Indicators, Haemoglobin and School Performance," *Cochrane Database Systematic Reviews*, vol. 11, no. 7 (2015), 1–157.

once established between six months and two years of age, are persistent.[41]

There were felt moral imperatives to continue the mass drug administration school programs nonetheless, particularly in Africa. Since the mid-1990s, in the Americas and Asia intestinal worm infections had dropped markedly in prevalence and in absolute numbers. These reductions were driven by rural-urban migration and social and economic development. Sub-Saharan Africa was the outlier. In Africa, prevalence rates had changed little, and because of population growth, there were dramatic increases in the absolute numbers of infections.[42]

ROTAVIRUS VACCINE

In the first decades of the twenty-first century, biomedical initiatives began to achieve robust success against viral intestinal pathogens. One of the major advances was against rotavirus. In the mid-1980s, rotavirus had caused approximately 20 percent of all diarrheal deaths in children under five years of age, and rotavirus had a global reach. Prevalence levels were similar in both economically advanced and developing countries. This suggested that the usual kinds of public health interventions would not lead to rotavirus control. An improved water supply and improved sanitation did not seem to make any appreciable difference.

In 2002 in the United States, experts recommended a live, attenuated virus vaccine for routine immunization of children, and a large-scale rollout commenced. It was then discovered that the rotavirus vaccine was associated with a telescoping of the intestine – an inversion of one part of the intestine within another – known as intussusception, and the program was halted immediately.[43] In 2006, an improved rotavirus vaccine, given in either two or three doses, was again rolled out, this time without complications. Rotavirus infections declined precipitously in the United States.[44] When rotavirus was included in recommended immunizations in

[41] D. W. T. Crompton and M. C. Nesheim, "Nutritional Impact of Intestinal Helminthiasis During the Human Life Cycle," *Annual Review of Nutrition*, vol. 22 (2002), 44.
[42] Nilanthi R. de Silva, Simon Brooker, Peter J. Hotez, Antonio Montresor, Dirk Engels, and Lorenzo Savioli, "Soil-Transmitted Helminth Infections: Updating the Global Picture," *Trends in Parasitology*, vol. 19, no. 12 (2003), 548.
[43] Umesh D. Parashar, Erik Hummelman, Joseph S. Bresee, Mark A. Miller, and Roger I. Glass, "Global Illness and Deaths Caused by Rotavirus Disease in Children," *Emerging Infectious Diseases*, vol. 9, no. 5 (2003), 565–72.
[44] Negar Aliabadi, Jacqueline E. Tate, Amber K. Haynes, Umesh D. Parashar, and Centers for Disease Control and Prevention (CDC), "Sustained Decrease in Laboratory

the developing world, in communities that received the vaccine, deaths declined rapidly. In 2008, rotavirus killed an estimated 453,000 children worldwide.[45] By 2013, the number was down to 215,000.[46] Access to the vaccine, however, was limited.

### THE SEVENTH CHOLERA PANDEMIC

As new programs for intestinal worms and intestinal viruses were rolled out, an old enemy reappeared. In 1991, the cholera strain known as El Tor exploded into the western hemisphere where cholera had been absent for more than a century. Cholera struck three coastal towns in Peru and then traveled north up the coast to Ecuador and Columbia and south to Chile. More than 400,000 people were afflicted, and there were roughly 4,000 deaths. The seventh cholera pandemic fleetingly raised awareness of the shockingly poor sanitation of impoverished peoples in South America, and the inability of the public health services to respond effectively to the epidemic. When El Tor sputtered out in South America, living conditions remained largely unchanged.[47] Cholera outbreaks could shock the conscience but not loosen the national and municipal purse strings. Even larger cholera outbreaks exploded in central Africa but generated little press coverage. Many died in refugee camps, uncounted in the greater maelstrom of political violence and displacement.[48]

In the early 2010s, cholera again flashed across global news screens, when UN peacekeepers from Pakistan inadvertently reintroduced cholera to the island of Haiti, whose populations were desperately poor, cursed with a corrupt government that tolerated violence toward its citizens, and trying to cope with the aftermath of a severe earthquake that struck in January 2010.[49] With people rendered homeless, and excreta disposal practices makeshift, cholera began to spread in the immunologically naïve populations, and the death tolls rose. From October 2010 through October 2012,

Detection of Rotavirus after Implementation of Routine Vaccination – United States, 2000–2014," *Morbidity and Mortality Weekly Report*, vol. 64, no. 13 (2015), 337–42.

[45] www.cdc.gov/rotavirus/surveillance.html.

[46] www.who.int/immunization/diseases/rotavirus/en/.

[47] Kelley Lee, "The Global Dimensions of Cholera," *Global Change and Human Health*, vol. 2, no. 1 (2001), 6–17.

[48] Myron Echenberg, *Africa in the Time of Cholera: A History of Pandemics from 1817 to the Present* (New York: Cambridge University Press, 2011).

[49] E. T. Ryan, "Haiti in the Context of the Current Global Cholera Pandemic," *Emerging Infectious Diseases*, vol. 17, no. 11 (2011), 2175–76, https://doi.org/10.3201/eid1711.110849.

the Haitian health ministry reported 604,634 cases of infection, 329,697 hospitalizations, and 7,436 cholera deaths.[50] These figures were probably a massive undercount. Doctors Without Borders suggested that in the initial phases of the epidemic (January–October 2010), the number of deaths was very high and underreported.[51] Thereafter, the numbers dropped dramatically, but cholera appeared to have become endemic on the island, with 6,000 cases and 37 deaths per month in 2015.[52] Cholera surged again on Haiti, in the aftermath of Hurricane Matthew in October 2016.[53]

### INFECTIOUS INTESTINAL DISEASE TODAY

Infectious intestinal disease continues to scourge human populations, although less extensively than in earlier decades. The absolute numbers of deaths from diarrheal disease are in steep decline from 4.2 million in 1982 to 3.0 million in 1992 to 2.5 million in 2000 to 1.4 million in 2010. This decline was part of an even broader success in reducing childhood deaths from all causes. Diarrheal disease, however, remained one of the principal killers of infants and children.[54]

Cholera and typhoid, major killers of adults as well as children, continue to exact a remarkable toll. Many of the deaths take place outside of the zones of media coverage. For cholera, experts in 2015 estimated that annually 1.3 billion people were at risk for infection, 2.9 million people were infected, mostly in endemic areas in sub-Saharan Africa and South Asia, and 95,000 died, mostly in Africa. Because cholera leaves survivors

[50] Ezra J. Barzilay, Nicolas Schaad, Roc Magloire, Kam S. Mung, Jacques Boncy, Georges A. Dahourou, Eric D. Mintz, Maria W. Steenland, John F. Vertefeuille, and Jordan W. Tappero, "Cholera Surveillance during the Haiti Epidemic – the First 2 Years," *New England Journal of Medicine*, vol. 368, no. 7 (2013), 599–609.

[51] Francisco J. Luquero, Marc Rondy, Jacques Boncy, André Munger, Helmi Mekaoui, Ellen Rymshaw, Anne-Laure Page et al., "Mortality Rates during Cholera Epidemic, Haiti, 2010–2011," *Emerging Infectious Diseases*, vol. 22, no. 3 (2016), 410–16.

[52] Rick Gladstone, "Cholera Deaths in Haiti Could Far Exceed Official Count," *New York Times*, March 18, 2016.

[53] Azam Ahmed, "Cholera Deepens Haiti's Misery after Hurricane," *New York Times*, October 15, 2016.

[54] Margaret Kosek, Caryn Bern, and Richard L. Guerrant, "The Global Burden of Diarrhoeal Disease, as Estimated from Studies Published between 1992 and 2000," *Bulletin of the World Health Organization*, vol. 81, no. 3 (2003), 197–204; Rafael Lozano, Mohsen Naghavi, Kyle Foreman, Stephen Lim, Kenji Shibuya, Victor Aboyans, Jerry Abraham et al., "Global and Regional Mortality from 235 Causes of Death for 20 Age Groups in 1990 and 2010: A Systematic Analysis for the Global Burden of Disease Study 2010," *Lancet*, vol. 380, no. 9859 (2013), 2105.

with an immunity that protected against reinfection with the same strain, most victims are children. Most do not receive medical treatment and their cases are not reported to the authorities.[55] For typhoid fever, experts estimated that in the year 2009 there were 21.6 million illnesses that killed about 1 percent – 216,000 people. Some died from typhoid fever because they did not have access to medical care. Others died because of the global emergence of multi-drug-resistant strains. Typhoid fever remained an important public health problem in South Asia, sub-Saharan Africa, and South America. To some analysts, the best lines of defense were to expand the immunization programs and, as ever, to improve sanitation. The *Salmonella typhi* bacteria are restricted to human beings, and thus the theoretical possibility existed for the global eradication of the pathogen.[56]

In the Global North, modern sanitation has triumphed. Cholera has disappeared, and typhoid fever is all but unknown. In communities with access to medical care, rotavirus infections can be prevented with a vaccine. Worm infections are no longer widespread. The water supplies are almost always potable. Young children and the elderly who fall ill with severe diarrhea can usually be successfully rehydrated at home with readily available over-the-counter remedies or in more extreme cases can be treated in clinics and hospitals. The advances are impressive.[57]

Challenges to intestinal systems in the Global North, however, continue to emerge. Some are rooted in the vulnerabilities of the industrial food systems. Consider, for example, the infectious intestinal disease known as campylobacteriosis. *Campylobacter* is probably an ancient bacterial infection of human beings, although it was identified only in

---

[55] M. Ali, A. R. Nelson, A. L. Lopez, and D. A. Sack, "Updated Global Burden of Cholera in Endemic Countries," *PLoS Neglected Tropical Diseases*, vol. 9, no. 6 (2015), e0003832, https://doi.org/10.1371/journal.pntd.0003832.

[56] M. K. Bhan, Rajiv Bahl, and Shinini Bhatnagar, "Typhoid and Paratyphoid Fever," *Lancet*, no. 366 (2005), 749–62.

[57] There are now effective vaccines against some of the deadliest infectious intestinal diseases: rotavirus, cholera, and typhoid. There is still, however, much more to be accomplished in the laboratory. There are as yet no effective vaccines against the dangerous *Escherichia coli* bacteria (Enterotoxigenic *E. coli* [ETEC], Enteropathogenic *E. coli* [EPEC], and Enterohemorrhagic *E. coli* [EHEC]) or *Shigella* spp., or against norovirus. Nor is there a vaccine against *Heliobacter pylori*, a bacterium that infects an estimated one-half of humanity and that causes peptic ulcers in ten percent of those infected. Cecil Czerkinsky and Jan Holmgren, "Vaccines against Enteric Infections for the Developing World," *Philosophical Transactions of the Royal Society, Part B*, vol. 379 (2015), 21050142.

the 1970s.[58] It is the most prevalent foodborne infection in the European Union and the United States, and it is proving difficult to check.[59]

The primary risk factor is exposure to contaminated poultry. In the United States, nearly 90 percent of the poultry flocks are infected with *Campylobacter*. There are, however, other sources of potential contamination, including unpasteurized milk and raw red meat, fruits, and vegetables. The bacteria are also found in dogs, cats, and in wild animal feces, particularly those of wild birds.[60] Cooking and heating will kill the bacterium. This is the best line of defense, although many infections are picked up through the inadvertent contamination of kitchen surfaces with *Campylobacter*-laden poultry and meats before cooking.

Other "new" bacterial threats have emerged. In 1980, *E. coli* infections were rare in developed countries, but during the course of the 1980s, a new *E. coli* bacterium, *E. coli* O157:H7 emerged, and the patterns of global risks from infection changed dramatically.[61] By the early twenty-first century, there was a marked difference between the Global North and the Global South. Enterotoxigenic *E. coli* (ETEC), Enteropathogenic *E. coli* (EPEC), and Enterohemorrhagic *E. coli* (EHEC) continued to pose a worldwide threat to human health, but ETEC and EPEC, human-to-human infections, were the more significant threats in low-income countries, and EHEC, a zoonotic infection, was more common in developed countries where it entered the food chain commonly through the fecal contamination of cattle meats.[62]

[58]  M. B. Skirrow, "Campylobacter Enteritis: A 'New' Disease," *British Medical Journal*, vol. 2, no. 6078 (1977), 9–11; P. Dekeyser, M. Gossuin-Detrain, J. P. Butzler, and J. Sternon, "Acute Enteritis due to Related Vibrio: First Positive Stool Cultures," *Journal of Infectious Diseases*, vol. 125, no. 4 (1972), 390–92.

[59]  Declan J. Boltan, "*Campylobacter* Virulence and Survival Factors," *Food Microbiology*, vol. 48 (2015), 99–108.

[60]  Harriet Whiley, Ben van den Akker, Steven Giglio, and Richard Bentham, "The Role of Environmental Reservoirs in Human Campylobacteriosis," *International Journal of Environmental Research and Public Health*, vol. 10 (2013), 5887–93.

[61]  Patricia M. Griffin and Robert V. Tauxe, "The Epidemiology of Infections Caused by Escherichia coli O157:H7, Other Enterohemorrhagic E. coli, and the Associated Hemolytic Uremic Syndrome," *Epidemiologic Reviews*, vol. 13, no. 1 (1991), 60–98.

[62]  F. Qadri, A.-M. Svennerholm, A. S. G. Faruque, and R. B. Sack, "Enterotoxigenic *Escherichia coli* in Developing Countries: Epidemiology, Microbiology, Clinical Features, Treatment, and Prevention," *Clinical Microbiology Reviews*, vol. 18, no. 3 (2005), 465–83, https://doi.org/10.1128/CMR.18.3.465-483.200; Elizabeth L. Heartland and John M. Leong, "Enteropathogenic and Enterohemorrhagic E. coli: Ecology, Pathogenesis, and Evolution," *Frontiers in Cellular and Infection Microbiology*, vol. 3 (2013), Article 15, https://doi.org/10.3389/fcimb.2013.00015.

Another "new" threat to human health is from infections in hospital and residential care facilities. The principal nosocomial infection is caused by the bacterium *Clostridium difficile*, transmitted by the fecal–oral route.[63] Once extremely rare, *C. difficile* infections now are common among the elderly, particularly those who have been on antibiotic treatments. In the United States, there were an estimated 27,300 deaths from *C. difficile* in 2011.[64] Hypervirulent infections are now common in the states bordering the North Atlantic, and the bacterium is now emerging in Asia.[65]

One of the core challenges in the twenty-first century will be to conceptualize new approaches to reducing the transmission of infectious intestinal diseases. Vaccination programs will continue to prevent large numbers of deaths, but some of the core intestinal pathogens cannot not be blocked in this way. Many of the world's poorest will not have modern waterborne sewage systems and clean drinking water within the foreseeable future.

In the second half of the twentieth century, medical advances against infectious intestinal disease improved the rates of survival of infants and young children. Oral rehydration therapy alone saved many tens of millions of young lives. The extension of childhood vaccination to developing countries saved tens of millions more. In the twenty-first century, the polio eradication campaign prevented a massive number of infections but was unable to get to zero. Efforts to reduce open defecation met with mixed success. The chasm in differential exposure to infectious intestinal disease between the Global North and Global South was not likely to be closed in the short or medium term.

---

[63] Ciarán P. Kelly and J. Thomas LaMont, "*Clostridium difficile* – More Difficult Than Ever," *New England Journal of Medicine*, vol. 359, no. 18 (2008), 1932–40.

[64] Fernanda C. Lessa, Yi Mu, Wendy M. Bamberg, Zintars G. Beldavs, Ghinwa K. Dumyati, John R. Dunn, Monica M. Farley et al., "Burden of *Clostridium difficile* Infection in the United States," *New England Journal of Medicine*, vol. 372, no. 9 (2015), 825–34.

[65] Kristin E. Burke and J. Thomas Lamont, "*Clostridium difficile* Infection: A Worldwide Disease," *Gut and Liver*, vol. 8, no. 1 (2014), 1–6.

# Conclusion

Shit has long endangered human health. Our earliest ancestors fell sick with diarrheal diseases, and many of their children tumbled into the grave. Over most of our time on earth, the situation did not improve. As we congregated in denser settlements, our environments became unhealthier. As we traveled to distant lands, our pathogens and parasites became global scourges.

This dire historical trajectory had its bright spots. Some early ancestors achieved modest successes in diarrheal disease control. The first advance was in water disinfection. In the distant era of early agriculture and proto-urbanization, some groups began to drink fermented grain or fruit beverages ("beer" or "wine") or plant infusions ("tea") steeped in boiled water. These practices lessened the damage from infectious intestinal disease, although death rates remained high. A second advance occurred when some early societies pioneered the use of cesspits and latrines. Their use diminished the prospects for the transmission of roundworm, hook-worm, and whipworm, and they had an even broader impact because communities could repurpose the concentrated fecal material as fertilizer, boosting crop yields and food security.

With the birth of cities, human waste accumulated in situ. For millennia, much of the urban excreta had been hauled to the farms nearby the cities or dumped into rivers, lakes, or oceans. Human waste, however, was not exceptionally rich in nutrients, and its market was limited by transport costs and seasonal demand. Fecal matter that was not evacuated from the cities seeped out of urban cesspits and contaminated wells. The cities stank. In the nineteenth century, many cities began to pipe river water to urban residents, inadvertently creating sewage, a new dilute pathogenic fluid that presented enormous problems of disposal. In some North Atlantic cities, a "sanitary movement" advocated for building sewers to banish objectionable waste and odors.

The first major advance in the control of infectious intestinal disease in the modern era was in the treatment of water supplies. It evolved in two stages: initially, sand filtration and settling ponds and, later, in some areas, mechanical filtration and treatment with anticoagulants reduced the pathogenic load. The definitive breakthrough arrived with the techniques of "water purification" by ozonation or chlorine treatment, which protected the communities with access to "clean" water.

The combined package of underground sewerage and purified water won broad cultural acceptance. In the first half of the twentieth century, in fully modernized cities with improved water supplies and excreta disposal systems, the threat of infectious intestinal diseases declined steeply, sometimes to a nuisance level. Sanitary advances in the rural areas of developed countries also brought declines, often to a rough parity. The North Atlantic sanitation model became a marker of European advancement in an era of rapid colonization and growing trade. It ultimately became the norm to which other political and cultural elites aspired.[1]

In states too poor to afford the full complement of modern sanitation infrastructure, a different pattern emerged. In the late twentieth and early twenty-first centuries, surrounding many urban cores in the Global South, migrants and displaced populations built massive informal settlements that frequently lacked clean water or a means of safe excreta disposal. As a result, those residing in the peri-urban fringe were far less healthy than those in the urban core.

Modern sanitation has reduced our exposure to an array of bacteria, viruses, protozoa, and intestinal worms. This ecological shift has had unintended consequences. Beginning in the last decades of the twentieth century, some biomedical researchers adopted the "hygiene hypothesis" to explain the greater prevalence of allergic and autoimmune diseases among populations who enjoy access to modern sanitation. The core idea is that modern hygienic conditions, divorced from the muck of the farm and urban fecal pollution and reinforced by the regular use of soaps

[1] Sanitation also became a metaphor with racial and political meanings, some of which reverberate into the present. Consider, for example, the US president's comment in January 2018 referring to El Salvador, Haiti, and African states – many of which have not fully adopted modern sanitation – as "shithole" countries.

and cleaning products, constitute a state of "biome depletion." According to this hypothesis, modern sanitation compromises normal immune responses and results in a heightened vulnerability to allergic and auto-immune diseases. The evidence is compelling. At the end of the twentieth century, an estimated one in five children in industrialized countries suffered from allergies such as asthma, allergic rhinitis, or atopic derma-titis. There was also a marked increase in the incidence of autoimmune diseases, such as Type 1 diabetes and multiple sclerosis.[2]

The success of modern sanitation has thus produced contrary health consequences. It has contributed to unanticipated disease processes, even as it has conveyed enormous population-level benefits in reducing infant and childhood mortality. From a public health perspective, the benefits have vastly outweighed the costs.[3]

Over the past several decades, oral rehydration therapy has saved the lives of hundreds of millions, and in the past decade, vaccination against rotavirus has also rung up major gains. These life-saving interventions have radically altered the global profile of diarrheal disease. For the first time in human history, most diarrheal deaths (roughly three-quarters) now occur in the age cohorts older than five.[4] Additional vaccines are in

---

[2] H. Okada, C. Kuhn, H. Feillet, and J.-F. Bach, "The 'Hygiene Hypothesis' for Autoimmune and Allergic Diseases: An Update," *Clinical & Experimental Immunology*, vol. 160, no. 1 (2010), 1–2.

   Some individuals who suffer from allergic and auto-immune diseases have become interested in possible health benefits from light helminthic infections. An underground economy has emerged that involves the order, sale, and delivery of hookworms to indivi-duals who intentionally infect themselves for therapeutic purposes. Some claim to have thereby cured themselves from allergic and auto-immune conditions. See Sophia Anne Strosberg, "The Human-Hookworm Assemblage: Contingency and the Practice of Helminthic Therapy" (master's thesis, Geography, University of Kentucky, 2014).

[3] As Marsha Wills-Karp and colleagues write: "It should not need saying that the current epidemic of allergic disease is a small price to pay for the marked suppression in infant mortality provided by measures such as improved sanitation, access to drinkable water and vaccination." Marsha Wills-Karp, Joanna Santeliz, and Christopher L. Karp, "Opinion: The Germless Theory of Allergic Disease: Revisiting the Hygiene Hypothesis," *Nature Reviews. Immunology*, vol. 1, no. 1 (2001), 74.

[4] Today, owing to the lengthening life-spans of most populations, there is a particularly high burden of diarrheal mortality in the over seventy age group. A word of caution, however, is in order. The data are poor in the areas with the highest burden of diarrheal disease. See Christopher Troeger, Mohammad Forouzanfar, Puja C. Rao, Ibrahim Khalil, Alexandria Brown, Robert C. Reiner Jr., Nancy Fullman et al., "Estimates of Global, Regional, and National Morbidity, Mortality, and Aetiologies of Diarrhoeal Diseases: A Systematic Analysis for the Global Burden of Disease Study 2015," *Lancet Infectious Diseases*, vol. 17, no. 9 (2017), 909–48.

the pipeline, and it is likely that further improvements in childhood survival rates will reinforce population growth, which has rocketed from roughly 2.5 billion in 1950 to more than 7.7 billion today.

Our soaring global population exacerbates the spate of ecological challenges that we face today. Among these is the conundrum of how to dispose of human waste. Using clean water to transport human waste to treatment plants that extract the bio-solids, partially detoxify the fluids using bacterial baths, and dump the effluent into adjacent water sources no long seems ecologically sound. When we discharge human waste, either raw or treated, into our rivers, lakes, and oceans, we contribute to the eutrophication and hypoxia of coastal waters.[5] Moreover, a return to ancient practices of integrating human waste in the soil is newly problematic. Today when we use human waste as fertilizer, we spread traces of pharmaceuticals and heavy metals that accumulate on our farmlands.[6]

The specter of more severe climate change translates into highly uncertain prospects for diarrheal disease transmission in the future. Projections are bedeviled by the sparsity of data as well as the contrasting effects of biophysical forces on different pathogens. Consider the issue of rising temperatures. Research suggests, for example, that higher temperatures decrease the incidence of rotavirus infections and increase that of shigellosis. Consider, too, the issue of changing rainfall intensities and distributions in different ecological settings. Some studies have found that rainfall does not affect the transmission of diarrheal diseases; others that dry seasons and flood recessions were associated with higher incidences of diarrhea; and yet others that heavy rainfall increased the opportunities for pathogenic transmission.[7]

---

[5] The major contributor to eutrophication and hypoxia is the nitrogen and phosphorus run-off from intensive agricultural activities. For an overview, see Mindy Selman, Suzie Greenhalgh, Robert Diaz, and Zachary Sugg, "Eutrophication and Hypoxia in Coastal Areas: A Global Assessment of the State of Knowledge," *World Resources Institute Policy Note*, no. 1 (2008), 1–6, www.wri.org/sites/default/files/pdf/eutrophicatio n_and_hypoxia_in_coastal_areas.pdf.

[6] Raymond A. Wuana and Felix E. Okieimen, "Heavy Metals in Contaminated Soils: A Review of Sources, Chemistry, Risks and Best Available Strategies for Remediation," *ISRN Ecology* (2011), 1–21, https://doi.org/10.5402/2011/402647.

[7] Erik W. Kolstad and Kjell Arne Johansson, "Uncertainties Associated with Quantifying Climate Change Impacts on Human Health: A Case Study for Diarrhea," *Environmental Health Perspectives*, vol. 119, no. 3 (2010), 299–305; Kathleen A. Alexander and Jason K. Blackburn, "Overcoming Barriers in Evaluating Outbreaks of Diarrheal Disease in Resource Poor Settings: Assessment of Recurrent Outbreaks in Chobe District, Botswana," *BMC Public Health*, vol. 13, no. 1 (2013), 775, https://bmcpubli chealth.biomedcentral.com/articles/10.1186/1471-2458-13-775; Elizabeth J. Carlton,

The prospects for capturing the energy potential of excreta before disposal are promising. In some villages, towns, and cities, septic tanks and other waste capture systems are channeling bio-gases to small- and large-scale power systems. The virtues of producing energy from gases emitted by decomposing human and animal wastes are both financial and ecological.[8] The small-scale systems can produce energy for home use inexpensively. Initial efforts to develop large-scale systems are promising, if not yet cost-competitive.[9] When these systems become profitable, they will open a new chapter in our species' struggle to deal with our own excrement.

Joseph N. S. Eisenberg, Jason Goldstick, William Cevallos, James Trostle, and Karen Levy, "Heavy Rainfall Events and Diarrhea Incidence: The Role of Social and Environmental Factors," *American Journal of Epidemiology*, vol. 179, no. 3 (2013), 344–52.

A parallel conundrum attends the efforts to estimate the health costs of increased migration that are projected to occur because of climate change. The health costs may well outweigh the health benefits, but any type of precision in these matters is elusive. Celia McMichael, Jon Barnett, and Anthony J. McMichael, "An Ill Wind? Climate Change, Migration, and Health," *Environmental Health Perspectives*, vol. 120, no. 5 (2012), 646–54.

The WHO, in its summary document on the relationship between climate change and human health, has held that heavy rainfall can cause the contamination of water supplies by cholera, cryptosporidium, *E. coli*, giardia, shigella, typhoid, and hepatitis A. World Health Organization, *Climate Change and Human Health: Risks and Responses Summary* (Geneva: WHO, 2003), 14.

[8] The global ratio of animal to human waste by weight in 2014 was 5:1 and is projected to increase to 6:1 by 2030. See David M. Berendes, Patricia J. Yang, Amanda Lai, David Hu, and Joe Brown, "Estimation of Global Recoverable Human and Animal Faecal Biomass," *Nature Sustainability*, vol. 1, no. 11 (2018), 679–85.

[9] Xiaotan Fu, Lijin Zhong, Vijay Jagannathan, and Wanli Fang, "Sludge to Energy: An Environment-Energy-Economic Assessment of Methane Capture from Sludge in Xiangyang City, Hubei Province," World Resources Center Working Paper, March 2017, 1–31.

# Bibliography

ARCHIVAL MATERIALS

I have consulted the archives of the World Health Organization (Geneva), the London School of Hygiene and Tropical Medicine, and the National Archives of the United Kingdom (Kew). Individual documents from these archives are cited in the footnotes.

UNPUBLISHED THESES

Berry, Greg. "Agricultural Sanitation: From Waste to Resource." Unpublished PhD thesis, University of Tasmania, 2000.
Strosberg, Sophia Anne. "The Human-Hookworm Assemblage: Contingency and the Practice of Helminthic Therapy." MA thesis, University of Kentucky, 2014.

PUBLISHED MATERIALS

Abel, Christopher. "Health, Hygiene and Sanitation in Latin America, c. 1870 to c. 1950," University of London, Institute for Latin American Studies, Research Paper no. 42 (1996).
Ackert, James E. "Some Influences of the American Hookworm," *American Midland Naturalist*, vol. 47, no. 3 (1952), 749–62.
Ahmad, Zahoor, Mohamed A.M. Abd-Elbasit, Shahid Javed Butt, Samiullah Khan, Muhammad Liaquat, Ali Raza Gurmani, Abdul Basir, Khair Muhammad Kakar, and Manzoor Qadir. "Spreading of Bio-wastes onto Soil Surfaces to Control Pathogens: Human Health and Environmental Consequences," *International Journal of Agriculture and Biology*, vol. 17, no. 4 (2015), 671–80.
Ahmed, Sharia M., Aron J. Hall, Anne E. Robinson, Linda Verhoef, Prasanna Premkumar, Umesh D. Parashar, Marion Koopmans, and Benjamin A. Lopman, "Global Prevalence of Norovirus in Cases of Gastroenteritis:

A Systematic Review and Meta-analysis," *Lancet Infectious Diseases*, vol. 14, no. 8 (2014), 725–30.

Alexander, Kathleen A., and Jason K. Blackburn. "Overcoming Barriers in Evaluating Outbreaks of Diarrheal Disease in Resource Poor Settings: Assessment of Recurrent Outbreaks in Chobe District, Botswana," *BMC Public Health*, vol. 13, no. 1 (2013), 775. https://bmcpublichealth .biomedcentral.com/articles/10.1186/1471-2458-13-775.

Aliabadi, Negar, Jacqueline E. Tate, Amber K. Haynes, Umesh D. Parashar, and Centers for Disease Control and Prevention (CDC). "Sustained Decrease in Laboratory Detection of Rotavirus after Implementation of Routine Vaccination – United States, 2000–2014," *Morbidity and Mortality Weekly Report*, vol. 64, no. 13 (2015), 337–42.

Allen, Arthur. *Vaccine: The Controversial Story of Medicine's Greatest Lifesaver*, New York: W. W. Norton, 2007.

Allen, Tim, and Melissa Parker. "The 'Other Diseases' of the Millennium Development Goals: Rhetoric and Reality of Free Drug Distribution to Cure the Poor's Parasites," *Third World Quarterly*, vol. 32, no. 1 (2011), 91–117.

Ali, Mohammed, Anna Lena Lopez, Young Ae You, Young Eun Kim, Binod Sah, Brian Maskery, and John Clemens. "The Global Burden of Cholera," *Bulletin of the World Health Organization*, vol. 90 (2012), 209–21. https://doi.org/10 .2471/BLT.11.993427.

Ali, M., A. R. Nelson, A. L. Lopez, and D. A. Sack. "Updated Global Burden of Cholera in Endemic Countries," *PLoS Neglected Tropical Diseases*, vol. 9, no. 6 (2015), e0003832. https://doi.org/10.1371/journal.pntd.0003832.

Anderson, Warwick. *Colonial Pathologies: American Tropical Medicine, Race, and Hygiene in the Philippines*. Durham, NC: Duke University Press, 2006.

Angelakis, A. N., D. Koutsoyiannis, and G. Tchobanoglous. "Urban Wastewater and Stormwater Technologies in Ancient Greece," *Water Research*, vol. 39 (2005), 210–20.

Angelakis, Andreas N., and Shane A. Snyder. "Wastewater Treatment and Reuse: Past, Present, and Future," *Water*, vol. 7 (2015), 4887–95.

Anonymous. "Enteric or Typhoid Fever in the Hot Climates," *Journal of Tropical Medicine*, 15 (1904), 27–30.

Anonymous. "Typhoid Fever and Its Prevention in Town and Country," *Virginia Health Bulletin*, vol. 3, no. 6 (1911), 75–88F.

Anonymous. "Typhoid: Beware the Black Hand," *Virginia Health Bulletin*, vol. 15, no. 9 (1923), 1–8.

Annett, H. E., et al. *Report of the Malaria Expedition to Nigeria of the London School of Tropical Medicine and Medical Parasitology*. Liverpool: University of Liverpool, 1901.

Antoniou, Georgios P., and Andreas N. Angelakis. "Latrines and Wastewater Sanitation Technologies in Ancient Greece," in Piers D. Mitchell (ed.), *Sanitation, Latrines and Intestinal Parasites in Past Populations*. Surrey: Ashgate, 2015, 41–67.

Anwar, E., E. Goldberg, A. Fraser, C. J. Acosta, M. Paul, and L. Leibovici. "Vaccines for Preventing Typhoid Fever," *Cochrane Database of Systematic*

*Reviews*, no. 1 (2014), Article No. CD001261. https://doi.org/10.1002/14651 858.CD001261.pub3.

Araújo, Adauto, Karl J. Reinhard, Luiz Fernando Ferreira, and Scott Lyell Gardner. "Parasites and Probes for Prehistoric Human Migrations," *Trends in Parasitology*, vol. 24, no. 3 (2008), 112–15. https://doi.org/10.1016/j .pt.2007.11.007.

Araújo, Adauto, Karl Reinhard, and Luiz Fernando Ferreira. "Paleoparasitology —Human Parasites in Ancient Material," *Advances in Parasitology*, vol. 89 (2015), 1–39.

Armstrong, Gregory L., Laura A. Conn, and Robert W. Pinner. "Trends in Infectious Disease Mortality in the United States during the 20th Century," *Journal of the American Medical Association*, vol. 281, no. 1 (1999), 61–66.

Arumugam, Manimozhiyan, Jeroen Raes, Eric Pelletier, Denis Le Paslier, Takuji Yamada, Daniel R. Mende, Gabriel R. Fernandes et al. "Enterotypes of the Human Gut Microbiome," *Nature*, vol. 473 (2011), 174–80. https://doi.org/10 .1038/nature09944.

Ashford, Bailey K., and Pedro Gutierrez Igaravidez. *Uncinariasis (Hookworm Disease) in Porto Rico: A Medical and Economic Problem*. Washington, DC: US Government Printing Office, 1911.

Association for Improving the Condition of the Poor. *Flies and Diarrheal Disease*. New York: Department of Health, 1914.

Atkins, P. J. "White Poison? The Social Consequences of Milk Consumption, 1850–1930," *Social History of Medicine*, vol. 5, no. 2 (1992), 207–27.

Avicenna. *A Treatise on the Canon of Medicine of Avicenna, Incorporating a Translation of the First Book*, by O. Cameron Gruner. London: Luzac, 1930.

Baity, H. G. "A Forward Look in World Sanitation," *Royal Society of Health Journal*, vol. 78, no. 4 (1958), 351–56.

Baker, M. N. *Sewerage and Sewage Purification*. New York, 1896.

Baker, Moses N. *The Quest for Pure Water: The History of Water Purification from the Earliest Records to the Twentieth Century*. Denver, CO: American Water Works Association, 1981.

Bardosh, Kevin. "Achieving 'Total Sanitation' in Rural African Geographies: Poverty, Participation, and Pit Latrines in Eastern Zambia," *Geoforum*, vol. 66 (2015), 53–63.

Banda, Kalyan, Rajiv Sarkar, Srila Gopal, Jeyanthi Govindarajan, Bhim Bahadur Harijan, Mary Benita Jeyakumar, Philip Mitta et al. "Water Handling, Sanitation and Defecation Practices in Rural Southern India: A Knowledge, Attitudes and Practices Study," *Transactions of the Royal Society of Tropical Medicine and Hygiene*, vol. 101, no. 11 (2007), 1124–30.

Banerjee, Sudeshna Ghosh, and Elvira Morella. *Africa's Water and Sanitation Infrastructure: Access, Affordability, and Alternatives*. Washington, DC: The World Bank, 2011.

Banwell, J. G. "Worldwide Impact of Oral Rehydration Therapy," *Clinical Therapy*, vol. 12, Suppl. A (1990), 29–37.

Barnes, David S. *The Great Stink of Paris and the Nineteenth-Century Struggle against Filth and Germs*. Baltimore: Johns Hopkins University Press, 2006.

Barzilay, Ezra J., Nicolas Schaad, Roc Magloire, Kam S. Mung, Jacques Boncy, Georges A. Dahourou, Eric D. Mintz, Maria W. Steenland, John F. Vertefeuille, and Jordan W. Tappero. "Cholera Surveillance during the Haiti Epidemic – The First 2 Years," *New England Journal of Medicine*, vol. 368, no. 7 (2013), 599–609.

Basu, Nilangshu Bhusan, Ayanangshu Dey, and P. G. D. B. M. Duke Ghosh. "Kolkata's Brick Sewer Renewal: History, Challenges and Benefits," *Proceedings of the Institution of Civil Engineers*, vol. 166, no. 2 (2013), 74–81.

Beaver, P. C. *Control of Soil-Transmitted Helminths*. Geneva: World Health Organization, 1961.

Begum, Sharifa, Mansur Ahmed, and Binayak Sen. "Do Water and Sanitation Interventions Reduce Childhood Diarrhoea? New Evidence from Bangladesh," *Bangladesh Development Studies*, vol. 34, no. 3 (2011), 1–30.

Belcher, John C. "Sanitation Norms in Rural Areas: A Cross-Cultural Comparison," *Bulletin of the Pan American Health Organization*, vol. 12, no. 1 (1978), 34–44.

Benidickson, Jamie. *The Culture of Flushing: A Social and Legal History of Sewage*. Vancouver: University of British Columbia Press, 2007.

Berendes, David M., Patricia J. Yang, Amanda Lai, David Hu, and Joe Brown. "Estimation of Global Recoverable Human and Animal Faecal Biomass," *Nature Sustainability*, vol. 1, no. 11 (2018), 679–85.

Bern, C., J. Martines, I. de Zoysa, and R. I. Glass. "The Magnitude of the Global Problem of Diarrhoeal Disease: A Ten-Year Update," *Bulletin of the World Health Organization*, vol. 70, no. 6 (1992), 705–14.

Bernier, Roger H. "Observations on Poliomyelitis Lameness Surveys," *Reviews of Infectious Diseases*, vol. 6, suppl. 2 (1984), S371–75.

Bethony, Jeffrey, Simon Brooker, Marco Albonico, Stefan M. Geiger, Alex Loukas, David Diemert, and Peter J. Hotez. "Soil-transmitted Helminth Infections: Ascariasis, Trichuriasis, and Hookworm," *Lancet*, vol. 367 (2006), 1521–32.

Bhan, M. K., Rajiv Bahl, and Shinjini Bhatnagar. "Typhoid and Paratyphoid Fever," *Lancet*, no. 366 (2005), 749–62.

Biehler, Dawn Day. *Pests in the City: Flies, Bedbugs, Cockroaches, and Rats*. Seattle: University of Washington Press, 2013.

Black, Maggie, and Ben Fawcett. *The Last Taboo: Opening the Door on the Global Sanitation Crisis*. London: Earthscan, 2008.

Black, R. E., J. H. Allen, Z. A. Bhutta, L. E. Caulfield, M. Onis, M. Ezzati, C. Mathers, and J. Rivera. "Maternal and Child Undernutrition: Global and Regional Exposures and Health Consequences," *Lancet*, vol. 371 (2008), 243–60.

Blackham, R. J. "The Goux System and Its Application to India," *Journal of the Royal Army Medical Corps*, vol. 6 (1906), 662–27.

Blaise, Nguendo, Yongsi Hénock, and Delali B. K. Dovie. "Diarrheal Diseases in the History of Public Health," *Archives of Medical Research*, vol. 38 (2007), 159–63.

Bleakley, Hoyt. "Disease and Development: Evidence from Hookworm Eradication in the American South," *Quarterly Journal of Economics*, vol. 122, no. 1 (2007), 73–117. https://doi.org/10.1162/qjec.121.1.73.

Blume, Stuart S. "Lock-In, the State and Vaccine Development: Lessons from the History of the Polio Vaccines," *Research Policy*, vol. 34 (2005), 159–73.

Bostoen, Kristof, and Barbara Evans. "Crossfire: Measures of Sanitation Coverage for the MDGs are Unreliable, Only Raising a False Sense of Achievement," *Waterlines*, vol. 27, no. 1 (2008), 5–11.

Bollet, Alfred Jay. "Scurvy and Chronic Diarrhea in Civil War Troops: Were They Both Nutritional Deficiency Syndromes?," *Journal of the History of Medicine and Allied Sciences*, vol. 47, no. 1 (1992), 49–67.

Boltan, Declan J. "*Campylobacter* Virulence and Survival Factors," *Food Microbiology*, vol. 48 (2015), 99–108.

Botero, David. "Persistence of the Endemic Intestinal Parasitoses in Latin America," *Bulletin of the Pan American Health Organization*, vol. 15, no. 3 (1981), 241–48.

Bourke, John Gregory. *Scatologic Rites of All Nations*. Washington, DC: W. H. Lowdermilk, 1891.

Bourke, John Gregory. *Compilation, Notes, and Memoranda Bearing upon the Use of Human Ordure and Human Urine*. Washington, DC, 1888.

Boyce, R., A. Evans, and H. H. Clarke. *Report on the Sanitation and Anti-Malarial Measures in Practice in Bathurst, Conakry, and Freetown*. London: University Press of Liverpool, 1905.

Boyd, Colin. "The Nestlé Infant Formula Controversy and a Strange Web of Subsequent Business Scandals," *Journal of Business Ethics*, vol. 106, no. 3 (2012), 283–93.

Bozzolo, Camillo. "Notes on the Treatment of Ankylostoma Anemia (Uncinariasis, Hookworm Disease) with Thymol," *Journal of the American Medical Association*, vol. 58, no. 23 (1912), 1744–46.

Brinkley, Garland L. "The Decline in Southern Agricultural Output, 1860–1940," *Journal of Economic History*, vol. 57, no. 1 (1997), 116–38.

Brioch, John. *London: Water and the Making of the Modern City*. Pittsburgh, PA: University of Pittsburgh Press, 2013.

Brooker, Simon, Archie C. A. Clements, and Don A. P. Bundy. "Global Epidemiology, Ecology and Control of Soil-Transmitted Helminths," *Advances in Parasitology*, vol. 62 (2006), 221–61.

Brooker, Simon. "Estimating the Global Distribution and Disease Burden of Intestinal Nematode Infections: Adding Up the Numbers – A Review," *International Journal of Parasitology*, vol. 40, no. 10 (2010), 1137–44.

Broom, George J. C. "On the Tub and Pail System," *Journal of the Sanitary Institute*, vol. 15 (1894), 664–74.

Brown, Theodore M., Marcos Cueto, and Elizabeth Fee. "The World Health Organization and the Transition from 'International' to 'Global' Public Health," *American Journal of Public Health*, vol. 96, no. 1 (2006), 62–72.

Bundy, D. A. P., and E. S. Cooper. "Trichuris and Trichuriasis in Humans," *Advances in Parasitology*, vol. 28 (1989), 107–73.

Burge, Wylie D., and Paul B. Marsh. "Infectious Hazards of Landspreading Sewage Waste," *Journal of Environmental Quality*, vol. 7 (1978), 1–9.

Burke, Kristin E., and J. Thomas Lamont. "*Clostridium difficile* Infection: A Worldwide Disease," *Gut and Liver*, vol. 8, no. 1 (2014), 1–6.

Burke, Timothy. *Lifebuoy Men, Lux Women: Commodification, Consumption, and Cleanliness in Modern Zimbabwe*. Durham, NC: Duke University Press, 1996.

Bushman, Richard L., and Claudia L. Bushman. "The Early History of Cleanliness in America," *Journal of American History*, vol. 74, no. 4 (1988), 1213–38.

Cacciò, Simone M., R. C. Andrew Thompson, Jim McLauchlin, and Huw V. Smith. "Unravelling Cryptosporidium and Giardia Epidemiology," *Trends in Parasitology*, vol. 21, no. 9 (2006), 430–37.

Cadwell, Ken. "Expanding the Role of the Virome: Commensalism in the Gut," *Journal of Virology*, vol. 89 (2015), 1951–53. https://doi.org/10.1128/JVI .02966-14.

Carlton, Elizabeth J., Joseph N. S. Eisenberg, Jason Goldstick, William Cevallos, James Trostle, and Karen Levy. "Heavy Rainfall Events and Diarrhea Incidence: The Role of Social and Environmental Factors," *American Journal of Epidemiology*, vol. 179, no. 3 (2013), 344–52.

Cash, R. A. "A History of the Development of Oral Rehydration Therapy," *Journal of Diarrhoeal Disease Research*, vol. 5, no. 4 (1987), 256–61.

Cassedy, James H. "The 'Germ of Laziness' in the South, 1900–1915: Charles Wardell Stiles and the Progressive Paradox," *Bulletin of the History of Medicine*, vol. 45, no. 2 (1971), 159–69.

Castro, José Esteban, and Leo Heller. "The Historical Development of Water and Sanitation in Brazil and Argentina," in Petri S. Juuti, Tapio S. Katko, and Heikki S. Vuorinen (eds.), *Environmental History of Water*. London: IWA, 2007, 429–45.

Chadwick, Edwin. *Report on the Sanitary Condition of the Labouring Population of Great Britain*. Edited by M. W. Flinn. Edinburgh: Edinburgh University Press, 1965.

Chambers, Robert. "Going to Scale with Community-Led Total Sanitation: Reflections on Experience, Issues and Ways Forward," *IDS Practice Papers*, no. 1 (2009), 1–50.

Chammartin, Frédérique, Ronaldo G. C. Scholte, Marcel Tanner, Jürg Utzinger, and Penelope Vounatsou. "Soil-Transmitted Helminth Infection in South America: A Systematic Review and Geostatistical Meta-Analysis," *Lancet Infectious Diseases*, vol. 13 (2013), 507–18. https://doi.org/10.1016/S1473-30 99(13)70071-9.

Chevallier, Fabienne. *Le Paris moderne: Histoire des politiques d'hygiène, 1855–1898*. Rennes: Presses Universitaires de Rennes, 2010.

Choffnes, Eileen R., and David A. Relman (rapporteurs). *The Causes and Impacts of Neglected Tropical and Zoonotic Diseases: Opportunities for Integrated Intervention Strategies: Workshop Summary*. Washington, DC: National Academies Press, 2011.

Cirillo, Vincent J. *Bullets and Bacilli: The Spanish-American War and Military Medicine*. New Brunswick, NJ: Rutgers University Press, 2004.

Cirillo, Vincent J. "Two Faces of Death: Fatalities from Disease and Combat in America's Principal Wars, 1775 to Present," *Perspectives in Biology and Medicine*, vol. 51, no. 1 (2008), 121–33.

Claesson, Marcus J., Siobhán Cusack, Orla O'Sullivan, Rachel Greene-Diniz, Heleen de Weerd, Edel Flannery, Julian R. Marchesi et al. "Composition, Variability, and Temporal Stability of the Intestinal Microbiota of the Elderly," *Proceedings of the National Academy of Sciences of the United States of America*, vol. 108, suppl. 1 (2011), 4586–91. https://doi.org/10.1073/pnas.1000097107.

Clemesha, William Wesley. *Sewage Disposal in the Tropics*. London: Thacker, Spink, 1910.

Coffey, J. Calvin, and D. Peter O'Leary. "The Mesentery: Structure, Function, and Role in Disease," *Lancet Gastroenterology and Hepatology*, vol. 1, no. 3 (2017), 238–47.

Coltman, Robert. *The Chinese, Their Present and Future: Medical, Political, and Social*. Philadelphia: F. A. Davis, 1891.

Connelly, Matthew. *Fatal Misconception: The Struggle to Control World Population*. Cambridge, MA: Harvard University Press, 2008.

Cook, G. C. "Influence of Diarrhoeal Disease on Military and Naval Campaigns," *Journal of the Royal Society of Medicine*, vol. 94 (2001), 95–97.

Corsi, Daniel J., Melissa Neuman, Jocelyn E. Finlay, and S. V. Subramanian, "Demographic and Health Surveys: A Profile," *International Journal of Epidemiology*, vol. 41, no. 6 (2012), 1602–13.

Cort, W. W., J. B. Grant, and N. R. Stoll. "General Summary of Results," in W. W. Cort, J. B. Grant, and N. R. Stoll (eds.), *Researches on Hookworm in China: Embodying the Results of the Work of the China Hookworm Commission, June, 1923 to November, 1924*, Monographic Series 7. Baltimore: The American Journal of Hygiene, 1926, 380–98.

Cort, W. W., and N. R. Stoll. "Studies on *Ascaris lumbricoides* and *Trichuris trichiura* in China," *American Journal of Hygiene*, vol. 14, no. 3 (1931), 655–89.

Cosgrove, John Joseph. *History of Sanitation*. Pittsburgh, PA: Standard Sanitary Manufacturing, 1909.

Coste, Christine, and R. Deschiens. "Données relative à l'histoire médicale des dysenteries avant la découverte de l'amibe dysenterique," *Bulletin de la Société de Pathologie Exotique*, nos. 1–2 (1945), 15–22.

Cotton, Andrew, and Jamie Bartram. "Sanitation: On- or Off-Track? Issues of Monitoring Sanitation and the Role of the Joint Monitoring Programme," *Waterlines*, vol. 27, no. 1 (2008), 12–29.

Courtwright, David T. *Forces of Habit: Drugs and the Making of the Modern World*. Cambridge, MA: Harvard University Press, 2002.

Crompton, D. W. T., and M. C. Nesheim. "Nutritional Impact of Intestinal Helminthiasis During the Human Life Cycle," *Annual Review of Nutrition*, vol. 22 (2002), 35–59.

Curtin, Philip D. *Death by Migration: Europe's Encounter with the Tropical World in the Nineteenth Century*. New York: Cambridge University Press, 1989.

Curtis, Valerie, Sandy Cairncross, and Raymond Yonli. "Domestic Hygiene and Diarrhoea – Pinpointing the Problem," *Tropical Medicine and International Health*, vol. 5, no. 1 (2000), 22–32.

Curtis, Valerie. "Talking Dirty: How to Save a Million Lives," *International Journal of Environmental Health Research*, vol. 13 (2003), S73–79.

Cushman, Gregory T. *Guano and the Opening of the Pacific World: A Global Ecological History*. New York: Cambridge University Press, 2013.

Cutler, David, and Grant Miller. "The Role of Public Health Improvements in Health Advances: The Twentieth-Century United States," *Demography*, vol. 42, no. 1 (2005), 1–22.

Czerkinsky, Cecil, and Jan Holmgren. "Vaccines against Enteric Infections for the Developing World," *Philosophical Transactions of the Royal Society, Part B*, vol. 379 (2015), 21050142.

da Cunha Ferreira, R. M., and R. A. Cash. "History of the Development of Oral Rehydration Therapy," *Clinical Therapy*, vol. 12, Suppl. A (1990), 2–11.

Darling, S. T., M. A. Barber, and H. P. Hacker. *Hookworm and Malaria Research in Malaya, Java, and the Fiji Islands. Report of Uncinariasis Commission to the Orient, 1915–1917*. New York: Rockefeller Foundation, International Health Board, 1920.

Darling, Samuel T. "Observations on the Geographical and Ethnological Distribution of Hookworms," *Parasitology*, vol. 12, no. 3 (1920), 217–33.

Darling, S. T., and W. G. Smillie. "Studies on Hookworm Infection in Brazil. First Paper," *Monograph of the Rockefeller Institute for Medical Research*, no. 14 (1921), 1–42.

Darling, Samuel T. "The Hookworm Index and Mass Treatment," *American Journal of Tropical Medicine*, vol. 2, no. 5 (1922), 397–447.

Davis, A. "Ascariasis: Drugs and Drug Policy," in D. W. T. Crompton, M. C. Nesheim, and Z. S. Pawlowski (eds.), *Ascariasis and Its Public Health Significance*. London: Taylor and Francis, 1985, 239–44.

de Silva, Nilanthi R., Simon Brooker, Peter J. Hotez, Antonio Montresor, Dirk Engels, and Lorenzo Savioli. "Soil-Transmitted Helminth Infections: Updating the Global Picture," *Trends in Parasitology*, vol. 19, no. 12 (2003), 547–51.

de Zoysa, I., and R. G. Feachem. "Interventions for the Control of Diarrhoeal Disease among Young Children: Rotavirus and Cholera Immunization," *Bulletin of the World Health Organization*, vol. 63 (1985), 569–83.

Dekeyser, P., M. Gossuin-Detrain, J. P. Butzler, and J. Sternon. "Acute Enteritis due to Related Vibrio: First Positive Stool Cultures," *Journal of Infectious Diseases*, vol. 125, no. 4 (1972), 390–92.

Dennis, Joseph M., and Abel Wolman. "1955–56 Infectious Hepatitis Epidemic in Delhi, India [with Discussion]," *Journal of the American Water Works Association*, vol. 51, no. 10 (1959), 1288–98.

Diamond, Jared. *Guns, Germs, and Steel*. New York: W. W. Norton, 1989.

Dixon, D. M. "A Note on Some Scavengers of Ancient Egypt," *World Archaeology*, vol. 21, no. 2 (1989), 193–97.

D'Olier, William L. *The Sanitation of Cities*. New York: Sanitation Corporation of New York, 1921.

Doré, Joël, and Hervé Blottière. "The Influence of Diet on the Gut Microbiota and Its Consequences for Health," *Current Opinion in Biotechnology*, vol. 32 (2015), 195–99. https://doi.org/10.1016/j.copbio.2015.01.002.

Donaldson, David. "Overview of Rural Water and Sanitation Programs for Latin America," *Journal of the American Water Works Association*, vol. 75, no. 5 (1983), 224–31.

Doron, Assa, and Robin Jeffrey, "Open Defecation in India," *Economic and Political Weekly*, December 6, 2014, 1–12.

Dubini, Angelo. "Nuovo Verme Intestinal Umano (Agchylostoma duodenale) Constituente un Sesto Genere dei Nematoidea Propri dell'Uomo," *Annali Universali de Medicina*, vol. 106 (1843), 5–13.

Dumett, Raymond E. "The Campaign against Malaria and the Expansion of Scientific Medical and Sanitary Services in British West Africa, 1898–1910," *African Historical Studies*, vol. 1, no. 2 (1968), 181–88.

Dunham, George C. "The Coöperative Health Program of the American Republics," *American Journal of Public Health and the Nation's Health*, vol. 34, no. 8 (1944), 817–27.

Dunn, James S. "The Borough of Kimberley," *Journal of the Sanitary Institute*, vol. 23 (1902), 366–71.

Echenberg, Myron. *Africa in the Time of Cholera: A History of Pandemics from 1817 to the Present*. New York: Cambridge University Press, 2011.

Eggers, Hans J. "Milestones in Early Poliomyelitis Research (1840 to 1949)," *Journal of Virology*, vol. 73, no. 6 (1999), 4533–35.

Enders, Guilia. *Gut: The Inside Story of Our Body's Most Underrated Organ*. Vancouver, BC: Greystone Books, 2015.

Epelboin, A. "Le péril fécal. Culture, environnement et péril fécal: réflexions anthropologiques," *Bulletin de la Société de Pathologie Exotique*, vol. 91, no. 5 (1998), 397–401.

Eppig, Christopher, Corey L. Fincher, and Randy Thornhill. "Parasite Prevalence and the Worldwide Distribution of Cognitive Ability," *Proceedings of the Royal Society: Biological Sciences*, vol. 277, no. 1701 (2010), 3801–8.

Erb, Claude C. "Prelude to Point Four: The Institute of Inter-American Affairs," *Diplomatic History*, vol. 9, no. 3 (1985), 249–69.

Esrey, S. A., J. B. Potash, L. Roberts, and C. Shiff. "Effects of Improved Water Supply and Sanitation on Ascariasis, Diarrhoea, Dracunculiasis, Hookworm Infection, Schistosomiasis, and Trachoma," *Bulletin of the World Health Organization*, vol. 69, no. 5 (1991), 609–21.

Ettling, John. *The Germ of Laziness: Rockefeller Philanthropy and Public Health in the New South*. Cambridge, MA: Harvard University Press, 1981.

Factura, H., T. Bettendorf, C. Buzie, H. Pieplow, J. Reckin, and R. Otterpohl, "Terra Preta Sanitation: Re-discovered from an Ancient Amazonian Civilisation–Integrating Sanitation, Bio-waste Management and Agriculture," *Water Science and Technology*, vol. 61, no. 10 (2010), 2673–79.

Faichnie, N. "Fly-Borne Enteric Fever; the Source of Infection," *Journal of the Royal Army Medical Corps*, vol. 13 (1909), 580–84.

Fan, Wenguang, Guicheng Huo, Xiaomin Li, Lijie Yang, Cuicui Duan, Tingting Wang, and Junliang Chen. "Diversity of the Intestinal Microbiota in

Different Patterns of Feeding Infants by Illumina High-Throughput Sequencing," *World Journal of Microbiology and Biotechnology*, vol. 29, no. 12 (2013), 2365–72.

Farley, John. *To Cast Out Disease: A History of the International Health Division of the Rockefeller Foundation (1913–1951)*. New York: Oxford University Press, 2004.

Faust, Ernest Carroll. "Preliminary Survey of the Intestinal Parasites of Man in the Central Yangtze Valley," *China Medical Journal*, vol. 35, no. 6 (1921), 1–30.

Faust, Ernest Carroll. "Some Facts Regarding the Relation between Nightsoil Disposal in China and the Propagation of Helminthic Diseases," *American Journal of Tropical Medicine and Hygiene*, 1–4 (November 1924), 487–505.

Fayrer, Sir Joseph. "Tropical Diarrhea," *Medical News*, November 25, 1893, 592–94.

Feacham, R. G. "Community Participation in Appropriate Water Supply and Sanitation Technologies: The Mythology for the Decade," *Proceedings of the Royal Society of London, Section B*, vol. 209 (1980), 15–29.

Feachem, R. G. "Preventing Diarrhoea: What Are the Policy Options?," *Health Policy Planning*, vol. 1, no. 2 (1986), 109–17.

Ferrell, John Atkinson. "The Rural School and Hookworm Disease," *U.S. Bureau of Education Bulletin*, no. 20 (1914).

Fieldhouse, David K. *Unilever Overseas: The Anatomy of a Multinational, 1895–1965*. London: Croom Helm, 1978.

Fomon, Samuel J. "Infant Feeding in the 20th Century: Formula and Beikost," *Journal of Nutrition*, vol. 131, no. 2 (2001), 409S–20S.

Forsberg, Birger Carl, Max G. Petzold, Göran Tomson, and Peter Allebeck. "Diarrhoea Case Management in Low- and Middle-Income Countries: An Unfinished Agenda," *Bulletin of the World Health Organization*, vol. 85, no. 1 (2007), 42–48.

Foster, Stanley O., Georges Kesseng-Maben, Hatib N'jie, and Emmou Coffi. "Control of Poliomyelitis in Africa," *Review of Infectious Diseases*, vol. 6, Suppl. 2 (1984), S433–37.

Foy, Henry, and Athena Kondi. "Hookworms in the Aetiology of Tropical Anaemia," *Transactions of the Royal Society of Tropical Medicine and Hygiene*, vol. 54, no. 5 (1960), 419–33.

Fuller, Dorian. "Pathways to Asian Civilizations: Tracing the Origins and Spread of Rice and Rice Cultures," *Rice*, vol. 4, no. 3 (2011), 78–92.

Furuse, Yuki, Akira Suzuki, and Hitoshi Oshitani. "Origin of Measles Virus: Divergence from Rinderpest Virus between the 11th and 12th Centuries," *Virology Journal*, vol. 7, no. 52 (2010). https://doi.org/10.1186/1743-422X-7-52.

Gale, Thomas S. "Lagos: The History of British Colonial Neglect of Traditional African Cities," *African Urban Studies*, vol. 5 (1979), 15–16.

Gale, Thomas S. "Segregation in British West Office," *Cahiers d'études africaines*, vol. 20 (1980), 495–508.

Gale, Thomas S. "The Struggle against Disease in the Gold Coast: Early Attempts at Urban Sanitary Reform," *Transactions of the Historical Society of Ghana*, vol. 16, no. 2 (1995), 185–203.

Garrison, Fielding H. "The History of Drainage, Irrigation, Sewage-Disposal and Water-Supply," *Bulletin of the New York Academy of Medicine*, vol. 5, no. 10 (1929), 887–938.

George, Rose. *The Big Necessity: The Unmentionable World of Human Waste and Why It Matters*. New York: Holt, 2008.

Gierlinger, Sylvia, Gertrud Haidvogl, Simone Gingrich, and Fridolin Krausmann. "Feeding and Cleaning the City: The Role of the Urban Waterscape in Provision and Disposal in Vienna during the Industrial Transformation," *Water History*, vol. 5, no. 2 (2013), 219–39.

Giles, Lieut. Colonel. *General Sanitation and Anti-Malarial Measures in Sekondi, the Goldfields and Kumassi*. London: Williams & Norgate for the University Press of Liverpool, 1905.

Glaser, Bruno, and Jago Jonathan Birk. "State of the Scientific Knowledge on Properties and Genesis of Anthropogenic Dark Earths in Central Amazonia (*terra preta de Índio*)," *Geochimica et Cosmochimica Acta*, vol. 82 (2012), 39–51.

Gonçalves, Marcelo, Luiz Carvalho, Adauto Araújo, and Luiz Fernando Ferreira. "Human Intestinal Parasites in the Past: New Findings and a Review," *Memórias do Instituto Oswaldo Cruz*, vol. 98, Suppl. I (2003), 103–18.

Gordon, John E., Moisés Béhar, and Nevin S. Scrimshaw. "Acute Diarrhoeal Disease in Less Developed Countries: 3. Methods for Prevention and Control," *Bulletin of the World Health Organization*, vol. 31, no. 1 (1964), 21–28.

Gordon, R. M. "The Effect of Ancylostome, Ascaris, and Trichuris Infections on the Health of the West African Native," *Annals of Tropical Medicine and Parasitology*, vol. 19 (1925), 429–60.

Gough, Ethan K., Erica E. M. Moodle, Andrew J. Prendergast, Sarasa M. A. Johnson, Jean H. Humphrey, Rebecca J. Stoltzhus et al. "The Impact of Antibiotics on Growth in Children in Low and Middle Income Countries: Systematic Review and Meta-Analysis of Randomised Controlled Trials," *British Medical Journal*, vol. 348 (2014), g2267.

Government of India. *Gazetteer of the Bombay Presidency*, vol. 12, *Khándesh*. Bombay: Government Central Press, 1880.

Gracey, Michael. "Oral Therapy for Acute Diarrhoea," *Medical Journal of Australia*, vol. 17 (1984), 348–49.

Grant, Charles Covell. *West African Hygiene; or Hints on the Preservation of Health, and the Treatment of Disease on the West Coast of Africa*. London: G. Wright for the Colonial Office, 1882.

Green, Monica (ed.). *Pandemic Disease in the Medieval World: Rethinking the Black Death*. Kalamazoo: Arc Medieval Press, 2015.

Greenberg, Bernard. *Flies and Disease*, vol. II, *Biology and Disease Transmission*. Princeton, NJ: Princeton University Press, 1973.

Greer, Frank R., and Rima D. Apple. "Physicians, Formula Companies, and Advertising: A Historical Perspective," *American Journal of Diseases of Children*, vol. 145, no. 3 (1991), 282–86.

Griffin, Patricia M., and Robert V. Tauxe. "The Epidemiology of Infections Caused by Escherichia coli 0157:H7, Other Enterohemorrhagic E. coli, and the Associated Hemolytic Uremic Syndrome," *Epidemiologic Reviews*, vol. 13, no. 1 (1991), 60–98.

Gröschel, Dieter H. M., and Richard B. Hornick. "Who Introduced Typhoid Vaccination: Almroth Wright or Richard Pfeiffer?," *Clinical Infectious Diseases*, vol. 3, no. 6 (1981), 1251–54.

Gross, Briana L., and Zhijun Zhao. "Archaeological and Genetic Insights into the Origins of Domesticated Rice," *Proceedings of the National Academy of Sciences*, vol. 111, no. 17 (2014), 6190–97.

Grove, David I. *A History of Human Helminthology*. Wallingford, UK: CAB International, 1990.

Guerrant, Richard L., Margaret Kosek, Sean Moore, Breyette Lorntz, Richard Brantley, and Aldo A. M. Lima. "Magnitude and Impact of Diarrheal Diseases," *Archives of Medical Research*, vol. 33 (2002), 351–55.

Halliday, Stephen. *The Great Stink of London: Sir Joseph Bazalgette and the Cleansing of the Victorian Metropolis*. Phoenix Mill, UK: Sutton, 1999.

Hamlin, Christopher. *Public Health and Social Justice in the Age of Chadwick: Britain, 1800–1854*. Cambridge: Cambridge University Press, 1998.

Hamlin, Christopher. *Cholera: The Biography*. Oxford: Oxford University Press, 2009.

Hamlin, Christopher. "'Cholera Forcing': The Myth of the Good Epidemic and the Coming of Good Water," *American Journal of Public Health*, vol. 99, no. 11 (2009), 1946–54.

Hanley, S. B. "Urban Sanitation in Preindustrial Japan," *Journal of Interdisciplinary History*, vol. 18, no. 1 (1987), 1–26.

Hardy, Albert V. "Diarrheal Diseases of Man: A Historical Review and Global Appraisal," *Annals of the New York Academy of Sciences*, vol. 66, no. 1 (1956), 5–13.

Hardy, Anne. "'Straight Back to Barbarism': Antithyphoid Inoculation and the Great War, 1914," *Bulletin of the History of Medicine*, vol. 74, no. 2 (2000), 265–90.

Harrison, Mark. *The Medical War: British Military Medicine in the First World War*. Oxford: Oxford University Press, 2010.

Harrison, Mark. *Contagion: How Commerce Has Spread Disease*. New Haven, CT: Yale University Press, 2012.

Hassan, J. A. "The Growth and Impact of the British Water Industry in the Nineteenth Century," *Economic History Review*, vol. 3, no. 4 (1985), 531–47.

Haudricourt, André G. "Le role des excrétats dans la domestication," *L'Homme*, vol. 17, nos. 2–3 (1977), 125–26.

Hawgood, Barbara J. "Waldemar Mordecai Haffkine, CIE (1860–1930), Prophylactic Vaccination against Cholera and Bubonic Plague in British India," *Journal of Medical Biography*, vol. 15, no. 1 (2007), 9–19.

Heartland, Elizabeth L., and John M. Leong. "Enteropathogenic and Enterohemorrhagic E. coli: Ecology, Pathogenesis, and Evolution," *Frontiers in Cellular and Infection Microbiology*, vol. 3 (2013), Article 15. https://doi.org/10.3389/fcimb.2013.00015.

Heiser, Victor G. "American Sanitation in the Philippines and Its Influence on the Orient," *Proceedings of the American Philosophical Society*, vol. 57, no. 1 (1918), 60–68.

Henderson, Donald. "Smallpox Eradication: A Cold War Victory," *World Health Forum*, vol. 19 (1998), 113–19.

Henning, John A. "The Summer Diarrhea of Children," *Ohio Medical Recorder*, vol. iv (1879–1880), 152–54.

Hewa, Soma. "The Hookworm Epidemic on the Plantations in Colonial Sri Lanka," *Medical History*, vol. 38, no. 1 (1994), 73–90.

Hewa, Soma. "Rockefeller Foundation's Typhoid Control Campaign at Kalutara-Totamune in Sri Lanka," *Galle Medical Journal*, vol. 16, no. 1 (2011), 29–32.

Hill, Rolla B. "Hookworm Reinfestation in Sanitated and Unsanitated Areas," *Southern Medical Journal*, vol. 18 (1925), 665–68.

Hoberg, Eric P., Nancy L. Alkire, Alan de Queiroz, and Arlene Jones. "Out of Africa: Origins of the Taenia Tapeworms in Humans," *Proceedings of the Royal Society of London B: Biological Sciences*, vol. 268 (2001), 781–87.

Hodge, C. F., and Jean Dawson. *Civic Biology*. Boston: Ginn, 1918.

Hoeppli, R. "The Knowledge of Parasites and Parasitic Infections from Ancient Times to the 17th Century," *Experimental Parasitology*, vol. 5, no. 4 (1956), 398–419.

Holt, L. Emmett. "The Antiseptic Treatment of Summer Diarrhea," *Archives of Pediatrics*, vol. 3 (1886), 726–51.

Hotez, Peter J. "Neglected Infections of Poverty among the Indigenous Peoples of the Arctic," *PLoS Neglected Tropical Diseases*, vol. 4, no. 1 (2010), e606. https://doi.org/10.1371/journal.pntd.0000606.

Hou, Tsung-Ch'ang, Huei-Lan Chung, Lien-yin Ho, and Hsin-Chin Weng. "Achievements in the Fight against Parasitic Diseases in New China," *China Medical Journal*, vol. 79 (1959), 493–520.

Howard, H. H. *The Control of Hookworm Disease by the Intensive Method*. New York: Rockefeller Foundation, International Health Board, 1919.

Howard-Jones, Norman. *The Scientific Background of the International Sanitary Conferences, 1851–1938*. Geneva: World Health Organization, 1975.

Howell, David L. "Fecal Matter: Prolegomenon to a History of Shit in Japan," in Ian Jared Miller, Julia Adeney Thomas, and Brett L. Walker (eds.), *Japan at Nature's Edge: The Environmental Context of a Global Power*. Honolulu: University of Hawaii Press, 2013, 137–51.

Humphrey, Jean H. "Underweight Malnutrition in Infants in Developing Countries: An Intractable Problem," *Archives of Pediatric Adolescent Medicine*, vol. 162, no. 7 (2008), 692–94.

Humphrey, Jean H. "Child Undernutrition, Tropical Enteropathy, Toilets, and Handwashing," *Lancet*, vol. 374 (2009), 1032–35.

Hürlimann, Eveline, Clarisse A. Houngbedji, Prisca B. N'Dri, Dominique Bänniger, Jean T. Coulibaly, Peiling Yap, Kigbafori D. Silué et al., "Effect of Deworming on School-Aged Children's Physical Fitness, Cognition and Clinical Parameters in a Malaria-Helminth Co-Endemic Area of Côte d'Ivoire," *BMC Infectious Diseases*, vol. 14, no. 441 (2014). www.biomedcentral.com/1471-2334/14/411.

Iwugo, K. O. "Factors Affecting the Implementation of Improved Sanitation in Africa," *Journal of the Royal Society for the Promotion of Health*, vol. 99, no. 1 (1979), 28–30.

Jacobsen, K. H., and S. T. Wiersma. "Hepatitis A Seroprevalence by Age and World Region, 1990 and 2005," *Vaccine*, vol. 28, no. 41 (2010), 6653–57. https://doi.org/10.1016/j.vaccine.2010.08.037.

Jacquemet, Gérard. "Urbanisme Parisien: La bataille du tout à l'égout à la fin du XIXe siècle," *Revue d'histoire modern et contemporaine*, vol. 46 (1979), 505–48.

Jannetta, Ann Bowman. *Epidemics and Mortality in Early Modern Japan.* Princeton, NJ: Princeton University Press, 1987.

Jansen, M. "Water Supply and Sewage Disposal at Mohenjo-Daro," *World Archaeology*, vol. 21, no. 2 (1989), 177–81.

Johnston, William. "The Shifting Epistemological Foundations of Cholera Control in Japan (1822–1900)," *Extrême-Orient Extrême-Occident*, no. 37 (2014), 171–96.

Jones, Richard (ed.). *Manure Matters: Historical, Archaeological, and Ethnographic Perspectives.* Surrey: Ashgate, 2012.

Jones, Richard. "Why Manure Matters," in Richard Jones (ed.), *Manure Matters.* Surrey: Ashgate, 2012, 1–11.

Jørgensen, Dolly. "Modernity and Medieval Muck," *Nature and Culture*, vol. 9, no. 3 (2014), 225–37.

Joseph, Stephen C. "The Anatomy of the Infant Formula Controversy," *American Journal of Diseases of Children*, vol. 135, no. 10 (1981), 889–92.

Juuti, Petri S., and Tapio S. Katko. "Birth and Expansion of Public Water Supply and Sanitation in Finland until World War II," in Petri S. Juuti, Tapio S. Katko, and Heikki S. Vuorinen (eds.), *Environmental History of Water.* London: IWA, 2007, 117–30.

Karagiannis-Voules, Dimitrios-Alexios, Patricia Biedermann, Uwem F. Ekpo, Amadou Garba, Erika Langer, Els Mathieu, Nicholas Midzi et al. "Spatial and Temporal Distribution of Soil-Transmitted Helminth Infection in Sub-Saharan Africa: A Systematic Review and Geostatistical Meta-Analysis," *Lancet Infectious Diseases*, vol. 15 (2015), 74–84. https://doi.org/10.1016/S1 473-3009(14)71004-7.

Kavadi, Shirish N. "'Parasites Lost and Parasites Regained': Rockefeller Foundation's Anti-Hookworm Campaign in Madras Presidency," *Economic and Political Weekly*, vol. 42, no. 2 (2007), 130–37.

Keller, A. E. "A State-Wide Study of the Human Intestinal Helminths in Tennessee," *Journal of Preventive Medicine*, vol. 6 (1932), 161–84.

Keller, A. E., W. S. Leathers, and H. C. Ricks. "An Investigation of the Incidence and Intensity of Infestation of Hookworm in Mississippi," *American Journal of Hygiene*, vol. 19 (1934), 629–56.

Keller, A. E., W. S. Leathers, and M. H. Jensen. "An Investigation of Hookworm Infestation in Thirty-Six Counties of Kentucky," *American Journal of Hygiene*, vol. 23 (1936), 33–45.

Keller, A. E., W. S. Leathers, and J. C. Knox. "The Present Status of Hookworm Infestation in North Carolina," *American Journal of Hygiene*, vol. 26 (1937), 437–54.

Keller, Alvin E., W. S. Leathers, and Paul M. Densen. "The Results of Recent Studies of Hookworm in Eight Southern States," *American Journal of Tropical Medicine*, vol. 20, no. 4 (1940), 493–509.

Kelley, Victoria. *Soap and Water: Cleanliness, Dirt and the Working Classes in Victorian and Edwardian Britain*. London: I. B. Taurus, 2010.

Kelly, Ciarán P., and J. Thomas LaMont. "*Clostridium difficile* – More Difficult Than Ever," *New England Journal of Medicine*, vol. 359, no. 18 (2008), 1932–40.

Kerr, J. Austin. "The Incidence and Intensity of Hookworm Infestation in the State of Florida," *Bulletin of the International Health Board*, vol. 7 (1927), 192–211.

Kerr, Harold. "Refuse Disposal in Relation to the Enteric Group of Diseases," *Proceedings of the Royal Society of Medicine*, vol. 17 (1924), 33–46.

Kesztenbaum, Lionel, and Jean-Laurent Rosenthal. "Sewers' Diffusion and the Decline of Mortality: The Case of Paris, 1880–1914," *Journal of Urban Economics*, vol. 98 (2017), 178–86.

Khalil, Ibrahim A., Christopher Troeger, Brigette F. Blacker, Puja C. Rao, Alexandria Brown, Deborah E. Atherly, Thomas G. Brewer et al. "Morbidity and Mortality due to Shigella and Enterotoxigenic Escherichia coli Diarrhoea: The Global Burden of Disease Study 1990–2016," *Lancet Infectious Diseases*, vol. 18, no. 11 (2018), 1229–40.

Khalil, M. "An Early Contribution to Medical Helminthology, Translated from the Writings of the Arabian Physician Ibn Sina (Avicenna) with a Short Biography," *Journal of Tropical Medicine and Hygiene*, vol. 25 (1922), 65–67.

King, Franklin H. *Farmers of Forty Centuries: Or Permanent Agriculture in China, Korea, and Japan*. Madison, WI: Mrs. F. H. King, 1911.

Kirchmann, H., and S. Pettersson. "Human Urine – Chemical Composition and Fertilizer Use Efficiency," *Fertilizer Research*, vol. 40, no. 2 (1995), 149–54.

Klein, Herbert S., Stanley L. Engerman, Robin Haines, and Ralph Shlomowitz. "Transoceanic Mortality: The Slave Trade in Comparative Perspective," *William and Mary Quarterly*, vol. 58, no. 1 (2001), 93–118.

Kliks, M. M. "Paleoparasitology: On the Origins and Impacts of Human-Helminth Relationships," in Neil A. Croll and John H. Cross (eds.), *Human Ecology and Infectious Diseases*. New York: Academic Press, 1983, 291–314.

Knox, J. H. M., Jr., and V. H. Bassett. "An Examination of Milk Supplied to Infants Suffering with Summer Diarrhea, with a Plea for a Purer Milk Supply Accessible to the Poor of Baltimore," *Maryland Medical Journal*, vol. 45, no. 6 (1902), 241–58.

Kofoid, Charles A., and John P. Tucker. "On the Relationship of Infection by Hookworm to the Incidence of Morbidity and Mortality in 22,842 Men of the United States Army," *American Journal of Hygiene*, vol. 1, no. 1 (1921), 79–117.

Kolstad, Erik W., and Kjell Arne Johansson. "Uncertainties Associated with Quantifying Climate Change Impacts on Human Health: A Case Study for Diarrhea," *Environmental Health Perspectives*, vol. 119, no. 3 (2010), 299–305.

Kosek, Margaret, Caryn Bern, and Richard L. Guerrant. "The Global Burden of Diarrhoeal Disease, as Estimated from Studies Published between 1992 and 2000," *Bulletin of the World Health Organization*, vol. 81, no. 3 (2003), 197–204.

Krain, Lisa J., Kenrad E. Nelson, and Alain B. Labrique. "Host Immune Status and Response to Hepatitis E Virus Infection," *Clinical Microbiology Reviews*, vol. 27, no. 1 (2014), 139–65.

Krasnoborodko, K. I., A. M. Alexeev, L. I. Tsvetkova, and L. I. Zhukova. "The Development of Water Supply and Sewerage Systems in St. Petersburg," *European Water Management*, vol. 2, no. 4 (1999), 51–61.

Kreitman, Paul. "Attacked by Excrement: The Political Ecology of Shit in Wartime and Postwar Tokyo," *Environmental History*, vol. 23 (2018), 342–66.

La Berge, Ann F. *Mission and Method: The Early Nineteenth-Century French Public Health Movement*. New York: Cambridge University Press, 1992.

Lahiri-Dutt, Kuntala. "Researching World Class Watering in Metropolitan Calcutta," *ACME: An International Journal for Critical Geographies*, vol. 14, no. 3 (2015), 700–720.

Lawn, Joy E., Jon Rohde, Susan Rifkin, Miriam Were, Vinod K. Paul, and Mickey Chopra. "Alma-Ata 30 Years On: Revolutionary, Relevant, and Time to Revitalise," *Lancet*, vol. 372, no. 9642 (2008), 917–27.

Layland, Laura E., and Sabine Specht. "Helpful or a Hindrance: Co-Infections with Helminths during Malaria," in William Horsnell (ed.), *How Helminths Alter Immunity to Infection*. New York: Springer, 2014, 99–129.

Leas, Eric C., Anne Dare, and Wael K. Al-Delaimy. "Is Gray Water the Key to Unlocking Water for Resource-Poor Areas of the Middle East, North Africa, and Other Arid Regions of the World?," *Ambio*, vol. 43, no. 6 (2014), 707–17.

Leathers, W. S., A. E. Keller, and B. F. Wyman. "A State-Wide Investigation of Hookworm in South Carolina," *American Journal of Epidemiology*, vol. 23, no. 3 (1936), 600–614.

Leathers, W. S., A. E. Keller, and W. A. McPhaul. "An Investigation Concerning the Status of Hookworm in Florida," *American Journal of Hygiene*, vol. 29, section D (1939), 1–16.

Leblanc, Ronald J., Peter Matthews, and Roland P. Richard (eds.). *Global Atlas of Excreta, Wastewater Sludge, and Biosolids Management*. Renouf, 2009.

Lee, Kelley. "The Global Dimensions of Cholera," *Global Change and Human Health*, vol. 2, no. 1 (2001), 6–17.

Lessa, Fernanda C., Yi Mu, Wendy M. Bamberg, Zintars G. Beldavs, Ghinwa K. Dumyati, John R. Dunn, Monica M. Farley et al. "Burden of *Clostridium difficile* Infection in the United States," *New England Journal of Medicine*, vol. 372, no. 9 (2015), 825–34.

Lewin, R. A. *Merde: Excursions in Scientific, Cultural, and Socio-historical Coprology*. New York: Random House, 1999.

Lewis, Brian. *"So Clean": Lord Leverhulme, Soap and Civilization*. Manchester: Manchester University Press, 2008.

Link, William A. "Privies, Progressivism, and Public Schools: Health Reform and Education in the Rural South, 1909–1920," *Journal of Southern History*, vol. 54, no. 4 (1988), 623–42.

Link, William A. "'The Harvest Is Ripe, but the Laborers Are Few': The Hookworm Crusade in North Carolina, 1909–1915," *North Carolina Historical Review*, vol. 67, no. 1 (1990), 1–27.

Linton, Derek S. "Was Typhoid Inoculation Safe and Effective during World War I? Debates within German Military Medicine," *Journal of the History of Medicine and Allied Sciences*, vol. 55, no. 2 (2000), 101–33.

Looss, A. "Notes on Intestinal Worms Found in African Pygmies," *Lancet*, August 12, 1905, 430–31.

Loreille, Odile, and Françoise Bouchet. "Evolution of Ascariasis in Humans and Pigs: A Multi-disciplinary Approach," *Memórias do Instituto Oswaldo Cruz*, vol. 98, Suppl. 1 (2003), 39–46.

Löwy, Ilana. "From Guinea Pigs to Man: The Development of Haffkine's Anticholera Vaccine," *Journal of the History of Medicine and Allied Sciences*, vol. 47, no. 3 (1992), 270–309.

Lozano, Rafael, Mohsen Naghavi, Kyle Foreman, Stephen Lim, Kenji Shibuya, Victor Aboyans, Jerry Abraham et al., "Global and Regional Mortality from 235 Causes of Death for 20 Age Groups in 1990 and 2010: A Systematic Analysis for the Global Burden of Disease Study 2010," *Lancet*, vol. 380, no. 9859 (2013), 2105.

Lun, Zhao-rong, Robin B. Gasser, De-Hua Lai, An-Xing Li, Xing-Quan Shu, Xing-Bing Yu, and Yue-Fi Yang. "Clonorchiasis: A Key Foodborne Zoonosis in China," *Lancet Infectious Diseases*, vol. 5, no. 1 (2005), 31–41.

Luquero, Francisco J., Marc Rondy, Jacques Boncy, André Munger, Helmi Mekaoui, Ellen Rymshaw, Anne-Laure Page et al. "Mortality Rates during Cholera Epidemic, Haiti, 2010–2011," *Emerging Infectious Diseases*, vol. 22, no. 3 (2016), 410–16.

Macfarlane, Alan. *Savage Wars of Peace: England, Japan, and the Malthusian Trap*. Oxford: Blackwell, 1997.

MacIntyre, Jessica, Jennifer McTaggert, Richard L. Guerrant, and David M. Goldfarb. "Early Childhood Diarrhoeal Diseases and Cognition: Are We Missing the Rest of the Iceberg?," *Paediatrics and International Child Health*, vol. 34, no. 4 (2014), 295–307.

Mahalanabis, D., A. B. Choudhari, N. G. Bagchi, A. K. Bhattacharya, and T. W. Simpson. "Oral Fluid Therapy of Cholera among Bangladesh Refugees," *Johns Hopkins Medical Journal*, vol. 132 (1973), 197–205.

Mann, Charles C. *1491: New Revelations of the Americas before Columbus*. New York: Vintage Books, 2006.

Mara, Duncan, and Sandy Cairncross. *Guidelines for the Safe Use of Wastewater and Excreta in Agriculture and Aquaculture: Measures for Public Health Protection*. Geneva: World Health Organization, 1989.

Marchoux, Émile. "Désinfection des matières fécales. Analyse du mémoire du docteur Vincent, médecin militaire," *Archives de médecine navale*, vol. 63 (1895), 365–69.

Martin, A. W. "The Influence of Privy-Middens and Water-Closets in Diarrhœa and Typhoid," *Public Health*, vol. 17 (1905), 709–14.

Martin, A. W. "Flies in Relation to Typhoid Fever and Summer Diarrhœa," *Public Health*, vol. 15 (1903), 652–53.

Mather, E., and J. F. Hart. "The Geography of Manure," *Land Economics*, vol. 32, no. 1 (1956), 25–38.

May, Charles D. "The 'Infant Formula Controversy': A Notorious Threat to Reason in Matters of Health," *Pediatrics*, vol. 68, no. 3 (1981), 428–30.

McDermott, Joseph P., and Shiba Yoshinobu. "Economic Change in China, 960–1279," in John W. Chaffee and Denis Twitchett (eds.), *The Cambridge History of China*, vol. 5, part II, *Sung China, 960–1279*. Cambridge: Cambridge University Press, 2015, 321–436.

McGuire, Michael J. "Eight Revolutions in the History of U.S. Drinking Water Disinfection," *Journal of the American Water Works Association*, vol. 98, no. 3 (2006), 123–49.

McGuire, Michael J. *The Chlorine Revolution: Water Disinfection and the Fight to Save Lives*. Denver, CO: American Water Works Association, 2013.

McIntosh, Roderick J. *Ancient Middle Niger: Urbanism and the Self-Organizing Landscape*. Cambridge: Cambridge University Press, 2005.

McLaughlin, Allan J. *Sewage Pollution of Interstate and International Waters with Special Reference to the Spread of Typhoid Fever*, Treasury Department, Public Health and Marine-Hospital Service of the United States, Hygienic Laboratory – Bulletin No. 77. Washington, DC: Government Printing Office, 1911.

McMahon, Augusta. "Waste Management in Early Urban Southern Mesopotamia," in Piers D. Mitchell (ed.), *Sanitation, Latrines and Intestinal Parasites in Past Populations*. Surrey: Ashgate, 2015, 19–39.

McMichael, Celia, Jon Barnett, and Anthony J. McMichael. "An Ill Wind? Climate Change, Migration, and Health," *Environmental Health Perspectives*, vol. 120, no. 5 (2012), 646–54.

McNeill, John R., and William H. McNeill. *The Human Web: A Bird's Eye View of World History*. New York: W. W. Norton, 2003.

Meckel, Richard A. *Save the Babies: American Public Health Reform and the Prevention of Infant Mortality, 1850–1929*. Baltimore: Johns Hopkins University Press, 1990.

Melosi, Martin V. "Environmental Crisis in the City: The Relationship between Industrialization and Urban Pollution," in M. V. Melosi (ed.), *Pollution and Reform in American Cities, 1870–1930*. Austin: University of Texas Press, 1980.

Melosi, Martin V. *The Sanitary City: Urban Infrastructure in America from Colonial Times to the Present*. Baltimore: Johns Hopkins University Press, 2000.

Melosi, Martin V. *Precious Commodity: Providing Water for America's Cities*. Pittsburgh, PA: University of Pittsburgh Press, 2011.

Mhaskar, K. S. "Hookworm Infection and Sanitation," *Indian Journal of Medical Research*, vol. 8 (1920), 398–406.

Mhaskar, K. S. "Mass Treatment of Hookworm Infection," *Indian Medical Gazette*, vol. 57 (1922), 208–10.

Mhaskar, K. S. "Report of the Ankylostomiasis Inquiry in Madras," *Indian Medical Research Memoirs*, no. 1 (1924), 1–95.

Miller, Shawn William. *An Environmental History of Latin America*. New York: Cambridge University Press, 2007.

Mitchell, Piers D. "The Origins of Human Parasites: Exploring the Evidence for Endoparasitism throughout Human Evolution," *International Journal of Paleopathology*, vol. 3 (2013), 191–98.

Mitchell, Piers D. "Human Parasites in Medieval Europe: Lifestyle, Sanitation, and Medical Treatment," *Advances in Parasitology*, vol. 90 (2015), 1–32.

Molyneux, David H., and Mwele N. Malecela. "Neglected Tropical Diseases and the Millennium Development Goals – Why the 'Other Diseases' Matter: Reality versus Rhetoric," *Parasites and Vectors*, vol. 4, no. 234 (2011), 1–13. www .parasitesandvectors.com/content/4/1/234.

Morris, A. "'Fight for Fertilizer!' Excrement, Public Health, and Mobilization in New China," *Journal of Unconventional History*, vol. 6, no. 3 (1995), 51–76.

Morse, Edward S. "Latrines of the East," *American Architect and Building News*, vol. 39, no. 899 (1893), 170–74.

Moule, Henry. *Earth Sewage versus Water Sewage or National Health and Wealth Instead of Disease and Waste*. Ottowa: G. E. Desbarats, 1868.

Mu, Cao. "The Public Lavatory of Tianjin: A Change in Urban Faeces Disposal in the Process of Modernization," *Global Environment*, vol. 9 (2016), 196–218.

Mutreja, Ankur, Dong Wook Kim, Nicholas R. Thomson, Thomas R. Connor, Je Hee Lee, Samuel Kariuki, Nicholas J. Croucher et al. "Evidence for Several Waves of Global Transmission in the Seventh Cholera Pandemic." *Nature*, vol. 477, no. 7365 (2011), 462–65.

Needham, Joseph, and Tsien Tsuen-Hsuin. *Science and Civilisation in China*, vol. 5, *Chemistry and Chemical Engineering, Part I, Paper and Printing*. Cambridge: Cambridge University Press, 1985.

Nesfield, V. B. "A Chemical Method of Sterilizing Water without Affecting Its Potability," *Public Health*, vol. 15, no. 7 (1903), 601–3.

Ngure, Francis M., Jean H. Humphrey, Mduduzi N. N. Mbuya, Florence Majo, Kuda Mutasa, Margaret Govha, Exevia Mazarura, Bernard Chasekwa, Andrew J. Prendergast, Valerie Curtis, Kathryn J. Boor, and Rebecca Stoltzfus. "Formative Research on Hygiene Behaviors and Geophagy among Infants and Young Children and Implications of Exposure to Fecal Bacteria," *American Journal of Tropical Medicine and Hygiene*, vol. 89, no. 4 (2013), 709–16.

Ngure, Francis M., Brianna M. Reid, Jean H. Humphrey, Mduduzi N. Mbuya, Gretel Pelto, and Rebecca J. Stoltfus. "Water, Sanitation, and Hygiene (WASH), Environmental Enteropathy, Nutrition, and Early Child Development: Making the Links," *Annals of the New York Academy of Sciences*, vol. 1308 (2014), 118–28. https://doi.org/10.1111/nyas.12330.

Nicholas, David D., James H. Kratzer, Samuel Ofosu-Amaah, and Donald W. Belcher. "Is Poliomyelitis a Serious Problem in Developing Countries? The Danfa Experience," *British Medical Journal*, vol. 1, no. 6067 (1977), 1009–12.

Nightingale, Florence. *Observations on the Sanitary State of the Army in India*. London: Edward Stanford, 1863.

Nilsson, David. "A Heritage of Unsustainability? Reviewing the Origin of the Large-Scale Water and Sanitation System in Kampala, Uganda," *Environment and Urbanization*, vol. 18, no. 2 (2006), 369–85.

Nilsson, David, and Arne Kaijser. "Discrimination by Default: The Post-colonial Heritage of Urban Water Provision in East Africa," in José Esteban Castro and

Léo Heller (eds.), *Water and Sanitation Services: Public Policy and Management*. New York: Earthscan, 2012, 275–91.

Njoh, Ambe J. "Colonization and Sanitation in Urban Africa: A Logistics Analysis of the Availability of Central Sewage Systems as a Function of Colonialism," *Habitat International*, vol. 38 (2013), 207–13.

Norfleet, Ernest. "Conservation of Filth in Chinese Cities and the Fruits Thereof," *The Sanitarian*, no. 270 (1892), 430–41.

North, Douglass. "Ocean Freight Rates and Economic Development 1730–1913," *Journal of Economic History*, vol. 18, no. 4 (1958), 537–55.

Northrup, R. "The Global Implementation of ORT," *Journal of Diarrhoeal Disease Research*, vol. 5, no. 4 (1987), 265–69.

Nyangeri, Ezekial, and Kenneth S. Ombongi. "History of Water Supply and Sanitation in Kenya, 1895–2002," in Petri S. Juuti, Tapio S. Katko, and Heikki S. Vuorinen (eds.), *Environmental History of Water*. London: IWA, 2007, 271–320.

Okada, H., C. Kuhn, H. Feillet, and J.-F. Bach. "The 'Hygiene Hypothesis' for Autoimmune and Allergic Diseases: An Update," *Clinical and Experimental Immunology*, vol. 160, no. 1 (2010), 1–9.

Otaki, Yurina, Masahiro Otaki, and Osamu Sakura. "Water Systems and Urban Sanitation: A Historical Comparison of Tokyo and Singapore," *Journal of Water and Health*, vol. 5, no. 2 (2007), 259–65.

Otto, G. F., and W. W. Cort. "The Distribution and Epidemiology of Human Ascariasis in the United States," *American Journal of Epidemiology*, vol. 19, no. 3 (1934), 657–712.

Paim, Jairnilson, Claudia Travassos, Celia Almeida, Ligia Bahia, and James Macinko. "The Brazilian Health System: History, Advances, and Challenges," *Lancet*, vol. 377, no. 9779 (2011), 1–86. https://doi.org/10.1016/S0140-6736(11)60054-8.

Palmer, Steven. *Launching Global Health: The Caribbean Odyssey of the Rockefeller Foundation*. Ann Arbor: University of Michigan Press, 2010.

Parashar, Umesh D., Erik Hummelman, Joseph S. Bresee, Mark A. Miller, and Roger I. Glass. "Global Illness and Deaths Caused by Rotavirus Disease in Children," *Emerging Infectious Diseases*, vol. 9, no. 5 (2003), 565–72.

Parker, Melissa, and Tim Allen. "Does Mass Drug Administration for the Integrated Treatment of Neglected Tropical Diseases Really Work? Assessing Evidence for the Control of Schistosomiasis and Soil-Transmitted Helminths in Uganda," *Health Research Policy and Systems*, vol. 9, no. 1 (2011), 1–20.

Parker, Melissa, and Tim Allen. "De-Politicizing Parasites: Reflections on Attempts to Control the Control of Neglected Tropical Diseases," *Medical Anthropology: Cross-Cultural Studies in Health and Illness*, vol. 33, no. 3 (2014), 223–39.

Pathak, Bindeswar. *Road to Freedom: A Sociological Study on the Abolition of Scavenging in India*. New Delhi: Motilal Benarsidass, 2000.

Paul, John R. "Poliomyelitis Attack Rates in American Troops, 1940–1948," *American Journal of Epidemiology*, vol. 50, no. 1 (1949), 57–62.

Paul, John R. "Endemic and Epidemic Trends of Poliomyelitis in Central and South America," *Bulletin of the World Health Organization*, vol. 19 (1958), 747–58.

Peduzzi, R., and J. C. Piffaretti. "Ancylostoma duodenale and the Saint Gothard Anaemia," *British Medical Journal*, vol. 287 (1983), 1942–45.

Peng, Weidong, and Charles D. Criscione. "Ascariasis in People and Pigs: New Inferences from DNA Analysis of Worm Populations," *Infection, Genetics, and Evolution*, vol. 12 (2012), 227–35.

Perabo, Franz E. "Poliomyelitis in the Ivory Coast," *Lancet*, October 31, 1970, 927–28.

Perroncito, Edoardo. "Helminthological Observations upon the Endemic Disease Developed among the Labourers in the Tunnel of Mount St Gothard," *Queckett Journal of Microscopical Club*, vol. 6 (1880), 141–50.

Peters, O. H. *Observations upon the Natural History of Epidemic Diarrhoea*. Cambridge: Cambridge University Press, 1911.

Pop, Mihai, Alan W. Walker, Joseph Paulson, Brianna Lindsay, Martin Antonio, M. Anowar Hossain, Joseph Oundo et al. "Diarrhea in Young Children from Low-Income Countries Leads to Large-Scale Alterations in Intestinal Microbiota Composition," *Genome Biology*, vol. 15, no. 6 (2014), R76. http://genomebiology.com/2014/15/6/R76.

Post, James E. "Assessing the Nestlé Boycott: Corporate Accountability and Human Rights," *California Management Review*, vol. 27, no. 2 (1985), 113–31.

Prignano, Ángel Ó. *El Inodoro y Sus Conexiones: La Indiscreta Historia del Lugar de Necesidad Que, Por Común, Excusado Es Nombrarlo*. Buenos Aires: Editorial Biblos, 2007.

Qadri, F., A.-M. Svennerholm, A.-S. G. Faruque, and R. B. Sack. "Enterotoxigenic *Escherichia coli* in Developing Countries: Epidemiology, Microbiology, Clinical Features, Treatment, and Prevention," *Clinical Microbiology Reviews*, vol. 18, no. 3 (2005), 465–83. https://doi.org/10.1128/CMR .18.3.465-483.200.

Race, Joseph. "Forty Years of Water Chlorination, 1910–1949," *Journal of the Institution of Water Engineers*, vol. 4 (1950), 479–505.

Rafter, George W., and M. N. Baker. *Sewage Disposal in the United States*. New York: D. Van Nostrand, 1894.

Ravel, Jacques, Martin J. Blazer, Jonathan Braun, Eric Brown, Frederic D. Bushman, Eugene B. Chang, Julian Davies et al. "Human Microbiome Science: Vision for the Future, Bethesda, MD, July 24 to 26, 2013," *Microbiome*, vol. 2 (2014), 16. www.microbiomejournal.com/content/2/1/16.

Ramprasad, Vanaja. "Manure, Soil and the Vedic Literature: Agricultural Knowledge and Practice on the Indian Subcontinent over the Last Two Millennia," in Richard Jones (ed.), *Manure Matters*. Surrey: Ashgate, 2012, 173–84.

Rees, Jonathan. *Refrigeration Nation: A History of Ice, Appliances, and Refrigeration in America*. Baltimore: Johns Hopkins University Press, 2013.

Reeve, Henry. "Water Supply of West African Towns," *Journal of the Royal Sanitary Institute*, vol. 24 (1904), 1057–67.

Reinhard, K. J., L. F. Ferreira, F. Bouchet, L. Sianto, J. M. F. Dutra, A. Iniguez, D. Leles, M. Le Bailly, M. Fugassa, E. Pucu, and A. Araújo. "Food, Parasites, and Epidemiological Transitions: A Broad Perspective," *International Journal of Paleopathology*, vol. 3 (2013), 150–57.

Reinhard, K. J., and E. Pucu de Araújo. "Comparative Parasitological Perspectives on Epidemiologic Transitions: The Americas and Europe," in M. K. Zuckerman (ed.), *Modern Environments and Human Health: Revisiting the Second Epidemiological Transition*. Hoboken, NJ: John Wiley, 2014, 321–37.

Renne, Elisha P. *The Politics of Polio in Northern Nigeria*. Bloomington: Indiana University Press, 2010.

Research Laboratories of the Army Medical School. *Immunization to Typhoid Fever*. Baltimore: Johns Hopkins University Press, 1941.

Riley, James C. *Rising Life Expectancy: A Global History*. New York: Cambridge University Press, 2001.

Rockefeller Foundation, International Health Board. *Report on the Control of Hookworm Disease in German East Africa and Other German Colonies*. New York, 1917.

Rockefeller Sanitary Commission for the Eradication of Hookworm Disease. *Hookworm Infection in Foreign Countries*. Washington, DC: Offices of the Commission, 1911.

Roechling, H. Alfred. "The Present Status of Sewage Irrigation in Europe and America," *Journal of the Sanitary Institute*, vol. 17 (1896), 483–504.

Roechling, H. Alfred. "The Berlin Sewage Farms (43,009 Acres)," *Journal of the Sanitary Institute*, vol. 32 (1912), 178–206.

Rogaski, Ruth. *Hygienic Modernity: Meanings of Health and Disease in Treaty-Port China*. Berkeley: University of California Press, 2014.

Rogers, Naomi. "Germs with Legs: Flies, Disease, and the New Public Health," *Bulletin of the History of Medicine*, vol. 63, no. 4 (1989), 599–617.

Rosenberg, Charles. *The Cholera Years: The United States in 1832, 1849, and 1866*. Chicago: University of Chicago Press, 1962.

Ross, Ronald. "New Bye-Laws on House Sanitation in Bangalore," *Indian Medical Gazette*, no. 32, no. 4 (1897), 121–23.

Ruxin, Joshua Nalibow. "Magic Bullet: The History of Oral Rehydration Therapy," *Medical History*, vol. 38 (1994), 363–97.

Ryan, E. T. "Haiti in the Context of the Current Global Cholera Pandemic," *Emerging Infectious Diseases*, vol. 17, no. 11 (2011), 2175–76. https://doi.org/10.3201/eid1711.110849.

Ryan, J. Charles. *Health Preservation in West Africa*. London: John Bale, Sons & Danielssons, 1914.

Sabin, Albert B. "Role of My Cooperation with Soviet Scientists in the Elimination of Polio: Possible Lessons for Relations between the USA and the USSR." *Perspectives in Biology and Medicine*, vol. 31, no. 1 (1987), 57–64.

Santosham, Mathuram, Aruna Chandran, Sean Fitzwater, Christa Fischer-Walker, Abdullah H. Baqui, and Robert Black. "Progress and Barriers for the Control of Diarrhoeal Disease," *Lancet*, vol. 376 (2010), 63–67.

Sartin, Jeffrey S. "Infectious Diseases during the Civil War: The Triumph of the 'Third Army,'" *Clinical Infectious Diseases*, vol. 16, no. 4 (1993), 580–84.

Savioli, Lorenzo. "Neglected Tropical Diseases: The Development of a Brand with No Copyright: A Shift from a Disease-Centered to a Tool-Centered Strategic

Approach," in Eileen R. Choffnes and David A. Relman (rapporteurs), *The Causes and Impacts of Neglected Tropical and Zoonotic Diseases: Opportunities for Integrated Intervention Strategies: Workshop Summary*. Washington, DC: National Academies Press, 2011, 481–89.

Schmidt, Luísa, Tiago Saraiva, and João Pato. "In Search of the (Hidden) Portuguese Urban Water Conflicts: The Lisbon Water Story (1856–2006)", in Bernard O. Barraqué (ed.), *Urban Water Conflicts*. Boca Raton, FL: CRC Press, 2011, 69–91.

Schneider, Daniel. *Hybrid Nature: Sewage Treatment and the Contradictions of the Industrial Ecosystem*. Boston: MIT Press, 2011.

Scobie, Alex. "Slums, Sanitation, and Mortality in the Roman World," *Klio*, vol. 86, no. 2 (1986), 399–433.

Scott, James C. *Against the Grain: A Deep History of the Earliest States*. New Haven, CT: Yale University Press, 2016.

Scrimshaw, Nevin S. "Historical Concepts of Interactions, Synergisms and Antagonism Between Nutrition and Infection," *Journal of Nutrition*, vol. 133 (2003), 316S–21S.

Sedgwick, William T. "On Recent Epidemics of Typhoid Fever in the Cities of Lowell and Lawrence due to Infected Water Supply: With Observations on Typhoid Fever in Other Cities and Towns of the Merrimack Valley, Especially Newburyport," in *State Board of Health of Massachusetts, Twenty-Fourth Annual Report*. Boston: State of Massachusetts, 1893, 667–704.

Sedgwick, William T. *Principles of Sanitary Science and the Public Health: With Special Reference to the Causation and Prevention of Infectious Diseases*. New York: Macmillan, 1902.

Sedgwick, William T., and J. Scott Macnutt. "On the Mills-Reincke Phenomenon and Hazen's Theorem Concerning the Decrease in Mortality from Diseases Other Than Typhoid Fever Following the Purification of Public Water-Supplies," *Journal of Infectious Diseases*, vol. 7, no. 4 (1910), 489–564.

Seeger, Hendrik. "The History of German Waste Water Treatment," *European Water Management*, vol. 2 (1999), 51–56.

Selman, Mindy, Suzie Greenhalgh, Robert Diaz, and Zachary Sugg. "Eutrophication and Hypoxia in Coastal Areas: A Global Assessment of the State of Knowledge," *World Resources Institute Policy Note*, no. 1 (2008), 1–6. www.wri.org/sites/default/files/pdf/eutrophication_and_hypoxia_in_coastal_areas.pdf.

Shchelkunov, S. "How Long Ago Did Smallpox Virus Emerge?," *Archives of Virology*, vol. 154, no. 12 (2009), 1865–71.

Shiel, Robert. "Science and Practice: The Ecology of Manure in Historical Retrospect," in Richard Jones (ed.), *Manure Matters*. Surrey: Ashgate, 2012, 13–23.

Shlomowitz, Ralph. "Epidemiology and the Pacific Labor Trade," *Journal of Interdisciplinary History*, vol. 19, no. 4 (1989), 585–610.

Siler, Joseph F., and John S. Lambie Jr. "Typhoid and the Paratyphoid Fevers," in *The Medical Department of the U.S. Army in the World War*, vol. IX, *Communicable and Other Diseases*. Washington, DC: US Government Printing Office, 1928, 15–60.

Simoons, Frederick J. *Eat Not This Flesh: Food Avoidances from Prehistory to the Present*. 2nd ed. Madison: University of Wisconsin Press, 1994.

Simpson, William J. R. *Report by Professor W. J. Simpson on Sanitary Matters in Various West African Colonies and the Outbreak of Plague in the Gold Coast*. London: HMSO, 1909.

Simpson, William J. R. *The Maintenance of Health in the Tropics*. 2nd ed. London: Bale & Danielsson, 1917.

Sisco, Dwight L. "Incidence of Hookworm Disease among Persons Who Were Cured Five Years Ago," *Journal of the American Medical Association*, vol. 80, no. 7 (1923), 451–54.

Skelton, Leona J. *Sanitation in Urban Britain, 1560–1700* New York: Routledge, 2016.

Skirrow, M. B. "Campylobacter Enteritis: A 'New' Disease," *British Medical Journal*, vol. 2, no. 6078 (1977), 9–11.

Smallman-Raynor, Matthew, and Andrew Cliff. *War Epidemics: An Historical Geography of Infectious Diseases in Military Conflict and Civil Strife, 1850–2000*. Oxford: Oxford University Press, 2004.

Smallman-Raynor, M. R., A. D. Cliff, B. Trevelyan, C. Nettleton, and S. Sneddon. *Poliomyelitis: Emergence to Eradication*. Oxford: Oxford University Press, 2006.

Smillie, Wilson G. "The Results of Hookworm Disease Prophylaxis in Brazil," *American Journal of Epidemiology*, vol. 2, no. 1 (1922), 77–95.

Smillie, Wilson G. "Studies on Hookworm Infection in Brazil, 1918–1920. Second Paper," *Monograph of the Rockefeller Institute for Medical Research*, no. 17 (1922), 1–73.

Smillie, W. G., and D. L. Augustine. "Intensity of Hookworm Infection in Alabama: Its Relationship to Residence, Occupation, Age, Sex, and Race," *Journal of the American Medical Association*, vol. 85 (1925), 1958–63.

Smillie, W. G., and D. L. Augustine. "Hookworm Infestation. The Effect of Varying Intensities on the Physical Condition of School Children," *American Journal of Diseases of Children*, vol. 31, no. 2 (1926), 151–68.

Smillie, W. G., and D. L. Augustine. "The Effect of Varying Intensities of Hookworm Infestations upon the Development of School Children," *Southern Medical Journal*, vol. 19 (1926), 19–28.

Smith, F. B. *The People's Health, 1830–1910*. London: Croom Helm, 1979.

Smith, Virginia. *Clean: A History of Personal Hygiene and Purity*. Oxford: Oxford University Press, 2007.

Smith, W. H. Y., D. G. Gill, and James G. McAlpine. "Intestinal Parasite Survey in Alabama. I. A Comparative Study of Two Anthelminthics," *Southern Medical Journal*, vol. 27 (1937), 471–75.

Snyder, J. D., and M. H. Merson. "The Magnitude of the Global Problem of Acute Diarrhoeal Disease: A Review of Active Surveillance Data," *Bulletin of the World Health Organization*, vol. 60, no. 4 (1982), 605–13.

Solomons, Noel W., Manolo Mazariegos, Kenneth H. Brown, and Kirk Klasing. "The Underprivileged, Developing Country Child: Environmental Contamination and Growth Failure Revisited," *Nutrition Reviews*, vol. 51, no. 11 (1993), 327–32.

Srivastava, B. N. *Manual Scavenging in India: A Disgrace to the Country*. New Delhi: Concept, 1997.

Stanwell-Smith, R. "The Infection Potential in the Home and the Role of Hygiene: Historical and Current Perspectives," *International Journal of Environmental Health Research*, vol. 13 (2003), S9–17.

Steckel, Richard H., and Richard A. Jensen. "New Evidence on the Causes of Slave and Crew Mortality in the Atlantic Slave Trade," *Journal of Economic History*, vol. 46, no. 1 (1986), 57–77.

Steiner, Theodore S., Amidou Samie, and Richard L. Guerrant. "Infectious Diarrhea: New Pathogens and New Challenges in Developed and Developing Areas," *Clinical Infectious Diseases*, vol. 43 (2006), 408–10.

Stephanson, Lani S. "Methods to Evaluate Nutritional and Economic Implications of Ascaris Infection," *Social Science and Medicine*, vol. 19, no. 10 (1984), 1061–65.

Stephanson, L. S., C. V. Holland, and E. S. Cooper. "The Public Health Significance of *Trichuris trichiura*," *Parasitology*, vol. 121 (2000), S73–95.

Stermer, Edy, Igor Sukhotnic, and Ron Shaoul. "Pruritus Ani: An Approach to an Itching Condition," *Journal of Pediatric Gastroenterology and Nutrition*, vol. 48, no. 5 (2009), 513–16.

Stiles, Charles Wardell. *The Significance of the Recent American Cases of the Hookworm Disease (Uncinariasis or Anchylostomiasis) in Man*. Washington, DC: Government Printing Office, 1902.

Stiles, Charles Wardell. *Report upon the Prevalence and Geographic Distribution of Hookworm Disease (Uncinariasis or Anchylostomiasis) in the United States*. No. 10. Washington, DC: US Government Printing Office, 1903.

Stiles, Charles Wardell. "Hookworm Disease and Its Relation to the Negro," *Public Health Reports (1896–1970)*, vol. 24, no. 31 (1909), 1083–89.

Stiles, C. W. *Report of the Scientific Secretary*. The Rockefeller Sanitary Commission for the Eradication of Hookworm Disease, Publication No. 2. New York, 1914.

Stiles, C. W. "Zooparasitic Intestinal Infections: An Analysis of Infections Found among 1,287 School Children (776 White, 511 Negro) in the City of X," *Public Health Reports*, vol. 30, no. 25 (1915), 1991–2002.

Stiles, C. W. "Decrease of Hookworm Disease in the United States," *Public Health Reports*, vol. 45, no. 1 (1930), 1763–81.

Stiles, Charles Wardell. "Some Practical Considerations in Regard to Control of Hookworm Disease in the United States under Present Conditions," *Journal of Parasitology*, vol. 18, no. 3 (1932), 169–72.

Stiles, Charles Wardell. "Early History, in Part Esoteric, of the Hookworm (Uncinariasis) Campaign in Our Southern United States," *Journal of Parasitology*, vol. 25, no. 4 (1939), 283–308.

Stiles, C. H. Wardell, W. L. Altman, and Robert Rinsky. "Hookworm Disease (1913) [with Commentary]," *Public Health Reports (1974–)*, vol. 121, Suppl. 1 (2006), 58–69.

Stoll, Norman R. "On the Economic Value of Nightsoil in China," in W. W. Cort, J. B. Grant, and N. R. Stoll (eds.), *Researches on Hookworm in China: Embodying the Results of the Work of the China Hookworm Commission,*

*June, 1923 to November, 1924*, Monographic Series no. 7. Baltimore: The American Journal of Hygiene, 1926, 257–64.

Stoll, N. R. "Investigations on the Control of Hookworm Disease. XV. An Effective Method for Counting Hookworm Eggs in Feces," *American Journal of Hygiene*, vol. 3 (1926), 59–70.

Stoll, N. R. "Investigations on the Control of Hookworm Disease. XVIII. On the Relation between the Number of Eggs Found in Human Feces and the Number of Hookworms in the Host," *American Journal of Hygiene*, vol. 3 (1923), 156–79.

Stoll, N. R. "This Wormy World," *Journal of Parasitology*, vol. 33, no. 1 (1947), 1–18.

Stoll, Steven. *Larding the Lean Earth: Soil and Society in Nineteenth-Century America*. New York: Hill and Wang, 2003.

Strachan, Henry. *Paper on the Health Conditions of West Africa*. Liverpool: African Trade Section, 1901.

Strunz, E. C., D. G. Addiss, M. E. Stocks, S. Ogden, J. Utzinger et al. "Water, Sanitation, Hygiene, and Soil-Transmitted Helminth Infection: A Systematic Review and Meta-Analysis," *PLoS Medicine*, vol. 11, no. 3 (2014), e1001620. https://doi.org/10.1371/journal.pmed.1001620.

Tan, Huizi, and Paul W. O'Toole. "Impact of Diet on the Human Intestinal Microbiota," *Current Opinion in Food Science*, vol. 2 (2015), 71–77. https://doi.org/10.1016/j.cofs.2015.01.005.

Tarr, Joel A. "From City to Farm: Urban Wastes and the American Farmer," *Agricultural History*, vol. 49, no. 4 (1975), 598–612.

Tarr, Joel A. "The Separate vs. Combined Sewer Problem: A Case Study in Urban Technology Design Choice," *Journal of Urban History*, vol. 5 (1979), 308–33.

Tarr, Joel A., James McCurley III, Francis C. McMichael, and Terry Yosie. "Water and Wastes: A Retrospective Assessment of Wastewater Technology in the United States, 1900–1932," *Technology and Culture*, vol. 25, no. 2 (1984), 226–63.

Tarr, Joel A. "The Evolution of the Urban Infrastructure in the Nineteenth and Twentieth Centuries," in Royce Hanson (ed.), *Perspectives on Urban Infrastructure*. Washington, DC: National Academy Press, 1984.

Tarr, Joel A. "The Horse: Polluter of the City," in Joel A. Tarr (ed.), *The Search for the Ultimate Sink: Urban Pollution in Historical Perspective*. Akron, OH: University of Akron Press, 1996, 323–33.

Tate, Jacqueline E., Anthony H. Burton, Cynthia Boschi-Pinto, Umesh D. Parashar, World Health Organization–Coordinated Global Rotavirus Surveillance Network, Mary Agocs, Fatima Serhan et al., "Global, Regional, and National Estimates of Rotavirus Mortality in Children < 5 Years of Age, 2000–2013," *Clinical Infectious Diseases*, vol. 62, Suppl. 2 (2016), S96–105.

Taylor, C. E., and X. Z. Yu. "Oral Rehydration in China," *American Journal of Public Health*, vol. 76, no. 2 (1986), 187–89.

Taylor, Craig. "A Tale of Two Cities: The Efficacy of Ancient and Medieval Sanitation Methods," in Piers D. Mitchell (ed.), *Sanitation, Latrines and Intestinal Parasites in Past Populations*. Surrey: Ashgate, 2015, 69–97.

Taylor-Robinson, David C., Nicola Maayan, Karla Soares-Weiser, Sarah Donegan, and Paul Garner. "Deworming Drugs for Soil-Transmitted Intestinal Worms in Children: Effects on Nutritional Indicators, Haemoglobin and School Performance," *Cochrane Database Systematic Reviews*, vol. 11, no. 7 (2015), 1–157.

Teh, Tse-Hui. "Bypassing the Flush, Creating New Resources: Analysing Alternative Sanitation Futures in London," *Local Environment: The International Journal of Justice and Sustainability*, vol. 20, no. 3 (2015), 335–49.

Thaman, Lauren A., and Lawrence F. Eichenfield. "Diapering Habits: A Global Perspective," *Pediatric Dermatology*, vol. 31, Suppl. 1 (2014), 15–18.

Thompson, R. C. Andrew, Carlysle S. Palmer, and Ryon O'Handley. "The Public Health and Clinical Significance of Giardia and Cryptosporidium in Domestic Animals," *The Veterinary Journal*, vol. 177, no. 1 (2008), 18–25.

Tidy, Charles Meymott. *The Treatment of Sewage*. New York: D. Van Nostrand, 1887.

Tisdale, E. S., and C. H. Atkins. "The Sanitary Privy and Its Relation to Public Health," *American Journal of Public Health*, vol. 33 (1943), 1319–22.

Tomes, Nancy. *The Gospel of Germs: Men, Women, and the Microbe in American Life*. Cambridge, MA: Harvard University Press, 1998.

Tomory, Leslie. *The History of the London Water Industry, 1580–1820*. Baltimore: Johns Hopkins University Press, 2017.

Trevelyan, Barry, Matthew Smallman-Raynor, and Andrew D. Cliff. "The Spatial Dynamics of Poliomyelitis in the United States: From Epidemic Emergence to Vaccine-Induced Retreat, 1910–1971," *Annals of the Association of American Geographers*, vol. 95, no. 2 (2005), 269–93.

Troeger, Christopher, Mohammad Forouzanfar, Puja C. Rao, Ibrahim Khalil, Alexandria Brown, Robert C. Reiner Jr., Nancy Fullman et al. "Estimates of Global, Regional, and National Morbidity, Mortality, and Aetiologies of Diarrhoeal Diseases: A Systematic Analysis for the Global Burden of Disease Study 2015," *Lancet Infectious Diseases*, vol. 17, no. 9 (2017), 909–48.

Uttley, K. H. "The Mortality and Epidemiology of Typhoid Fever in the Colored Inhabitants of Antigua, West Indies over the Last Hundred Years," *West Indian Medical Journal*, vol. 9 (1960), 114–16.

Utzinger, Jürg. "A Research and Development Agenda for the Control and Elimination of Human Helminthiases," *PLoS Neglected Tropical Diseases*, vol. 6, no. 4 (2012), e1646.

Vågene, Å. J., M. G. Campana, N. M. R. García, C. G. Warinner, M. A. Spyrou, A. Andrades Valtueña, D. Huson et al. "*Salmonella enterica* Genomes Recovered from Victims of a Major 16th Century Epidemic in Mexico," *bioRxiv* (2017), 106740. https://doi.org/10.1101/106740.

Valence, Deborah M. *Milk: A Local and Global History*. New Haven, CT: Yale University Press, 2011.

Van Zile Hyde, Henry. "Sanitation in the International Health Field," *American Journal of Public Health*, vol. 41, no. 1 (1951), 1–6.

Varisco, Daniel. "Zibl and Zira'a: Coming to Terms with Manure in Arab Agriculture," in Richard Jones (ed.), *Manure Matters*. Surrey: Ashgate, 2012, 129–43.

Velten, Hannah. *Milk: A Global History*. London: Reaktion Books, 2010.

Victora, César G., Peter G. Smith, J. Patrick Vaughan, Leticia C. Nobre, C. Lombard, Ana Maria B. Teixeira, Sandra Costa Fuchs, L. B. Moreira, L. P. Gigante, and Fernando C. Barros. "Water Supply, Sanitation and Housing in Relation to the Risk of Infant Mortality from Diarrhoea," *International Journal of Epidemiology*, vol. 17, no. 3 (1988), 651–54.

Vinten-Johansen, Peter, Howard Brody, Nigel Paneth, Stephen Rachman, and Michael Rip. *Cholera, Chloroform, and the Science of Medicine: A Life of John Snow*. New York: Oxford University Press, 2003.

Virchow, Rudolf. *Infection-Diseases in the Army, Chiefly Wound Fever, Typhoid, Dysentery and Diptheria*. Translated by John James. London: H. K. Lewis, 1879.

Waddington, Claire S., Thomas C. Darton, and Andrew J. Pollard. "The Challenge of Enteric Fever," *Journal of Infection*, vol. 68 (2014), S38–50.

Wagner, E. G., and J. Lanoix. *Excreta Disposal for Rural Areas and Small Countries*. WHO Monograph Series no. 39. Geneva: World Health Organization, 1958.

Waisley, Thomas. "Public Health Programs in Early Twentieth-Century Louisiana," *Louisiana History: The Journal of the Louisiana Historical Association*, vol. 41, no. 1 (2000), 41–69.

Waltner-Toews, David. *The Origin of Feces*. Toronto: ECW Press, 2013.

Wammes, Linda J., Harriet Mpairwe, Alison M. Elliott, and Maria Yazdanbakhsh. "Helminth Therapy or Elimination: Epidemiological, Immunological, and Clinical Considerations," *Lancet Infectious Diseases*, vol. 14 (2014), 1150–62.

Waring, George Edwin. *Earth Closets and Earth Sewage*. New York: The Tribune Association, 1870.

Warner, Dennis B., and Louis Laugeri. "Health for All: The Legacy of the Water Decade," *Water International*, vol. 16, no. 3 (1991), 135–41.

Watson, Malcolm. *Rural Sanitation in the Tropics: Being Notes and Observations in the Malay Archipelago, Panama and Other Lands*. New York: E. P. Dutton, 1915.

Watt, James, and Dale R. Lindsay. "Diarrheal Disease Control Studies. I. Effect of Fly Control in a High Morbidity Area," *Public Health Reports*, vol. 63, no. 41 (1948), 1319–49.

Webb, James L. A., Jr. *Humanity's Burden: A Global History of Malaria*. New York: Cambridge University Press, 2009.

Webb, James L. A., Jr. *The Long Struggle against Malaria in Tropical Africa*. New York: Cambridge University Press, 2014.

Webb, James L. A., Jr. "The Historical Epidemiology of Global Disease Challenges," *Lancet*, vol. 385, no. 9965 (2015), 322–23.

Webb, James L. A., Jr. "Early Malarial Infections and the First Epidemiological Transition," in Michael Petraglia, Nicole Boivin, and Rémy Cressard (eds.), *From Colonization to Globalization: Species Movements in Human History*. New York: Cambridge University Press, 2017, 477–93.

Webb, James L. A., Jr. "Battling Intestinal Worm Disease: From the Hookworm Campaigns of the Rockefeller Foundation to Contemporary Mass Drug

Administration," *Gesnerus: Swiss Journal of the History of Medicine and Sciences*, vol. 74, no. 2 (2017), 229–39.

Weiss, M. G. "Cultural Models of Diarrheal Illness: Conceptual Framework and Review," *Social Science and Medicine*, vol. 27, no. 1 (1988), 5–16.

Whiley, Harriet, Ben van den Akker, Steven Giglio, and Richard Bentham. "The Role of Environmental Reservoirs in Human Campylobacteriosis," *International Journal of Environmental Research and Public Health*, vol. 10 (2013), 5887–93.

Wilson, Charles. *The History of Unilever*. 2 vols. London: Cassell, 1954.

Winblad, Uno, and Wen Kilama. *Sanitation without Water*. London: Macmillan, 1985.

Wines, Richard. *Fertilizer in America: From Waste Recycling to Resource Exploitation*. Philadelphia: Temple University Press, 1985.

Wolf, Jacqueline H. *Don't Kill Your Baby: Public Health and the Decline of Breastfeeding in the Nineteenth and Twentieth Centuries*. Columbus: Ohio State University Press, 2001.

Wolman, Abel, and A. E. Gorman. *The Significance of Waterborne Typhoid Fever Outbreaks 1920–1931*. Baltimore: Williams and Wilkins, 1931.

Wolman, Abel. "Environmental Sanitation in Urban and Rural Areas: Its Importance in the Control of Enteric Infections," *Bulletin of the Pan American Health Organization*, vol. 9, no. 2 (1975), 157–59.

Woods, Robert. "Urban-Rural Mortality Differentials: An Unresolved Debate," *Population and Development Review*, vol. 29, no. 1 (2003), 29–46.

World Health Organization. *Climate Change and Human Health: Risks and Responses Summary*. Geneva: WHO, 2003.

Worster, Donald. "The Good Muck: Toward an Excremental History of China," *RCC Perspectives: Transformations in Environment and Society*, no. 5 (2017). https://doi.org/10.5282/rcc/8135.

Wright, Almroth E. *A Short Treatise on Anti-Typhoid Inoculation*. Westminster: Archibald Constable, 1904.

Wright, Lawrence. *Clean and Decent: The Fascinating History of the Bathroom and the Water Closet*. New York: Viking Press, 1960.

Woods, R. I., P. A. Watterson, and J. H. Woodward. "The Causes of Rapid Infant Mortality Decline in England and Wales, 1861–1921 Part I," *Population Studies*, vol. 42, no. 3 (1988), 343–66.

Woods, R. I., P. A. Watterson, and J. H. Woodward. "The Causes of Rapid Infant Mortality Decline in England and Wales, 1861–1921 Part II," *Population Studies*, vol. 43, no. 1 (1989), 113–32.

Wuana, Raymond A., and Felix E. Okieimen. "Heavy Metals in Contaminated Soils: A Review of Sources, Chemistry, Risks and Best Available Strategies for Remediation," *ISRN Ecology*, vol. 2011 (2011), Article 402647. https://doi.org/10.5402/2011/402647.

Xiang, Hai, Jianqiang Gao, Baoquan Yu, Hui Zhou, Dawei Cai, Youwen Zhang, Xiaoyong Chen, Xi Wang, Michael Hofreiter, and Xingbo Zhao. "Early Holocene Chicken Domestication in Northern China," *Proceedings of the National Academy of Sciences*, vol. 111, no. 49 (2014), 17564–69.

Xinzhong, Yu. "The Treatment of Night Soil and Waste in Modern China," in Angela Ki Che Leung and Charlotte Furth (eds.), *Health and Hygiene in Chinese East Asia*. Durham, NC: Duke University Press, 2010, 51–72.

Xu, L. Q., S. H. Yu, Z. X. Jiang, L. Q. Lai, X. J. Zhang, and C. Q. Zheng. "Soil-Transmitted Helminthiases: Nationwide Survey in China," *Bulletin of the World Health Organization*, vol. 73, no. 4 (1995), 507–13.

Xue, Yong. "Treasure Nightsoil as If It Were Gold: Economic and Ecological Links between Urban and Rural Areas in Late Imperial Jiangnan," *Late Imperial China*, vol. 26, no. 1 (2005), 41–71.

Yatsunenko, Tanya, Frederico E. Ray, Mark J. Manary, Indi Trehan, Maria Gloria Dominguez-Bello, Monica Contreras, Magda Magris et al. "Human Gut Microbiome Viewed across Age and Geography," *Nature*, vol. 486, no. 7402 (2012), 222–27. https://doi.org/10.1038/nature11053.

Yellen, John E., Alison S. Brooks, Els Cornelissen, Michael J. Mehlman, and Kathlyn Stewart, "A Middle Stone Age Worked Bone Industry from Katanda, Upper Semliki Valley, Zaire," *Science*, Vol. 268, No. 5210 (1995), 553–56.

Yokogawa, M. "JOICFP'S Experience in the Control of Ascariasis within an Integrated Programme," in D. W. T. Crompton, M. C. Nesheim, and Z. S. Pawlowski (eds.), *Ascariasis and Its Public Health Significance*. London: Taylor & Francis, 1985, 265–77.

Young, Sera L., Paul W. Sherman, Julius B. Lucks, and Gretel H. Pelto. "Why on Earth? Evaluating Hypotheses about the Physiological Functions of Human Geophagy," *Quarterly Review of Biology*, vol. 86, no. 2 (2011), 97–120.

Zeder, Melinda A. "Domestication and Early Agriculture in the Mediterranean Basin: Origins, Diffusion, and Impact," *Proceedings of the National Academy of Sciences*, vol. 105, no. 33 (2008), 11597–604.

Zeheter, Michael. *Epidemics, Empire, and Environments: Cholera in Madras and Quebec City, 1818–1910*. Pittsburgh, PA: University of Pittsburgh Press, 2015.

Ziegelbauer, Kathrin, Benjamin Speich, Daniel Mäusezahl, Robert Bos, Jennifer Keiser, and Jürg Utzinger. "Effect of Sanitation on Soil-Transmitted Helminth Infection: Systematic Review and Meta-analysis," *PLoS Medicine*, vol. 9, no. 1 (2012), e1001162. https://doi.org/10.1371/journal.pmed.1001162.

Zhou, Zhemin, Angela McCann, François-Xavier Weill, Camille Blin, Satheesh Nair, John Wain, Gordon Douglass, and Mark Achtman. "Transient Darwinian Selection in Salmonella Enterica Serovar Parathyphi A during 450 Years of Global Spread of Enteric Fever," *Proceedings of the National Academy of Sciences*, vol. 111, no. 33 (2014), 12199–204.

Zwane, Alix Peterson, and Michael Kremer. "What Works in Fighting Diarrheal Diseases in Developing Countries? A Critical Review," *The World Bank Research Observer*, vol. 22, no. 1 (2007), 1–24.

# Index

African slave trade, 45
African slave workers, 44
agriculture
  early zones in Eurasia, 33–34
  paracultivation of tubers, 26
Al-Awqati, Qais, 136
Alma-Ata. *See* Primary Health Care
amoebic dysentery, 9, 53, 140
*Ancylostoma duodenale*, 12, 103, *See also* hookworm epidemiology
anemia, 115, 161
  and intensity of hookworm infection, 116
  as symptom of hookworm disease, 105, 106
  as symptom of malaria, 113
animal dung for fuel, 52–53
animal waste
  composted with human waste, 48
  in cities, 57
  pathogens propagated in horse manure, 75
anthroponoses, 30
*Ascaris lumbricöides. See* roundworm
*Ascaris suum*, 26, 27
attitudes toward human waste
  in East and Southeast Asia, 35
  in Japan, 50
  in the Indic world, 35
  in western Eurasia, 35–36
auto-immune diseases, 171

bacterial infections, 8–9
Bao Shichen (1785–1855), 53

Bazalgette, Joseph, 68
boiled water, 91, 169
  Ayurvedic medical knowledge, 37
  Chinese use, 47
  recommended in Susruta Samhita, 37
bottle-feeding, 149
Bozzolo, Camillo, 104
Brandon, W.L., 107
breast-feeding, 149
brucellosis, 30

*Campylobacter*, 9, 166, 167
cattlepox, 29
cesspits, 15, 39, 55, 57, 69, 72, 86, 124, 143, 169
cesspools in London, 53, 56, 66, 69
Chadwick, Edwin, 66
*champa. See* wet rice cultivation
Chatterjee, Hemendra Nath, 136
chicken feces, 15, 16
chickenpox, 29, 30
chickens, 14, 33
child survival revolution, 152–53
  explanations, 21–23
childhood diarrheal disease, 15–17
  and malnutrition, 17
  and water availability, 16–17, 146
  declines in, as public health success, 138
  differential death rates, 141
  mortality rates in Britain, 69
childhood diseases, 30
China Hookworm Commission, 121
chlorination, 9, 82–84, 170